# Acclaim for Engaged Teaching

*"Impressive in its command of the research literature, masterful in its writing, and innovative in its organization, Engaged Teaching offers us the best, most comprehensive collection currently available of the essential concepts of good teaching in higher education. Most books on this subject focus on only one aspect of a highly complex and interconnected process. Barkley and Major have written the first book that combines these big themes into one volume. It is a beautifully crafted guidebook on how to be a better, more engaged teacher, providing a structured pathway through the essential elements of good university pedagogy with a combination of accessible and relevant theoretical discussions and practical tips. At its heart, this book is an extended and meaningful tribute to the work of K. Patricia Cross, giving her due credit for the indelible impact she has had on teaching and learning in higher education and translating her ideas into a contemporary context. Whether you are an educational developer looking for one book to share with your teaching staff, or a university teacher wanting to choose one book to help improve your teaching, this is the book you've been searching for. It's a book I've been searching for for years."*

**— ROBERT GRAY**
Associate Professor of University Pedagogy, University of Bergen, Norway

*"In this fabulously comprehensive introduction to better teaching, Barkley and Major provide a clear framework and practical tools for improvement. They have somehow managed to survey everything from learning theories and assessment strategies to inclusion and visual design succinctly in this brief but substantial handbook. Here, the vast literature on teaching and learning is made engaging and manageable for all faculty."*

**— JOSÉ ANTONIO BOWEN**
Senior Fellow, American Association of Colleges and Universities (AAC&U)

*"Inspired by K. Patricia Cross's groundbreaking leadership in pedagogical innovation, Barkley and Major provide an invaluable resource for catalyzing the engaged teaching essential to preparing students for success in work, citizenship, and life in the 21st century."*

**— LYNN PASQUERELLA**
President, American Association of Colleges and Universities (AAC&U)

*The two foremost scholars of college teaching, Barkley and Major, have produced a user-friendly treasure trove of research-based information on engaged teaching in higher education. Their volume equips college and university faculty members with the pedagogical knowledge to complement disciplinary knowledge and belongs on the desks of novice and experienced college teachers as a ready reference to guide teaching practice.*

**— JOHN M. BRAXTON**

Professor Emeritus, Higher Education Leadership and Policy Program, Peabody College of Education and Human Development, Vanderbilt University

*Higher education is teeming with new ideas about effective teaching and learning. What's sometimes missing, however, is a framework, an integrative vision, that pulls together the many promising insights and innovations from the last few decades. That is the gift that Barkley and Major give us in their latest volume. Designed to work in tandem with the K. Patricia Cross Academy, Engaged Teaching combines thoughtful summaries of relevant research along with descriptions of promising practices that educators can use right now — and build on. The volume concludes with a call for reflective practice and pedagogical inquiry in pursuit of ongoing improvement — for individual educators, the profession of teaching, and our students' learning.*

**— PAT HUTCHINGS**

Senior Scholar, National Institute for Learning Outcomes Assessment (NILOA)
Senior Scholar, Bay View Alliance (BVA)

*This elegant synthesis of scholarship on college-level teaching and learning is a fitting tribute to one of the field's most influential founders, K. Patricia Cross. Written to accompany the rich collection of materials now available through the K. Patricia Cross Academy website, Engaged Teaching is a practical guide to the art and science of teaching well in higher education today. Authors Barkley and Major are master mapmakers. Those who wish to get their bearings in the vast and various landscape of pedagogical theory and practice will do well to consult this welcome book.*

**— MARY TAYLOR HUBER**

Contributing Editor, *Change: The Magazine of Higher Learning*
Senior Scholar, Bay View Alliance: Leadership for Learning in Higher Education
Senior Scholar Emerita, Carnegie Foundation for the Advancement of Teaching

*Effective teaching is fundamental to high quality learning and success for all students. Educators seeking ways to deepen their knowledge about teaching will find trusted tools and techniques in Engaged Learning, the newest resource from the K. Patricia Cross Academy that promises to enhance teaching in today's shifting learning context.*

**— JILLIAN KINZIE**
Interim Co-Director, National Survey of Student Engagement,
Indiana University Center for Postsecondary Research

*Engaged Teaching clearly and concisely synthesizes a wide range of teaching and learning topics. The book is an excellent go-to resource for all instructors in higher education.*

**— TRACIE ADDY**
Associate Dean of Teaching & Learning, Lafayette College
Co-author, *What Inclusive Instructors Do: Principles & Practices for Excellence in College Teaching*

*Barkley and Major's Engaged Teaching is a timely, thorough resource that provides an array of helpful suggestions and tools to promote high-quality instruction in face-to-face, online, and hybrid classrooms. The handbook is adaptable to many fields and disciplines. With its focus on the what, why, and how of engaged teaching, it can serve as an excellent source of support for learners and instructors in higher education.*

**— STEPHANIE BLACKMON**
Associate Professor of Higher Education, William & Mary

*Enlightened common sense supported by significant research is the hallmark of Engaged Teaching. Barkley and Major were mentored by one of the most influential educators of our time, K. Patricia Cross, and her spirit permeates this book, which is peppered with her cogent quotes. Those who dream of becoming great teachers need wait no longer; the answer is here.*

**— TERRY O'BANION**
President Emeritus, League for Innovation in the Community College
Senior Professor of Practice, Kansas State University

*Traditional teaching approaches are more focused on teaching than learning. Engaged Teaching is a must-read for anyone genuinely interested in understanding how students learn and how best to engage students, particularly our nontraditional, first-gen, and underserved populations.*

**— BERNADINE CHUCK FONG**
Acting President, Foothill College
Senior Scholar and Director of Leadership Initiatives, Stanford University

*Engaged Teaching moves beyond particular instructional techniques to examine the entire eco-system of college teaching, from its foundations to classroom climate to the reflective habits of mind that will deepen our pedagogical practice. Instructors at every level will come away with critical insights into creating powerful learning environments for their students.*

**— PAUL HANSTEDT**
Director of the Houston H. Harte Center for Teaching and Learning,
Professor of Education Studies, Washington and Lee University

*Barkley and Major have once again demonstrated they are worthy keepers of K. Patricia Cross's legacy. With Engaged Teaching, they continue Pat's long-standing contributions to faculty professional development, offering practical applications of theory and research for real-world teaching and learning settings.*

**— CYNTHIA WILSON**
Vice President for Learning and Chief Impact Officer,
League for Innovation in the Community College

*Engaged Teaching approaches the essence of teaching from a practical perspective. The teaching process presented here will not only allow you to discuss what constitutes teaching effectiveness but will also help you to reflect directly and concretely upon your own teaching methods and improve them.*

**— JUN-ICHI IMURA**
Executive Officer and Vice-President for Teaching and Learning,
Tokyo Institute of Technology

*Barkley and Major have compiled the essential college teaching handbook for novice and seasoned faculty alike, covering topics from student motivation and engagement to instructional strategies and evaluations for in-person and online modalities. Accessible, practical, and evidence-based, the handbook captures the essence of engaged college teaching, with the wisdom and inspiration of K. Patricia Cross ever-present throughout the text.*

**— MARILYN J. AMEY**

Interim Associate Provost for Faculty and Academic, Staff Development;
Mildred B. Erickson Endowed Chair Emerita and Professor of Higher, Adult, and Lifelong Education, Michigan State University

*Engaged Teaching pays homage to K. Patricia Cross, a legendary leader in higher education. Throughout the book, Barkley and Major aptly exemplify Cross's deeply held pedagogical values and principles: engaging and motivating students to succeed and offering practical and accessible research-based strategies for teaching improvement that apply to both beginning and experienced instructors. The authors' carefully articulated model of engaged teaching describes the core elements of what it means to be and how to become an effective college teacher and fittingly honors and encompasses Cross's ideals and her distinguished contributions to the field.*

**— BARBARA GROSS DAVIS**

Author, *Tools for Teaching*

*With a new handbook that complements the free resources available from the K. Patricia Cross Academy, Barkley and Major delve into their experiences and scholarly work to frame engaged teaching as an intellectual process. With particular relevance to the context of teaching and learning in 2022 and beyond, they bridge new ways for college instructors of all levels to experience engaged teaching as a necessary process for creating high-quality learning experiences that will be valued by students and teachers alike.*

**— LINDA M. BOLAND**

Associate Provost for Faculty, University of Richmond

*Engaged Teaching is a masterpiece of practical pedagogical advice steeped in scholarship — the book you dream of writing. Recommended reading for all, especially early career teachers and those undertaking higher education teaching qualifications and recognition.*

**— DANIELLE HINTON**

Educational Developer, University of Birmingham, United Kingdom

*This inspiring and practical book connects the dots between engaged teaching and meaningful learning. By integrating the authors' extraordinary knowledge of research and their decades of teaching experience, this book is a go-to resource for engaging and equitable teaching in higher education.*

**— PETER FELTEN**

Professor of History; Executive Director, Center for Engaged Learning;
Assistant Provost for Teaching and Learning, Elon University
Co-author, *Relationship-Rich Education: How Human Connections Drive Success in College*

*In this illuminating, incisive, and superbly clear volume, Barkley and Major reflect the genius of their mentor K. Patricia Cross who taught several generations of teachers at all levels of education that instruction is ultimately a partnership between teacher and student. However, this partnership only works when the participants learn to listen to one another with care, respect, and a sense of discovery. From quick deep dives into the minds of learners to broad systematic approaches to design and evaluation, Cross created theory-grounded practices that any instructor could grasp and implement. This book both honors and builds upon that legacy.*

**— LEE S. SHULMAN**

Charles E. Ducommun Professor of Education Emeritus, Stanford University
President Emeritus, Carnegie Foundation for the Advancement of Teaching

We wrote *Engaged Teaching: A Handbook for College Faculty* to support the K. Patricia Cross Academy. The Academy is a nonprofit professional development website (*kpcrossacademy.org*) founded to honor and preserve the legacy of Pat Cross while providing free, accessible, and substantive resources for college teachers. Although written solely by us, *Engaged Teaching* is the culmination of our career-long collaboration with Pat, and her voice and values are woven throughout. It is dedicated to college educators who strive to strengthen their teaching skills in the service of promoting student learning. All proceeds directly subsidize the Academy and its ongoing development.

Published by SocialGood
PO Box 5473
Richmond, CA 94805
510.621.7223
(EIN) TAX ID: 46-1323531
socialgood@socialgoodfund.org
socialgoodfund.org



Library of Congress Cataloging-in-Publication Data is Available:
2022902777 (Paperback)

Cover Design: 20|20 Creative Group
Cover Image: © Zffoto / Envato Elements
Proofing and Copyediting: Tracy Skipper
Indexing: Varsha Venkatasubramanian

ISBN 979-8-9857742-0-7

Printed in the United States of America
FIRST EDITION

# Engaged Teaching

A HANDBOOK FOR COLLEGE FACULTY

ELIZABETH F. BARKLEY

CLAIRE HOWELL MAJOR

# Contents

PART 1

# Foundations

*While learning has many ends, teaching has only one:*
*to enable or cause learning.*

**—K. PATRICIA CROSS**

CHAPTER 1

# Engaged Teaching—What It Is and Why It Matters

The two of us have talked with thousands of college educators over the past four decades, and while we acknowledge that college teaching has always had its difficulties, never has it been tougher or mattered more than at this moment. Today's teachers face era-defining challenges. We are trying to teach in sometimes suddenly shifting learning contexts that also require us to quickly learn new tools and technologies. We are struggling to promote substantive discourse among students who may have deep differences in views and values and who have been shaped by a society torn apart by anger, hatred, and incivility. We are seeking to prove to a variety of stakeholders that what we do is both cost-effective and that it results in significant learning.

There's no question that teaching today is tough, but it also remains one of the world's most rewarding professions for several reasons:

- **College teaching allows us to pursue our passions.** Most of us were drawn to our academic discipline because somewhere along the line we became fascinated by it. Academia encourages us to deepen our knowedge about our chosen subject matter and offers us incentives for doing so.
- **College teaching is important work.** Many of us know how influential a teacher can be because we had a teacher who inspired us personally, who changed our lives for the better. Teaching is our chance potentially to have a simlarly profound effect on others.
- **College teaching is intellectually and emotionally engaging.** How often have you looked at other jobs and thought: that must be crushingly

boring? For those of us who teach at the college level, there is constant novelty as we keep up with our disciplines, problem-solve in our classrooms, and interact with peers who have far-ranging interests and expertise.

- **College teaching offers us opportunities for community.** Humans have a basic need for social connection, and our academic institutions are comprised of multiple avenues for supporting both formal and informal communities. With a little effort, most of us can find colleagues with whom we can form bonds around shared values and interests.
- **College teaching allows us to help solve the world's problems.** Through our teaching, we can help students resist misinformation, conspiracy theories, and cloudy thinking. We can model the open exchange of ideas and the civil debate of opposing viewpoints. We can support institutional efforts to promote inclusion and equity. We can incorporate experiential learning into our courses to address pressing problems in both local and international communities. And we can preserve the best aspects of civilization by inspiring and passing the torch to the next generation.

Thus, although college teaching today can be tough, it can also be extraordinarily rewarding because *what we do matters*. It matters most when we recognize this and truly engage with our work to best ensure student learning. In this chapter, we outline our framework for how to be an engaged teacher who effectively prepares students to think creatively, critically, and courageously in a rapidly changing world.

## KNOWING WHAT: ABOUT ENGAGED TEACHING

While the need for effective college teaching is clear, we also know that some college teachers are simply better at it than others. They are better at planning their courses, connecting with students, creating a positive climate, choosing teaching methods, assessing learning, and communicating the value of what they do to others. In our current observations of colleagues on every campus, including our own, some professors demonstrate extraordinary ability to motivate and engage students. Others, not so much. What is it that makes some teachers so good?

### Definition of Effective Teaching

This quality of being particularly good at teaching is often referred to as "teaching effectiveness." This unwieldy and imprecise term gained traction in the higher education community in the 1980s and early 1990s amid the extensive work then being done on student ratings.

Even now, the phrase is frequently connected to student evaluations of teaching, as higher education administrators around the country attempt to promote teaching effectiveness while still relying primarily on end-of-course student surveys as evidence of its existence.

Multiple definitions for teaching effectiveness exist, which makes it difficult to find any one of them to be definitive. Nevertheless, they all can help to shed some light on what it means to be an effective teacher. Following is a sample of the numerous definitions of teaching effectiveness:

- "a level of performance evidenced by high quality teaching practices (including classroom teaching, assessment practices, module development, range of teaching, supervision of student projects) and activities in professional self-development" (Pan et al., 2009, p. 79);
- "a situation in which a teacher strives to "deliver concrete, explicit, and engaging instruction, implement evidence-based classroom management and teaching strategies; and build strong relationships with their students" (Macsuga-Gage et al., 2012, p. 14); and
- "the manner in which the course is designed, content is selected and delivered, students are engaged in learning activities, and the conditions under which the course is taught (i.e., technology, physical setting, and students who typically enroll in the course)" (Palmquist, 2011, p. 2).

These three definitions focus on teacher performance as well as on the quality of the act of teaching itself. Other definitions, however, highlight the importance of learning outcomes as key indicators of effective teaching. Some of these definitions of teaching effectiveness include the following:

- "teaching that results in student achievement" (Rink, 2013, p. 408);
- "the ability to produce gains on student achievement scores; taking account of a baseline measure of students' prior attainment and other characteristics of student intake, the teacher effect is identified in relation to students' progress measured by later attainment" (Little et al., 2009, as cited in Ko et al., 2013, p. 8); and
- "the effectiveness with which the teacher is producing the desired learning outcomes for the given student population" (Weiman, 2015, p. 8).

Taking these definitions together, we believe that teaching effectiveness can be described as the high-quality practices that teachers enact during performance of their roles and responsibilities evidenced by their subsequent effects on student learning.

## The Engaged Teaching Model

There is frequently an underlying assumption that effective teachers are just naturally so, that they have been endowed with a special combination of personal and professional characteristics that equip them to effortlessly excel in their role. But we think there is more to it than simply being a "born teacher" or passively enjoying the state of "being effective." We propose that it is largely engagement in the teaching process that gets teachers to the state of teaching effectiveness.

We find the term *engaged teaching* a particularly useful conception, as it emphasizes the investment that excellent teachers put into their teaching to be "effective." Thus, engaged teaching is the path to teaching effectiveness, and fortunately, taking that path is something over which we teachers have direct control. Engaged teaching is a complex process that centers on the intellectual effort that teachers willingly invest in the service of teaching. Thus, engaged teaching is comprised of a *foundation* and a *process* that leads to the desirable result of effective teaching. In the following sections, we share our Model for Engaged Teaching.

## The Model Foundation: Intellectual Effort

Whether an instructor is teaching onsite or online or a hybrid of the two, this intellectual investment requires a full range of effort. Engaged teachers employ the core functions of the mind — thinking, feeling, doing — as they fulfill their instructional roles and responsibilities. This allows them to engage with their work not only cognitively but also affectively and conatively.

- The *cognitive element* of engaged teaching is connected to thinking. Cognition refers to the conscious mental processes of coming to know and understand as we encode, store, process, and retrieve information. This element is related to "Knowing What," since knowing more about something can help one better understand it.

- The *affective element* of engaged teaching is connected to emotions or feelings. Affect refers to the emotional interpretation of perceptions, information, or knowledge. It means coming to value or appreciate something. This element is related to "Knowing Why," since knowing why something is useful or valuable can improve one's feelings about it.

- The *conative element* of engaged teaching is connected to the intention or plan to do something. Conation is closely associated with the concept of volition, defined as the use of will, or the freedom to make choices about what to do. It includes the intentional, deliberate, goal-oriented, or striving component of motivation and behavior and is critical for engaging in self-direction and self-regulation. This element is related to "Knowing How," since knowing how to do something can affect one's intention to engage with it.

Engaged teaching requires effort in all three of these core mental areas: cognition (thinking), affect (feeling), and conation (doing). Put simply, engaged teachers work to deepen their knowledge of the what, why, and how of effective teaching.

These three elements combine in an interconnected process to create a unified whole. As an engaged teacher invests the intellectual effort to increase their knowledge of any single element, that knowledge influences and enriches knowledge of the other elements. We use the trefoil knot in Figure 1.1: The Engaged Teaching Model Foundation to illustrate the intertwining nature of our conception of the effort involved in engaged teaching.

| **KNOWING WHAT**<br>What is this particular concept that applies to teaching? In what ways does it contribute to effective teaching? |
|---|
| **KNOWING WHY**<br>Why should I do this? What is my purpose? What value can it add to student learning? |
| **KNOWING HOW**<br>How can I do this? How can I take action to achieve this concept in ways that improve student learning? |

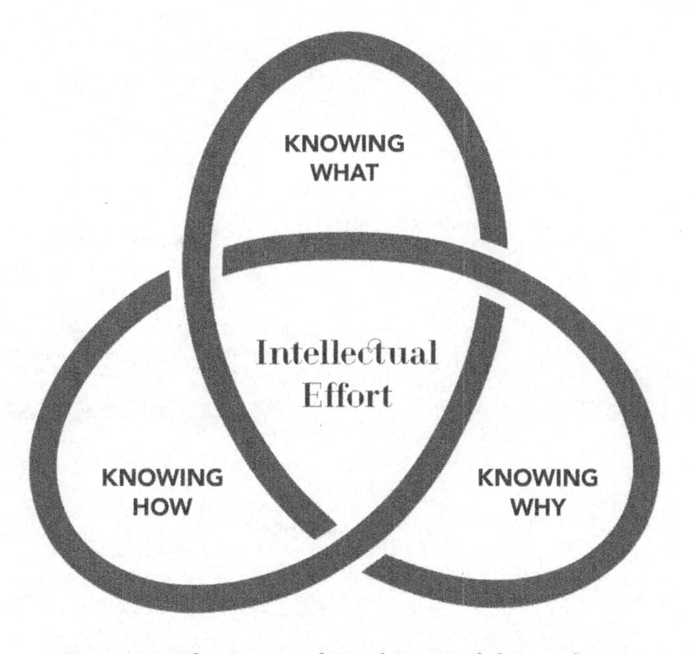


**Figure 1.1. The Engaged Teaching Model Foundation**

## The Model Process: Applying Intellectual Effort to Five Core Elements of Teaching

Engaged teaching happens when teachers work to deepen their knowledge of the what, why, and how of effective teaching in five core elements.

1. **Foundations:** Engaged teachers develop foundational knowledge of teaching and learning.

2. **Planning:** Engaged teachers produce a plan for instruction by setting significant learning goals and selecting coordinated assessments.

3. **Climate:** Engaged teachers establish a positive learning climate by striving to motivate students, to teach for equity and inclusion, and to create community.

4. **Methods:** Engaged teachers identify and select the best mix of instructional methods to meet their learning goals.

5. **Improvement:** Engaged teachers seek to improve their teaching.

We illustrate our conception of this in Figure 1.2: The Engaged Teaching Model Process.

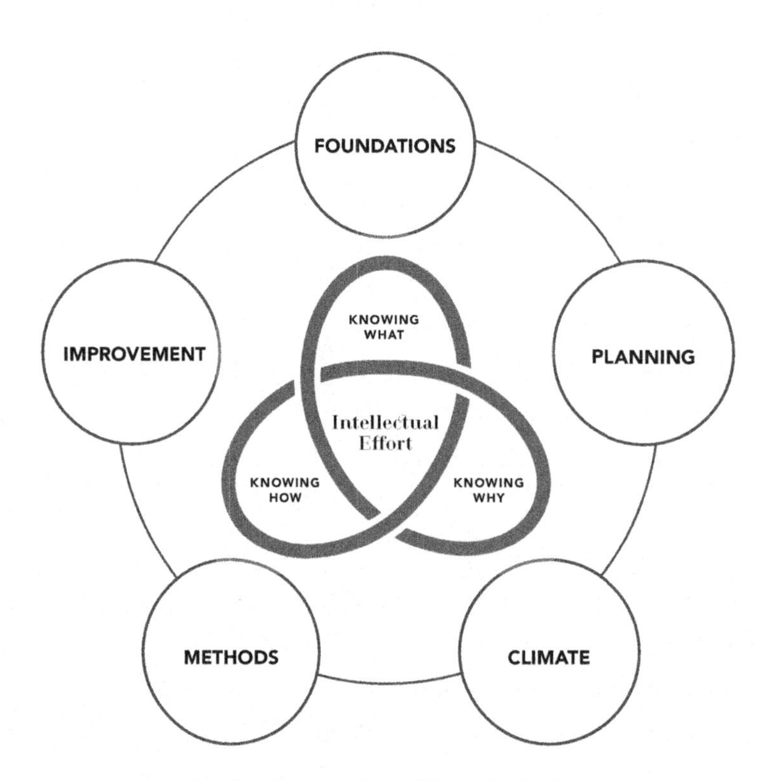


**Figure 1.2. The Engaged Teaching Model Process**

## KNOWING WHY: RESEARCH ON VIEWS OF TEACHING EFFECTIVENESS

Engaged teaching as we define it is a new concept that we set forth with the publication of this book. Thus, researchers have not yet studied engaged teaching directly, particularly the intellectual effort that goes into it. However, researchers have studied the processes involved in engaged teaching, and we discuss these findings in depth in the associated chapters of this book. Researchers have also examined the qualities, characteristics, and habits of effective teachers, which provides us with insights about engaged teaching.

### Are Engaged Teaching and Effective Teaching Really Related?

The literature on excellent teaching suggests that engaged teaching and effective teaching are related, as research focuses on and highlights many of the same domains we have identified as critical for engaged teaching, including faculty knowledge, instructional design, course environment, instructional methods, and teaching improvement. We illustrate overlaps in the core elements of engaged teaching and several key studies on effective teaching in Table 1.1: Research-Based Qualities of Effective/Engaged Teachers.

| | BUSKIST (2018) | BAIN (2004) | CHICKERING & GAMSON (1987) |
|---|---|---|---|
| RESEARCH QUESTION | WHAT IS A "MASTER" COLLEGE TEACHER? | WHAT DO THE "BEST" COLLEGE TEACHERS DO? | WHAT ARE THE PRINCIPLES OF EFFECTIVE UNDERGRADUATE TEACHING? |
| TEACHER KNOWLEDGE | ✓ | ✓ | |
| COURSE AND INSTRUCTIONAL DESIGN | ✓ | ✓ | ✓ |
| COURSE ENVIRONMENT | | ✓ | ✓ |
| INSTRUCTIONAL METHODS | ✓ | ✓ | ✓ |
| TEACHING IMPROVEMENT | ✓ | ✓ | |

**Table 1.1. Research-Based Qualities of Effective/Engaged Teachers**

Clearly, there are overlaps in our conception of engaged teaching and the literature on teaching effectiveness. We offer this distinction: Engaged teaching is a process while effective teaching is an outcome. Thus, it is worthwhile for those who strive for engaged teaching to know what the research says on effective teaching.

## Teacher and Student Views of Effective Teaching

Several researchers have investigated whether teachers and students agree on what constitutes effective teaching. In an early study attempting to answer this question, Feldman (1988) examined 31 previous research reports in which instructors and students listed descriptors associated with effective teaching. Teachers placed emphasis on setting high standards, being academically challenging, motivating students, and pushing self-directed learning. On the other hand, the top three words students used to describe effective teachers were these: interesting, approachable, and clear. Teachers largely valued the technical skills of teaching. Students, however, more highly valued social skills.

In a similarly focused study, Layne (2012) examined contrasting student and teacher definitions of teaching effectiveness. Layne argued that understanding differing viewpoints "is crucial to faculty and administrators when interpreting student survey results" (p. 43). To identify the diverging faculty and student definitions, Layne used teacher and student responses to form a list of 30 potential definitions of teaching effectiveness. Then, following additional rounds of revision and pretesting, she instructed student and faculty cohorts to determine which four definitions best reflected effective teaching.

How did faculty definitions differ from student responses? Below are the top definitions identified by teachers as well as the percentage of respondents who identified the description as one of their four best definitions (also noted in Weimer, 2014):

- loves the subject; knows the subject material well (50%);
- is organized, well-prepared for class (44%);
- uses a variety of teaching methods and formats (41%);
- cares about the success of students (31%);
- motivates students to do well in the course (25%);
- outlines course expectations clearly and accurately (22%); and
- encourages questions and feedback from students (22%).

In contrast, these are the top definitions listed by students and the percentage who identified the description as one of their top four definitions:

- keeps students interested for the whole class period; makes the class enjoyable (45%);
- loves the subject; knows the subject material well (34%);
- interacts with students; takes a hands-on approach to the subject (29%);
- uses a variety of teaching methods or formats (24%);
- is accessible to students (23%); and
- is patient and flexible when dealing with students' problems (21%).

Where did student and teacher definitions overlap? Both groups identified the importance of knowing and loving their subject matter. And both groups championed the use of a variety of teaching methods.

And where did student and teacher definitions diverge? While the most popular definition among students was "keeps students interested for the whole period," just 6% of teachers listed that description among their top definitions. And while 44% of teachers answered that an effective teacher "is organized, well-prepared for class," this definition was important to just 13% of student respondents. The differences identified by Layne (2012) affirm Feldman's (1988) research, suggesting that students place a premium on the social, relational, and communication aspects of teaching, while instructors most highly value academic rigor and the instructional process. Of course, both groups are likely correct. Academic rigor and social processes may legitimately improve college-level learning. It's interesting, however, that neither teachers nor students ranked the achievement of learning outcomes highly among their descriptions.

## Teacher and Student Views of Ineffective Teaching

Research on *ineffective* teaching supports Feldman's (1988) and Layne's (2012) findings as well. For example, Zayac et al. (2021) reported on the results from two studies. In the first study, researchers surveyed 70 students and 105 faculty at a small private university. For the second study, they surveyed 621 students and 59 faculty from a regional comprehensive university. Table 1.2: Student and Teacher Ratings of the Worst Qualities for Teachers summarizes the results.

| RATINGS OF THE WORST QUALITIES FOR TEACHERS | | | | | | | |
|---|---|---|---|---|---|---|---|
| **STUDENTS** | | | | **TEACHERS** | | | |
| **STUDY 1 • SMALL PRIVATE UNIVERSITY** | | **STUDY 2 • REGIONAL COMPREHENSIVE** | | **STUDY 1 • SMALL PRIVATE UNIVERSITY** | | **STUDY 2 • REGIONAL COMPREHENSIVE** | |
| Disrespectful | 64% | Disrespectful | 57% | Disrespectful | 69% | Disrespectful | 70% |
| Having Unrealistically High Expectations | 53% | Having Unrealistically High Expectations | 47% | Lack of Knowledge | 51% | Poor Communication Skills | 57% |
| Not Caring | 51% | Not Being Accessible/ Helpful | 44% | Not Caring | 45% | Lack of Knowledge | 54% |
| **SOURCE:** Zayac, R. M., Poole, B. D., Gray, C., Sargent, M., Paulk, A., & Haynes, E. (2021). No disrespect: Student and faculty perceptions of the qualities of ineffective teachers. Teaching of Psychology, 48(1), 55-62. | | | | | | | |

**Table 1.2. Student and Teacher Ratings of the Worst Qualities for Teachers**

Thus, while faculty and students alike rated being disrespectful as the biggest indicator of poor teaching, students focused more on caring, while faculty focused more on knowledge. Once again, this finding highlights that faculty were more concerned about cognitive and technical skills, while students cared more about affective and social skills.

When taken together, all of this research suggests that engaged teachers can be effective teachers when they employ the three core functions of the mind — thinking, feeling, doing — as they invest effort in effectively completing teaching's essential tasks.

## KNOWING HOW: ABOUT THIS BOOK

While many of us likely recognize the value of an engaged teaching approach, it can be a challenge to determine exactly how to go about the process. To accomplish the goal of engaged teaching, we encourage you to continue with this book, as it has been carefully designed and written to support you in your efforts.

## Book Organization

The book is organized into five parts that correspond to the five core elements of the engaged teaching model identified in the "Knowing What" section above. The five parts are further subdivided into three chapters that address topics that support each of the parts. Our conception of the integration of the engaged teaching model and the book organization is displayed in Figure 1.3: Integration of Engaged Teaching Model and Book Organization.

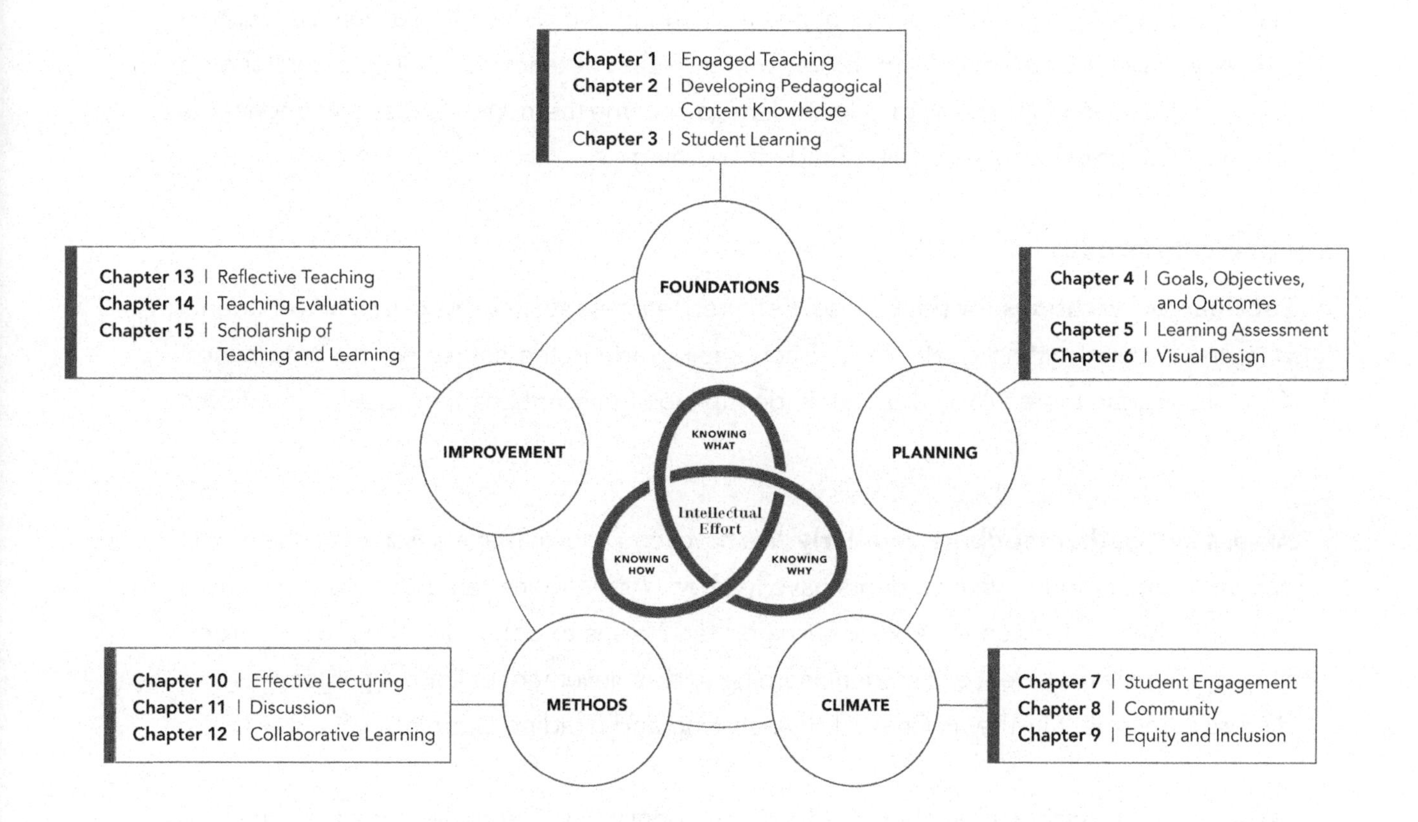


**Figure 1.3. Integration of Engaged Teaching Model and Book Organization**

In preview, we offer the following advice and information about each topic along with the corresponding book chapter and title where you can learn more.

## Part 1: Foundations

**Understand what "engaged teaching" is.** To work efficiently and effectively toward becoming an engaged teacher, it is helpful to understand what it is. In Chapter 1 (the chapter you are currently reading) we offer our argument for what engaged teaching is, why it is important, and how you can achieve it in your own teaching.

**Learn about teaching.** To be an engaged and ultimately effective teacher, it is essential to develop and maintain expertise in your content area. Knowing about pedagogy is equally important. But where engaged teaching really happens is when these two are best combined to improve student learning. We discuss teacher knowledge in Chapter 2: Developing Pedagogical Content Knowledge.

**Understand how students learn.** Being an engaged teacher means developing and maintaining expertise in the theories of human learning and developing a clear conception of how you believe students learn. Moreover, engaging in teaching means understanding challenges to learning and how to help students overcome them. We discuss these concepts further in Chapter 3: Understanding Student Learning.

## Part 2: Planning

**Set clear expectations for the course.** Engaged teachers strive to make it clear to students what the course learning goals are and how their grade in the course will be determined. We discuss goals more fully in Chapter 4: Identifying Significant Learning Goals, Objectives, and Outcomes.

**Assess and gather feedback regularly.** We have long known that assessment can provide rich information about what students have learned. Assessment can also help to promote learning. Thus, one essential task for engaged teachers is to determine the most appropriate ways to collect evidence of student learning and achievement of learning objectives. We discuss assessment further in Chapter 5: Assessing and Grading Learning.

**Work on visual design.** One often overlooked responsibility of engaged instructors is visual design. Yet is it critical to determine the most effective ways to improve the clarity, aesthetic appeal, usability, and function of instructional products. If we don't, we may impede learning, but if we do invest the time in effective visual design, we can promote it. We discuss visual design concepts further in Chapter 6: Attending to Visual Elements in Teaching.

## Part 3: Climate

**Strive to engage students.** Student engagement is a watchword today. Drawing upon the knowledge base to create learning environments and select learning activities that encourage students to value learning and to expect to succeed at it is an essential goal for engaged instructors. We discuss this concept further in Chapter 7: Engaging Students.

**Develop a community of learners.** Students flourish in courses where they bond with their classmates and work together productively. When engaging in your work, strive to build a vibrant learning community. This helps promote positive social skills and academic achievement. We discuss the concept of community further in Chapter 8: Supporting Community.

**Promote equity and inclusion.** All students need to be encouraged and empowered to learn. It is important for the engaged teacher to try to inspire all students intellectually, socially, emotionally, and politically in the service of learning. We discuss these concepts in Chapter 9: Promoting Equity and Inclusion.

## Part 4: Methods

**Use lectures effectively.** Most college instructors lecture at some point; the challenge is to do it well. Good lecturers share information with students in a way that draws upon physical presence, verbal message, and visual message. We discuss lecturing further in Chapter 10: Lecturing Effectively.

**Facilitate discussions.** Many college instructors use discussions in class. Discussions can take a variety of forms. Good discussions are an open-ended, collaborative exchange of ideas and information among a teacher and students or among students for the purpose of furthering students' learning. We discuss this concept more fully in Chapter 11: Facilitating Discussion.

**Use collaborative learning techniques.** Engaged teachers often design strategies for two or more learners working together to solve problems, complete tasks, or learn new concepts to enhance learning through working together. We discuss collaborative learning more fully in Chapter 12: Implementing Collaborative Learning.

## Part 5: Improvement

Reflect on teaching. One of the more challenging tasks for engaged instructors is to examine underlying beliefs about teaching and learning and their alignment with actual classroom practice before, during and after a course is taught. We may not feel we have time to engage with reflection, yet it can make a critical difference in our teaching. We discuss this idea further in Chapter 13: Reflecting on Teaching.

**Assess and evaluate teaching.** It can be important to gather evidence on our teaching. Knowing how what we're doing affects student learning can help us improve for the next time. We discuss this further in Chapter 14: Assessing and Evaluating Teaching.

**Engage in the scholarship of teaching and learning.** After we gather information, it is important to further our profession by adding back to the knowledge base. Scholarship of Teaching and Learning (SoTL) can allow us to do so. We discuss SoTL further in Chapter 15: Engaging in the Scholarship of Teaching and Learning.

## Chapter Organization

As you read this book, you will notice that each chapter is organized into three main sections, each corresponding to one of the three core functions of intellectual effort for engaged teaching that is at the core of our model.

- **Knowing what:** In this section, we provide information to develop and deepen your understanding of the chapter topic. This knowledge can enhance awareness and readiness to engage.
- **Knowing why:** This section highlights the critical research on the topic. It is intended to help you appreciate the value of understanding, engaging with, and applying this concept in your own courses. Knowing why brings desire and willingness to engage.
- **Knowing how:** This section focuses on the topic with an intent to help you plan practical approaches to implementing the concept in your own courses. You will also find references to The K. Patricia Cross Academy (Cross Academy). In particular, we will refer to Cross Academy Techniques (CATs). CATs are 50 practical, research-based teaching tools that can be adapted to fit a wide variety of disciplines, instructional goals, and learning contexts. You can find short 2- to 3-minute videos that provide information about how to implement a teaching technique in both onsite and online course environments. We will also refer to Cross Academy blog posts. These references may be found at the K. Patricia Cross Academy web site: *kpcrossacademy.org*. Each video is also accompanied by a downloadable information sheet/template for you to adapt the technique in your own courses. Knowing how increases the abilities and skills necessary to engage.

Thus, the book is carefully constructed to guide you through the necessary steps to become a fully engaged teacher.

## CONCLUSION

Perhaps more than at any other time in history, we need effective college teachers. One way to become an effective teacher is to begin by being an engaged teacher. This means intellectually, emotionally, and conatively engaging with the complicated art and craft of teaching. We define this process as intellectual inquiry into the what/why/how of five core elements of teaching. These five elements include:

1. developing a foundational knowledge base,
2. planning the course,
3. establishing the climate,
4. choosing the best instructional methods, and
5. continuously improving your teaching.

This book and its companion website — The K. Patricia Cross Academy — provide a carefully constructed framework to support you in your efforts. Together, we can reexamine the conditions that promote student learning and find creative solutions to the complex challenges involved in teaching effectively. We can acknowledge the powerful influence we teachers have on student learning and find the best ways to capitalize on that. With its focus on Knowing What, Knowing Why, and Knowing How in relation to key aspects of college teaching, this book is intended to help current and future college teachers become effective, engaged teachers.

## FOCUS ON ONLINE TEACHING

The information we share in the main body of this chapter applies to both onsite and online teaching, but here we provide additional insights focused specifically on teaching online, hybrid, and blended courses.

### What: Engaged Teaching Online

Engaged online teaching isn't based solely on the ability to navigate a learning management system (LMS), hold a Zoom class session, or create a Google doc or Padlet page. Rather, engaged teaching online relies on how instructors develop the knowledge they need to teach online, design courses and materials, respond to and engage with students, select instructional approaches, and seek to learn and improve on what they've done.

### Why: Engaged and Effective Teaching Online

As one might predict, research indicates similarities between effective teaching online and onsite. A study by Young (2006) investigated student opinions of online instruction in higher education courses. Seven items emerged as key components from this survey of 199 online students. Effective teaching online involved:

- adapting to student needs,
- motivating students to do their best,
- showing concern for student learning,
- providing meaningful examples,
- delivering a valuable course,
- facilitating the course effectively, and
- communicating effectively.

The research indicated that, while social and relational factors are important, students also valued academic processes. In response to open-ended questions, students wrote that effective online instructors are visibly involved in education, work diligently to gain students' trust, and establish a structured, but adaptable online classroom environment.

In a study examining the validity of a tool for gauging online teaching effectiveness, Ravenscroft et al. (2017) affirmed some of Young's (2006) findings. In this study, researchers examined focus group data from 6 department heads, 4 faculty, and 11 students, in addition to survey data from 871 students. Students and teachers agreed that effective communication and teacher responsiveness in online teaching were important evaluation criteria, but their respective roles as instructor and student also led to differences. Students placed a premium on course design, whereas teachers were less likely to consider that among their evaluation criteria, perhaps because some online teachers did not design the structure of the course.

### How: Engaged Teaching Online

Many of us have had to move our teaching online. And what we learned from this move is that a good number of the things that we believed about onsite teaching hold true in an online space. They may play out differently, but the basic elements of engaged teaching are the same. Thus, when we write about the different aspects of engaged teaching in each chapter, the information holds true for both onsite and online teaching. In each chapter of this book, however, we also include a section that focuses specifically on teaching online. In these sections, we consider the "what," "why," and "how" of engaged teaching online and offer practical suggestions and advice for engaging in online teaching.

**RELATED CROSS ACADEMY RESOURCES**

- **Cross Academy** (video library)
  *kpcrossacademy.org*
- **Cross Academy Downloads** (template library)
  *kpcrossacademy.org/downloads*
- **Cross Currents** (blog)
  *kpcrossacademy.org/news*

*Faculty who understand their discipline and observe student learning have an excellent chance of making a contribution to knowledge as well as to the improvement of their own teaching.*

**—K. PATRICIA CROSS**

CHAPTER 2

# Developing Pedagogical Content Knowledge

We were hired as college professors because our institutions deemed we had acquired sufficient specialized knowledge to be qualified to profess it. Higher education's guild-based classification of degrees was designed to certify the progression from novice to expert, and possessing these credentials remains a required first step toward becoming a member of the professoriate. This deep, disciplinary expertise is one of the critical factors distinguishing us from other avenues students currently have for accessing knowledge. We are therefore expected to enter the classroom as subject matter experts.

While it is generally accepted that we must have in-depth disciplinary content knowledge, it is less universally accepted that we should also have deep knowledge of teaching. Every other profession prepares its people for practice. As students pursue legal, medical, engineering, and a host of other professional and vocational degrees, they are given ample opportunities to perform the tasks they will do in their future careers — if not during their education, then after completion in the form of apprentices, internships, and mentorships. In marked contrast, when many of us first entered a classroom or started to teach online, it was a daunting experience for which we were ill-prepared, and we were most often expected to go it alone. This makes us likely to use the same approaches that our teachers used, thus perpetuating the potentially poor or outdated teaching methods that may have worked for us, but may be ineffective with a large number of students today.

As engaged teachers, we strive to bridge this knowledge gap. We recognize that not only should we have deep knowledge about our disciplines, but we should also have deep knowledge about teaching. Lacking such knowledge, we cannot be truly effective in our teaching roles. Thus, as engaged faculty, we strive to balance our subject matter expertise with knowledge about teaching and learning.

## KNOWING WHAT: ABOUT PEDAGOGICAL CONTENT KNOWLEDGE

Disciplinary content knowledge is the essential element that qualifies a college profess or to teach. But effective teachers also know how to guide students in their own acquisition of this knowledge. The method and practice by which teachers impart this knowledge to students in an educational context is called pedagogy. Most educators today recognize that in order to be effective, teachers need two types of knowledge:

- **Disciplinary content knowledge**, which consists of the theories, principles, and concepts of a given subject as well as the syntactic and substantive structures of the subject.
- **Pedagogical knowledge**, which includes knowledge of how students learn, effective teaching strategies, assessment methods, and classroom management.

These two types of knowledge have traditionally been thought of as separate entities, each existing in isolation from the other. Renowned educator Lee Shulman (1986, 1987), one of the first researchers to investigate what teachers should know to be effective, challenged this division.

Recognizing the importance of preparing teachers in both content knowledge and pedagogical knowledge, Shulman (1986) asked "[w]hy this sharp distinction between content and pedagogical process" existed (p. 6). He argued that instead of being separate concepts, effective teaching actually is borne out of the overlap between subject matter knowledge and pedagogical knowledge. The blending of these two bases of knowledge helps teachers identify the best ways of presenting their subjects so that they can transform them into something that learners can comprehend.

Shulman (1986) referred to this overlap as *pedagogical content knowledge* (PCK) and defined it as "that special amalgam of content and pedagogy that is uniquely the province of teachers, their own special form of professional understanding" (p. 8). PCK is the combination of "content and pedagogy into an understanding of how particular topics, problems, or issues are organized, represented, and adapted to the diverse interests and abilities of learners, and presented for instruction" (Shulman, 1987, p. 8). Shulman further described pedagogical content knowledge as "an understanding of what makes the learning of specific topics easy or difficult: the conceptions and preconceptions that students of different ages and background bring with them to the learning of those most frequently taught topics and lessons" (1987, pp. 9-10).

PCK involves "the skill to transfer the topic from the teacher's knowing to the student's knowing" (Fernandez-Balboa & Stiehl, 1995). The act of examining content and identifying how best to communicate it to students begins the knowledge transformation and communication process that is the core of teaching. This concept of PCK as the interaction between disciplinary knowledge and pedagogical knowledge suggests that the most effective teaching is that which is performed within the space where the two types of knowledge overlap. We illustrate PCK in Figure 2.1: Pedagogical Content Knowledge (PCK).

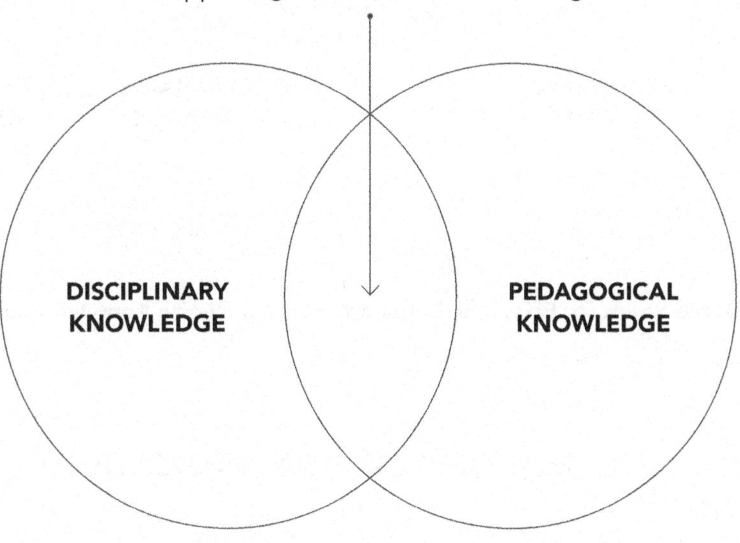


**Figure 2.1. Pedagogical Content Knowledge (PCK)**

As we have argued elsewhere (Barkley & Major, 2016), this interaction also suggests that when there is insufficient disciplinary or pedagogical knowledge, the capacity for effective teaching shrinks, as indicated in Figure 2.2: Reduced Space for Effective, Engaged Teaching Due to Knowledge Imbalance.

The best teachers usually have robust knowledge, of both their discipline and pedagogy. We recognize that some teachers have acquired pedagogical knowledge without formal instruction and that they make good teaching choices based primarily on replicating or avoiding practices they observed as former students themselves. We also acknowledge that for centuries, students have been able to learn from professors who possessed deep knowledge of their discipline but did not give a hoot about teaching. (We suspect, however, that many of these students were already capable learners or quickly learned to become capable). Accepting that there are exceptions, we propose that, as a general rule, one needs both disciplinary and pedagogical knowledge to be an excellent and effective college professor today.

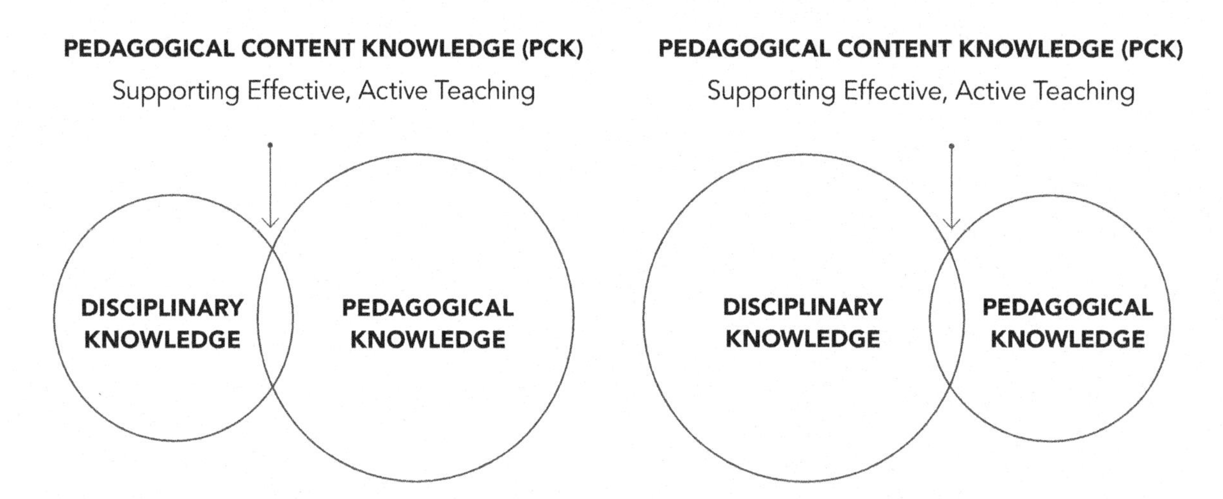


**Figure 2.2. Reduced Space for Effective, Engaged Teaching Due to Knowledge Imbalance**

## KNOWING WHY: RESEARCH ON PCK AND IMPLICATIONS FOR EDUCATION

The concept of pedagogical content knowledge suggests that instructors' disciplinary content knowledge pairs with pedagogical knowledge to develop a new knowledge form that has practical application for teaching. Examinations of faculty knowledge have generally focused on this evolution. For instance, Grossman et al. (1989) found that instructors' beliefs about their discipline along with beliefs about students, schools, and the nature of teaching and learning combine to "powerfully affect their teaching" (p. 31). Stark (2000) determined that teachers' beliefs about knowledge related to their discipline had the greatest effect on their lesson planning and course design. Other researchers have focused on how experienced teachers differ from less experienced instructors in their understanding of their disciplines and the differences in teachers' ability to plan instruction and share information effectively; experienced teachers are better able to plan and deliver instruction (Grant, 1988; Hashweh, 1987; Leinhardt & Smith, 1985; Lenze & Dinham, 1994, 1999). Additionally, faculty members' expectations for how their students will learn and what students should learn has a direct influence on how they approach teaching, even in a narrowly defined subject matter context (Martin et al., 2000).

What research generally indicates is that teachers' pedagogical choices are influenced by what teachers know, and their choices affect student engagement and learning. To illustrate, Andrews et al. (2019) examined how PCK was used to plan, implement, and reflect on engaged learning tasks. The researchers determined that expert instructors were more likely to display their pedagogical knowledge than novice teachers. They also ascertained that a lack of pedagogical knowledge inhibited a teacher's effectiveness as well as the development of new pedagogical content knowledge (Andrews et al., 2019).

Additionally, Hativa (2000) found that improvements to pedagogical content knowledge can increase student satisfaction. For example, in a case study of two law professors who had consistently received poor student evaluations for several years, their student surveys improved and remained at higher levels for 18 months after they participated in professional development. Furthermore, researchers have suggested that "due to the intersection and integrative character of PCK, enhancing any [single PCK component] will also enhance PCK as a whole" (Fernandez-Balboa & Stiehl, 1995, p. 294).

Researchers have also found that pedagogical content knowledge doesn't just happen; rather, it takes time and effort to develop. As Shulman (1987) noted, experienced instructors have practical knowledge that they have developed through their years of teaching such that they have accumulated the "wisdom of practice." Qualitative research involving interviews with faculty has shown that teachers learn not only from intentionally studying (as you are doing by reading this book) but also from action and reflection, collaboration with other faculty, and careful examination of students and their work (Major & Dolly, 2003).

## KNOWING HOW: AN ENGAGED APPROACH TO DEVELOPING AND USING PCK

While pedagogical content knowledge is an interesting theoretical construct that clearly influences the act of teaching, how can teachers intentionally develop this knowledge? We recommend a combination of inventorying and refreshing both disciplinary and pedagogical knowledge bases and then striving to ensure they align.

### Inventory and Refresh Content Knowledge

A teacher's content knowledge is difficult to categorize or to articulate and record. As college teachers, we usually have spent years, even decades, developing our content knowledge bases, and as such, much of our knowledge is tacit rather than explicit. It can be useful, therefore, to take stock of our existing content knowledge base related to a specific topic prior to teaching it. Taking an inventory can help you to identify and locate knowledge assets or gaps. Lundvall and Johnson (1994) identified several different kinds of knowledge that provide a good starting place for an inventory:

- **Knowledge about facts.** This knowledge is explicit and can be standardized and formalized.
- **Knowledge of scientific principles and laws of nature.** This knowledge may involve individual interpretation that is based upon experience and intuition, and hence it is not standardized. It differs among individuals and reflects prior knowledge and the personal experiences that help them understand why things work the way that they do.
- **Knowledge about how to do something.** This knowledge consists of a set of practical or theoretical skills, which tends to be discipline- or field- specific.
- **Knowledge about who can help.** This knowledge involves knowing who knows what and who knows how to do what. It is not standardized or formalized; rather, it is highly localized and individualized. To take stock of this knowledge, consider developing a Personal Learning Environment of your own (CAT 19).

It can be a useful exercise to simply walk through these different types of knowledge bases to examine what you already know about a topic you are about to teach. Such a review likely means rereading the chapter or article you assigned or revisiting your lecture notes or any videos you have produced. Also, identify any gaps and update your knowledge accordingly. The goal is not only to remember but also to refresh and replenish.

## Review Your Pedagogical Options

Faculty members' beliefs either legitimize or exclude a variety of pedagogical techniques that teachers find appropriate or inappropriate for their field and with their students. In Part 4 of this book, we address three key instructional activities and outline specific techniques for carrying them out.

- **Lecture:** an educational talk to an audience; particularly useful for helping students develop foundational knowledge
- **Discussion:** a conversation or debate about a certain topic; useful for developing foundational knowledge and for helping students integrate and apply knowledge

- **Collaborative learning:** a strategy that encourages small groups of students to work together for the achievement of a common goal; particularly helpful for having students apply knowledge and use higher order thinking skills

## Conduct an Instructional Alignment Analysis for Fit Between Content and Pedagogy

In an Instructional Alignment Analysis, a teacher determines that the content to be taught and the methods used to teach it are aligned. For example, focusing on the three key instructional activities identified above, a lecture may be most appropriate for helping students learn information and ideas. Whole-class discussion may be particularly effective for helping students see different perspectives or make connections between concepts or opinions. Collaborative learning may be the best choice for ensuring that students apply their newly acquired knowledge to real situations through critical and creative thinking, problem solving, or performance. For a more comprehensive approach, consider Figure 2.3: Instructional Alignment Analysis as a guide for your analysis.

To summarize, your purpose in developing pedagogical content knowledge is to teach in ways that clearly enhance student learning. This requires considering how students learn and then using this information to guide adjustment of your teaching approach. While creating a broad Instructional Alignment Analysis can be a worthy long-term goal, there are many small steps you can take that make an immediate impact and contribute considerably to aligning content and pedagogy. For example, you can take time to clarify what is really important for students to learn about your content as opposed to thinking primarily about what you want to teach. You can establish what students already know and believe about your subject so that you can determine the best starting place for instruction. You can also try to understand who your students are so that you can better adjust for the differences that could arise from cultural backgrounds, preparation for college-level work, learning preferences, and interests.

Visit the K. Patricia Cross Academy (*kpcrossacademy.org*) for videos, downloads, and regular blogs on current trends and issues to help you increase your PCK. Taking stock of both the disciplinary and pedagogical knowledge bases you possess and then striving to ensure alignment can have a significant impact on the effectiveness of your teaching.

**Figure 2.3. Instructional Alignment Analysis**

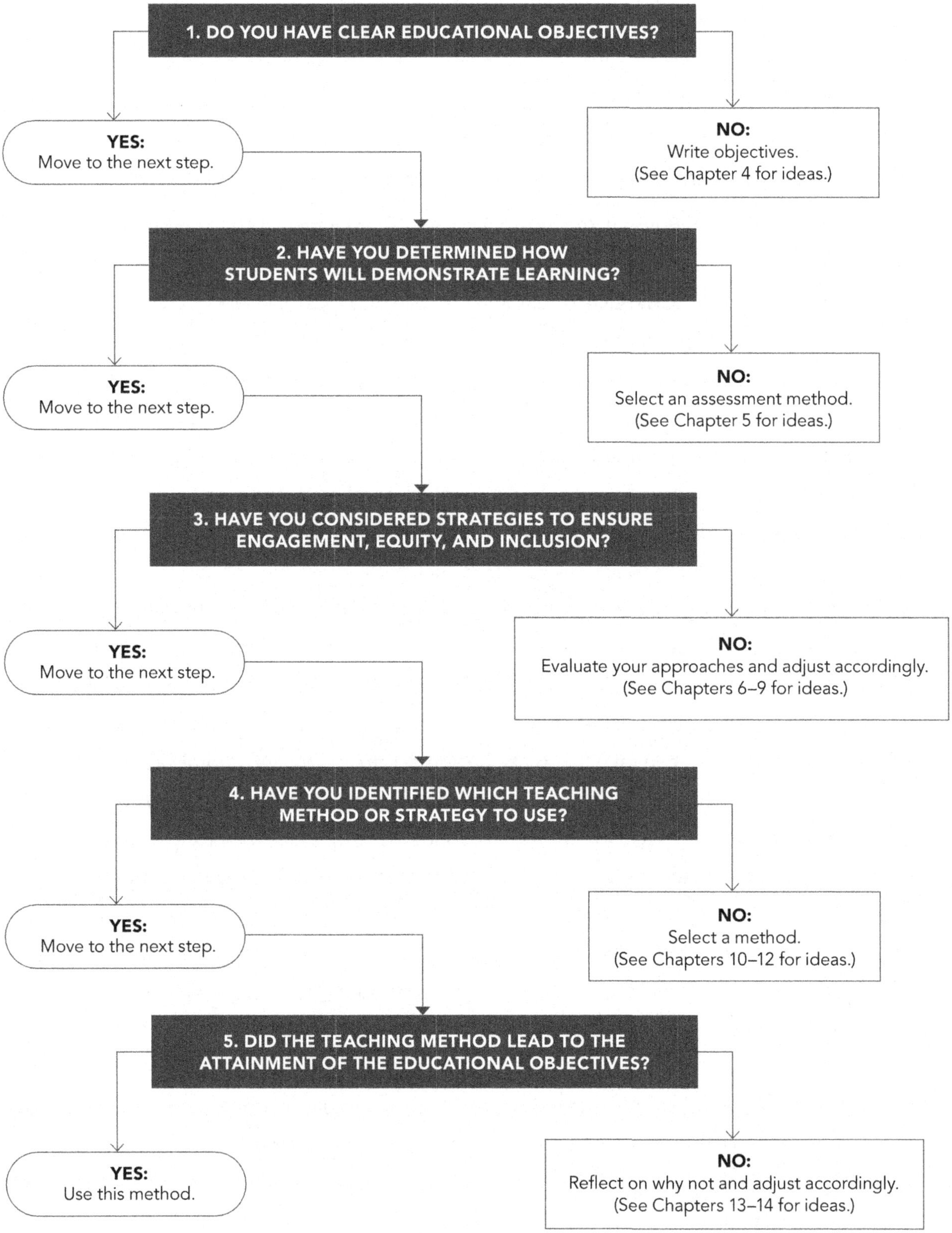

**1. DO YOU HAVE CLEAR EDUCATIONAL OBJECTIVES?**

**YES:**
Move to the next step.

**NO:**
Write objectives.
(See Chapter 4 for ideas.)

**2. HAVE YOU DETERMINED HOW STUDENTS WILL DEMONSTRATE LEARNING?**

**YES:**
Move to the next step.

**NO:**
Select an assessment method.
(See Chapter 5 for ideas.)

**3. HAVE YOU CONSIDERED STRATEGIES TO ENSURE ENGAGEMENT, EQUITY, AND INCLUSION?**

**YES:**
Move to the next step.

**NO:**
Evaluate your approaches and adjust accordingly.
(See Chapters 6–9 for ideas.)

**4. HAVE YOU IDENTIFIED WHICH TEACHING METHOD OR STRATEGY TO USE?**

**YES:**
Move to the next step.

**NO:**
Select a method.
(See Chapters 10–12 for ideas.)

**5. DID THE TEACHING METHOD LEAD TO THE ATTAINMENT OF THE EDUCATIONAL OBJECTIVES?**

**YES:**
Use this method.

**NO:**
Reflect on why not and adjust accordingly.
(See Chapters 13–14 for ideas.)

## CONCLUSION

One key to effective teaching is to be intentional about one's development of both disciplinary and pedagogical knowledge. Deficits in either knowledge base can undermine success in promoting student learning. As engaged teachers, we strive to stay up to date in our disciplinary knowledge, but we also keep trying to expand our pedagogical content knowledge. We must consider how best to teach a given unit of content to a specific group of students in a particular educational environment. Given that very few of us have had formal training on how to teach, applying pedagogical knowledge is not an easy task, but it is both a necessary and a rewarding one.

## FOCUS ON TEACHING ONLINE

The information we share in the main body of this chapter applies to both onsite and online teaching, but here we provide additional insights focused specifically on teaching online, hybrid, and blended courses.

College instructors today invariably use technology to support their teaching, and more and more often, instructors are teaching fully online or blended/hybrid courses. Technology has become an integral part of college teaching. So, in addition to developing general pedagogical content knowledge, to best ensure student learning and success, college teachers need to develop an adequate level of knowledge about technology (Major, 2015).

### What: Technological Pedagogical Content Knowledge

Furthering Shulman's (1986, 1987, 1991) ideas, education technologists Mishra and Koehler (2006) identified an additional concept: technological knowledge (TK). Their definition of TK includes knowledge about — and how to use — standard technologies (e.g., dry erase boards and markers), mid-range technologies (e.g., presentation slides), as well as more advanced web-based technologies (e.g., cloud file sharing). The researchers considered the interaction among the three knowledge components (pedagogical knowledge, content knowledge, and technological knowledge) so important that they suggested that the interactions form a new kind of knowledge: technological pedagogical content knowledge (TPACK). They demonstrate their idea in Figure 2.4: Technological Pedagogical Content Knowledge.

Thus, the authors' concept of technological knowledge and TPACK introduces three new combinations of knowledge bases to Shulman's model.

TPACK advances the idea that instructors who teach online need knowledge and expertise that differs from onsite teachers. While all faculty need basic technological knowledge, faculty who teach online must acquire this type of knowledge at a more complex and sophisticated level. They must become familiar with (and perhaps even master) an increasingly large number of newer technology-based tools.

Along with knowledge of what these technologies are and how to use them, online teachers need to develop knowledge about how technology and content interact with pedagogy so that they can choose the technology that best applies to a given learning goal. If, for example, online instructors wish to facilitate discussion, they should be familiar with how discussion

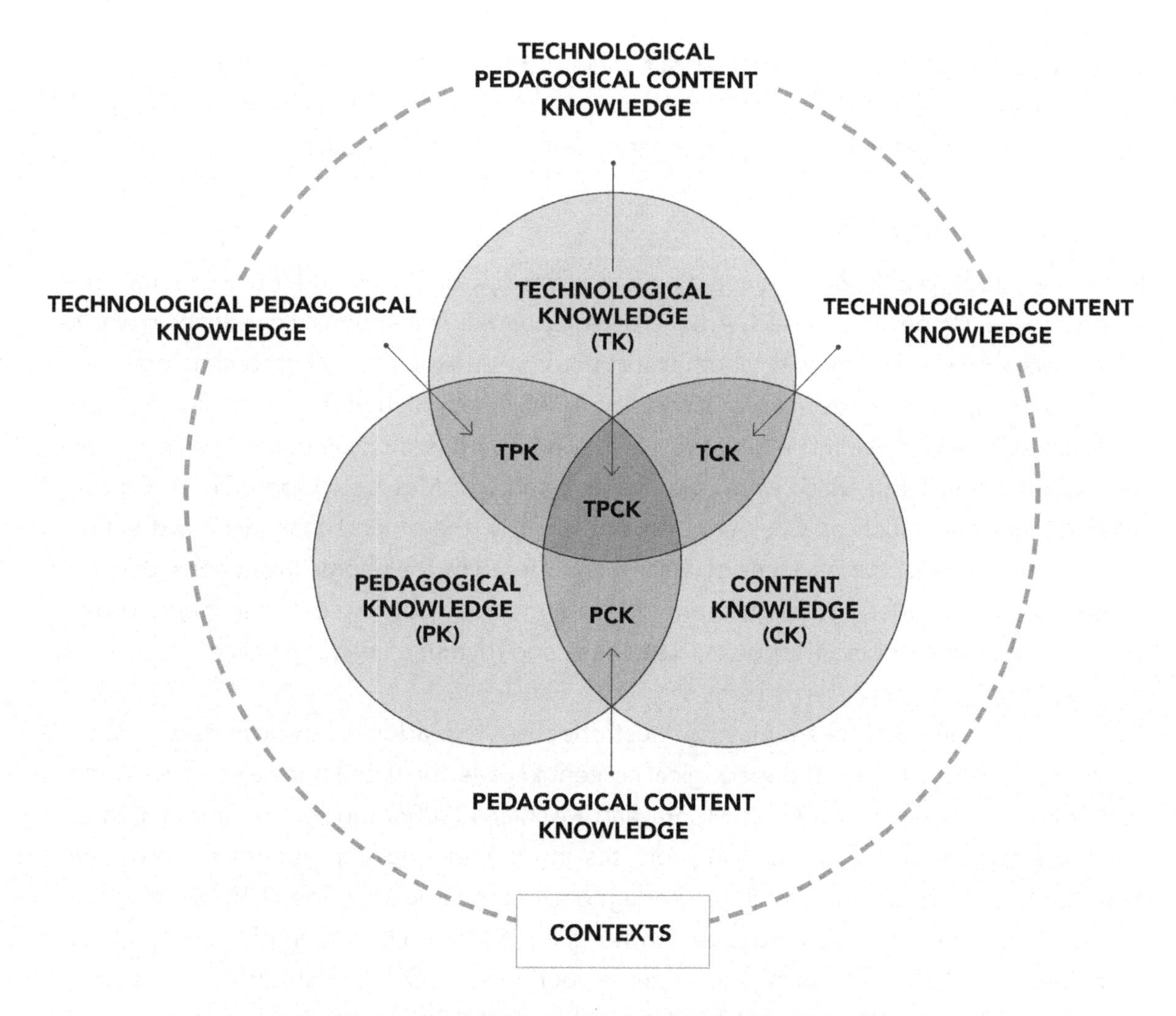


**Figure 2.4. Technological Pedagogical Content Knowledge**
**(Reproduced by permission of the publisher, © 2012 by *tpack.org*)**

can work using various chat, messaging, discussion forum, and videoconferencing methods, as some formats draw out quick reactions while others may lead to deeper thought and reflection. Either result may be effective depending upon the learning goal.

## Why: Research on TPACK

The research suggests that there is a relationship between an instructor's well-developed TPACK and student gains in learning. In examining TPACK specifically, Eichelberger and Leong (2019), for example, compiled a multiple-case study to investigate how faculty beliefs about students' digital literacy and preparation for college in combination with faculty beliefs about teaching online influenced the efficacy of their online teaching. Their results suggested that instructors' beliefs about their students influenced online education in several ways, and that the teaching choices instructors made led to differing results, with stronger knowledge leading to stronger achievement of learning goals.

## How: Developing TPACK

Major and McDonald (2021) conducted a literature review of TPACK and found several studies on how faculty develop TPACK. Among these options is instructional consulting, in which instructors worked directly with another instructor with experience with technology and teaching online. Another avenue for increasing TPACK was through formal faculty development workshops and events held by the institution. A third was online courses, which many institutions offered, but which were also available through Massively Open Online Course (MOOC) providers such as Coursera and EdX. Finally, they found that many instructors enrolled in for-credit courses, some of which were offered by their home institutions. Beyond these more formal offerings, we recommend reading about teaching online and enrolling in an online course to begin to understand the pace and rhythm of learning online.

To summarize, online teachers may be most effective if, in addition to possessing robust content knowledge (CK) and pedagogical content knowledge (PCK), they also have strong technological knowledge (TK). In Mishra and Koehler's (2006) model, the interaction of the three basic forms of knowledge produces three additional categories of knowledge that combine to create technological pedagogical content knowledge (TPACK). Visit the K. Patricia Cross Academy (*kpcrossacademy.org*) for videos on how to implement teaching techniques in your online courses to improve your TPACK. Online instructors with strong TPACK are likely to feel confident teaching online and to make the kind of instructional decisions that result in improved student learning.

*Learning is not so much an additive process, with new learning simply piling up on top of existing knowledge, as it is an active, dynamic process in which the connections are constantly changing and the structure reformatted.*

**—K. PATRICIA CROSS**

CHAPTER 3

# Understanding Student Learning

Learning does not inherently require teaching. Indeed, being "self-taught" is a bit of a badge of honor. Those who were purported to be autodidacts include Buckminster Fuller, Ernest Hemingway, Karl Marx, Herman Melville, George Bernard Shaw, and Frank Lloyd Wright (Barkley & Major, 2016). That list would certainly be longer if we included non-White males and females. While it is possible to learn without the aid of a teacher, no self-respecting teacher should be proud if students did not learn from their instruction. While one can learn without the help of a teacher, one cannot be an effective teacher if there is no student learning.

To ensure their teaching is as effective as possible, engaged teachers endeavor to understand the basics of human learning. They familiarize themselves with different perspectives about how people learn. They clarify their personal views on learning, recognizing that if they articulate and own their views about learning, they have the potential to make better instructional decisions. They recognize that when they are knowledgeable about learning's inherent challenges, they can use this understanding to help students overcome these challenges. In this chapter, we share four prominent models of learning developed primarily through educational psychology, as well as a neuroscientific perspective on learning. We then identify common learning challenges and offer practical advice on how to address them in ways that can improve both teaching and learning.

## KNOWING WHAT: ABOUT LEARNING

Information about learning is voluminous. Scholars have debated for centuries what comprises learning, what catalyzes it, and what criteria should be used to judge whether it has occurred. There are now many opinions about learning, but despite diverging viewpoints, the majority of scholars agree that learning consists of developing new (or altering prior) knowledge, attitudes, values, skills, or behavior. At its core, then, learning is a process that leads to change.

## Educational Psychology Perspectives on Learning

Theories of learning provide concise descriptions of what learning is, how it happens, and what it involves. Among the key theories of learning from the field of psychology are behaviorism, cognitivism, and constructivism. These theories can guide us as we strive to be engaged teachers by providing us with context and structure for our own understandings of what constitutes learning and how we can best promote it in a given course.

### BEHAVIORISM

Behaviorism is the theory that learning results in an observable, outward change in behavior resulting from the positive and negative reinforcement students receive from their actions and decisions. Behaviorists argue that every behavior can be measured, altered, and developed. Teachers who adhere to a behaviorist approach facilitate student learning by positively reinforcing desired behavior (such as paying attention in class or contributing thoughtfully to classroom discussion), thus promoting the continuation of these behaviors. Even if students don't demonstrate these behaviors early in the course, behaviorists argue that students will improve over time if the behavior is reinforced and undesired behavior is limited through non-reinforcement or, if necessary, extinguished by disincentives or punishment (such as poor grades or point penalties).

Behaviorists propose that the purpose of learning activities is to further the development of skills and accretion of content knowledge. Additionally, behaviorists suggest that learning is reinforced through repetition; therefore, students should be given multiple chances to practice and develop new skills. In behaviorist classrooms, learning occurs when students are able to generalize and use their newly developed knowledge, skills, and understanding in new environments. It is demonstrated, for example, when students provide correct or best answers on their assignments or exams. We see the influence of behaviorism throughout the educational system in the form of grades, detention, praise, awards, and so on.

## COGNITIVISM

The cognitivist learning theory proposes that the mind is a black box that can be opened, analyzed, and understood. To cognitivists, learning is mainly a permanent alteration in learners' brains. Cognitivists are concerned with how the mind receives, processes, and stores information. Learning involves the encoding of new information into the mind in an organized form that allows for retrieval. Meaningful learning occurs when new information is able to connect with pre-existing knowledge and remap neural networks. For cognitivist teachers, learning is content-driven and both linear and sequential.

Effective teaching from a cognitivist perspective involves understanding a student's stage of development and then meeting them where they are. It also means designing coursework in such a way that it helps students transfer knowledge from short-term memory to long-term memory. One strategy a cognitivist might employ is to have students access their prior knowledge so that they are better prepared to process new information. Other approaches might include helping students adopt effective learning strategies or scaffolding student learning by providing temporary supports until students become proficient and no longer require them.

## CONSTRUCTIVISM

Constructivists suggest individual learners build their own knowledge and perception of the world. Students learn through experience and reflection as they engage in a process known as "knowledge construction." Instead of knowledge being an absolute, it is more fluid and personalized, as individuals filter new information through their own realities to make sense of their interactions with others and their environment (Driscoll, 2000). Students bring pre-existing schemata (or schema in the individual form) consisting of their previously learned ideas and facts that have been organized into a meaningful cognitive structure. Thus, students do not enter the classroom tabula rasa (as a blank slate) but instead bring with them their own experiences, backgrounds, and cultural contexts.

Constructivists contend that knowledge changes as a result of exposure to new situations and ideas. In this tradition, a teacher's primary responsibility is to facilitate student learning, not to deliver information. Constructivist teachers propose that effective teaching involves structuring and sequencing learning activities to mimic real-world experiences and to help learners apply their knowledge outside the classroom. In this way, students are encouraged to build their knowledge as they select, interpret, and create meaning in ways that link their various lived experiences into something that is important to them. Students demonstrate what they have learned by completing an authentic task that has personal significance.

## Other Perspectives on Learning

While behaviorism, cognitivism, and constructivism are the three main theories of learning from a psychological perspective, there are other views of how learning happens, including the humanistic perspective from philosophy and new work in educational neuroscience.

### HUMANISM

For humanists, learning is a personal act in which individuals seek knowledge and understanding to fulfill their own potential and expand their awareness of the human condition. Humanists suggest that we learn by watching the behavior of others or by studying significant works of the human intellect and imagination. As we do so, we cultivate an appreciation of human values and achievement. The overarching purpose of teaching is to enable learners to participate in social and cultural communities, understand and empathize with others, and appreciate the variety of perspectives and responses to the human condition.

Effective teachers in the humanist tradition design opportunities for learners to increase their self-awareness and to practice critical thinking, especially by learning to make reasoned judgments that reflect ethical and aesthetic human values. A humanist teacher might, for example, ask students to participate in a role play so that they can experience the emotional and intellectual responses of an assumed identity or imagined circumstance. Several instructional approaches have been developed that reflect humanist values, including approaches such as critical pedagogy (Freire, 1970), service learning, and authentic learning activities.

### NEUROSCIENCE

Beginning in the 1990s, researchers began to observe the brain directly during learning events using tools such as magnetic resonance imaging (MRIs). With these developments and their attendant findings, we have seen a rise of research that focuses on the biological changes that take place in the brain while new information is processed. Neuroscientists continue to make discoveries that help us understand what happens within our brains when we learn.

Brain cells are called neurons. They begin as round cell bodies and then grow as many as 100,000 short branches called dendrites as well as a single long root known as an axon. Neurons receive information through the dendrites and then send the information as a signal down the axon, whereupon chemicals called neurotransmitters are fired across a gap called the synapse to a neighboring neuron. As the neurotransmitter enters the dendrites of this new neuron, it sparks a series of electrochemical reactions that cause the receiving neuron to fire through its axon. Dendrites, therefore, are the main way by which neurons get information (learn), and the axon is the main way the neuron sends the information (teach).

Our brain's neurons are bombarded with thousands of stimuli every moment of our lives. Once stimulated, a neuron stays in a state of readiness for hours or even days, and if the associated network of neurons fires together again, the combination of connections becomes more permanent. As connections are repeated, they are strengthened and we learn. Connections that are not stimulated again decay and we forget. The product of this pattern of neuronal connections firing together and then either being reinforced or decaying is the formation of an extraordinarily complex, interconnected web of about 100 trillion constantly changing connections.

Educational neuroscientists posit that everything we know and understand is preserved as a network of neuronal connections in our brain. As adults, we build on or modify networks that were created through previous learning and experience. If new information connects easily with existing understandings, the information is said to be assimilated. If new information challenges existing understandings, such that the neuronal network needs to be revised, it is said to be accommodated (Svinicki, 2004, p. 11).

As we learn, our neurons grow more dendrites. The more dendrites we have, the better equipped our brains are for learning and retaining new information. Additionally, the greater number of basic neuronal networks we have, the easier it is to form more complex networks. This is why it is so challenging for us to learn things that are brand new, while much easier for us to learn more about something we already know. From a neuroscientific viewpoint, therefore, learning is long-lasting change in neurons and existing neuronal networks. When we promote learning, we are helping students grow dendrites and activate and build on existing neuronal networks.

This work has given birth to a new field of educational neuroscience, one that focuses on the brain and strengths and weaknesses of an individual learner. While the work has seen some criticism (for example, see Bruer, 1997), many believe that the bridge between neuroscience and education has much to offer both fields (for example, see Mason, 2009).

## KNOWING WHY: RESEARCH ON CHALLENGES TO LEARNING

Though most of the research on learning has been framed by cognitive science, most learning challenges apply across a variety of perspectives and theories. In this section, we offer an overview of some of the key challenges to learning. In so doing, we aggregate and integrate several sources, including Ambrose et al., 2010; Chew and Cerbin, 2021; Bransford et al., 1999; and work from our own texts (Barkley & Major, 2016, 2018, 2020; Barkley et al., 2014). Our hope is that by helping you understand these challenges, you can better appreciate how complicated learning is and why it can be difficult for students to accomplish.

### Insufficient Prior Knowledge

Learning requires students to integrate new information or ideas into what they already know. It is not surprising that students' capacity to learn is improved if they have accurate and sufficient prior knowledge (Ambrose et al., 2010). Similarly, their capacity to learn is challenged if there are gaps in prior knowledge relevant to the task at hand (Chew & Cerbin, 2021). For example, a student may be able to define words or provide basic descriptions of concepts but then not be able to apply this knowledge to real-world situations. Students are not always able to identity insufficiencies in their prior knowledge (Dunning, 2007), so it can be important for teachers to help them to figure out where the gaps exist.

### Misconceptions

Misconceptions arise when students' existing knowledge is incorrect. As a result, students may misunderstand or even disregard new concepts if the concepts do not align with their prior knowledge. Misconceptions are often exceedingly resistant to correction (Taylor & Kowalski, 2014). Furthermore, in some cases, students may briefly give up their misconceptions only to regress into them once they've completed the course (Chew & Cerbin, 2021). Mistaken ideas, while resistant to change, must be corrected or everything that is learned subsequently will be built upon a faulty foundation.

### Unhelpful Mental Mindsets

Dweck et al. (1995) researched views of intelligence and found that they fall along a spectrum (Yeager & Dweck, 2012; Yeager et al., 2019). At one extreme, individuals view intelligence as a set entity, unalterable by personal effort. These individuals may define themselves by their setbacks and subsequently avoid challenging work because they believe they will be unable to overcome their failures. Unhelpful mindsets extend to other situations as well. For example, if students don't believe the course content is relevant or important, they may not invest the effort required to learn it. Or if they have heard the course is overly difficult, they may enter the classroom with self-fulfilling expectations that they will not succeed.

## Ineffective Learning Strategies

There is considerable research on the relationship between learning strategies and learning outcomes. Marton and Säljö (1976), for example, identified qualitative differences in approaches to reading that were directly related to learning outcomes. They described *deep learning approaches* as the methods by which students focused on what the authors of the text meant and also tried hard to connect that information to their pre-existing knowledge. The researchers described *surface learning approaches* as the methods in which students focused on individual elements of the reading, attempted to memorize facts, and viewed the reading task as an external imposition to be undertaken only for passing the assessment.

## Attention Limits

Attention refers to the cognitive and behavioral process of an individual selectively concentrating on a discrete stimulus while ignoring other stimuli. Without sustained attention, students cannot make connections with course material nor store it in short-term memory. That said, it can be difficult for students to pay attention, with multiple studies indicating that student attention may wane during learning, especially throughout long lectures (for example, see Farley et al., 2013; Risko et al., 2012; Scerbo et al., 1992). Students who engage in non-academic activities during class or while studying, such as browsing the web or texting (Hora & Oleson, 2017) potentially undermine their learning (Favizza et al., 2017; Glass & Kang, 2019; Levitin, 2014; Patterson, 2017).

## Memory Challenges

While there are many models describing memory, one broadly accepted definition divides memory into short-term and long-term. Short-term memory occurs when the brain stores new information temporarily before determining if it should be stored permanently. Elements that can contribute to long-term retention include whether the information makes sense or has meaning within the student's understanding of the world. If the information we teach is understandable (makes sense) and students can connect it to their lives and experiences (has meaning), they are more likely to retain it in their long-term memory. Conversely, if the information doesn't make sense and/or becomes or does not have meaning to the students, they will be unlikely to remember it (Sousa, 2006).

## Issues Related to Cognitive Load

The term *cognitive load* refers to how much information can be maintained in short-term memory at one time. Citing Blikstein and Wilensky (2010), Schwartz et al. (2016) found that lectures often contain too much material. Cognitive load also increases when students are unfamiliar with the material, the lecture is disorganized or too fast, or when the classroom is filled with frequent distractions. Cognitive overload happens when the demands of the task exceed learners' cognitive capacities. Harp and Maslich (2005), for example, determined that students listening to a lecture with numerous details exhibited hindered recall and problem-solving skills compared to those who listened to a less detailed lecture. Cognitive overload is common in college classrooms because instructors feel compelled to "cover the content." Yet, students can only process so much information at a given time and quickly forget information that they are unable to process (Chandler & Sweller, 1991).

## Transfer of Learning Challenges

Transfer of learning occurs when students are able to apply their learning in different contexts or situations. Research indicates that knowledge learned in the classroom is not often used beyond its immediate context (Bransford et al., 1999). Svinicki (2004) observed several means of transfer in the literature but identified two means as the most important for teaching (p. 99). One is positive versus negative transfer, which suggests that when students make accurate connections, they experience a "positive" transfer of learning that enables them to understand and integrate new information. However, if students make incorrect connections, it results in a "negative" transfer of learning, which may breed confusion and mistakes. The other relevant type of transfer for instruction is near transfer versus far transfer, which refers to the type of task. In near transfer settings, tasks look similar and follow the same rules of response, whereas in far transfer settings, which require more thinking by the student, the same rules may apply but in a different environment. The ability of learners to transfer information to new learning depends on the quality of original learning. Original learning that is deep, accurate, and comprehensive will be more beneficial than shallow original learning.

## Metacognition and Self-Regulation Issues

Learners who are self-aware and consistently monitor their own aptitude are demonstrating *metacognition*, a term used by cognitive psychologists to describe the mind's executive function. As we outlined in our 2016 book *Learning Assessment Techniques*, there are two key aspects of metacognition: the knowledge of cognition and the ability to self-regulate cognition. Nilson (2013) regarded metacognition as an essential aspect of the larger concept of self-regulation. Tasks such as outlining the steps required to complete a course activity, self-assessing comprehension, and evaluating personal progress play an important role in successful learning in a collegiate setting. However, many students have not yet developed such skills, impairing their ability to learn.

## KNOWING HOW: MITIGATING LEARNING CHALLENGES

Recognizing the challenges students face as they try to learn is the first step toward identifying solutions. We offer a wide range of strategies and techniques below to guide you in your efforts to mitigate common learning challenges. Where appropriate, we suggest a Cross Academy Technique (CAT). For more information on each CAT, visit our companion site, The K. Patricia Cross Academy, where you will find videos and downloadable templates to guide implementation in both onsite and online classrooms.

### Activate and Identify Relevant Prior Knowledge

- Ask learners to respond to an open-ended prompt, such as, "Please describe what you remember and understand about __________." (CAT 10: Quick Write)
- Craft a short, simple, focused questionnaire that students complete at the beginning of a course or start of a new unit to identify the best starting point for the class as a whole. (CAT 31: Background Knowledge Probe)
- Create an assignment in which students write a memo to a real or fictional student who missed class the day before to describe what was taught and explain why it might be important. (CAT 14: Update Your Classmate)

### Correct Misconceptions

- Help students recognize differences between their misconceptions and correct explanations. For example, have students participate in groups in an adaptation of CAT 50: Sentence Stem Predictions. Students complete a partial sentence that is structured to prompt them to draw upon their prior knowledge to foretell a result or consequence.
- Make sure students have the correct explanation to replace their faulty misconception. Fill in gaps in students' knowledge base by returning to the facts or discussing how misconceptions develop. And make sure that the information you're offering to replace misinformation is believable and plausible. Emphasize the facts and highlight why right is right and actively refute misinformation by emphasizing why wrong is wrong. Consider CAT 12: Fact or Opinion, which encourages students to critically evaluate information by questioning what they read.

- Try to find a balance between allowing learners time to build up the strength of the new conception while also avoiding focusing on the misconception, to minimize the chances of a familiarity backfire effect. Point out logical fallacies that students may face from others when they discuss the misconceptions in personal conversations. Remember to emphasize what's correct, why it's correct, and why the misconception is incorrect. End the class by helping students retain information. Consider CAT 2: 3-2-1, in which students write about 3 things they learned in the lecture, 2 things they found particularly interesting, and 1 question they still have about the lecture content.

## Tackle Unhelpful Mindsets

- Encourage students to accept and embrace their imperfections. Share notable quotes or anecdotes that help students think of obstacles as opportunities.

- Demonstrate to students how tough material and tasks are and then offer a path to self-improvement. For example, consider having students construct a Personal Learning Environment (CAT 19), which consists of a set of people and digital resources they can access for the specific intent of learning.

- Experiment with different learning strategies. Inform students that there is no perfect model for learning. Reassure them that what works for a class-mate may not work for them, and encourage them to experiment with various tactics until one works.

- Prioritize process over conclusion. At times, the most important aspect of an activity is the process, not getting the right answer. Ask students to show their work so that even if their conclusions are incorrect, you can still acknowledge their effort.

- Develop students' sense of purpose. According to Dweck (2006), students who have growth mindsets have a more developed sense of purpose. Advise students to focus on the big picture.

- Prioritize growth, not speed. Help students remember they aren't in a race and that learning well is more important than learning fast.

- Praise actions, not individual attributes. When commending students, tell them they're doing something intelligent, not simply being intelligent.

- Help students to recognize that criticism is positive. Remind students how important feedback is to the learning process and assure them that your comments are meant to help them grow, not to belittle them.
- Give students several chances to reflect on what they've learned. Consider assigning CAT 47: What? So What? Now What? Journals, in which students reflect on their recent course-related activities as they respond to each prompt in a journal entry.
- Suggest that students learn from the mistakes of others. Explain that while it is not always beneficial to compare themselves to others, recognizing that everyone is flawed can be reassuring and also offer opportunities to learn from each other's mistakes.

## Help Students Acquire Effective Learning Strategies

- Urge students to take ownership of their educations so that they are more likely to seek out deep learning. Wherever possible, give them choices, or explain why the material is important or relevant. Consider CAT 21: Post-Test Analysis, a two-stage process that is divided into several steps designed to help students develop greater awareness of their test-preparing and test-taking skills.
- Offer guidance on how to make good choices about workload so that students are in a better position to learn rather than defaulting to a superficial learning approach simply to survive.
- Model and mentor students on how to learn efficiently and effectively.
- Design assessment tasks to mirror and reward deep learning objectives rather than recall.
- Encourage students' enthusiasm and interest in the subject matter by demonstrating your own enthusiasm and interest in the subject.
- Design fewer but higher quality assessments — ones that require students to engage with problems and apply their learning rather than encouraging them to memorize facts.

## Adjust for Attention Limits

- Share research findings with students on how multi-tasking will make learning more difficult.
- Encourage students to take responsibility for using their time on coursework efficiently and effectively.
- Create a course policy that limits technology use for activities that are not related to coursework to reduce distractions in class.
- Take brief breaks between segments of long classes. Even a few moments in which students get up and stretch can help them refocus.

## Help Improve Memory

- Break information up into digestible chunks so that students remember material better.
- Have students create a graphic organizer for new course material. For example, consider CAT 5: Group Grid, in which group members are given pieces of information and asked to place them in the blank cells of a grid according to category rubrics, which helps them clarify and remember conceptual categories.
- Help students stay focused on their work and not be distracted by worries or concerns outside the classroom. Focused students better retain information and are more productive.
- Give students opportunities to retrieve and recall information in practice tests that lead up to exams.
- Create an assignment in which students are asked to create their own questions or practice tests, which improves their retention and memory.

## Address Issues Related to Cognitive Load

- Avoid giving students extraneous load in the classroom by stripping out activities that are not essential to the learning process.
- Offer students information in an easily understood manner. For example, consider using one integrated and self-explanatory source of information rather than having scattered bits and pieces of information throughout

the course. This approach ensures that learners don't have to dig for the information. Additionally, avoid having audio, text, and graphics on-screen simultaneously.

- Provide numerous opportunities for students to practice so that they hone their skills and apply their knowledge throughout the course.
- Break the material up into bite-sized chunks with evident connections between the segments so students better understand and retain information.
- Use a simple-to-complex method. Help students master the core principles of the material before moving on to problems of greater complexity.
- Use a low-to-high intensity method. Let students master the key tenets of a task in a low-intensity environment before weaving in more complex activities.
- Examine your own actions to determine whether they may distract students and add to their cognitive load.

## Design Material for Transfer of Learning

- Design coursework with the intention of improving the transfer of learning to next contexts. For example, help students to learn material in environments and through methods that correspond to how they will use the material. Consider CAT 15: Translate That! in which you pause your lecture and call on a student at random to "translate" the information you just provided into plain English for an imagined audience that you specify.
- Consider what types of questions make up your learning modules. It is important to include open-ended questions that encourage higher order thinking.
- Give students multiple opportunities to collaborate with their peers. During the process, they will both generate and encounter new ideas.
- Design tasks so that students make connections across content areas.
- Consider whether your testing requires students to apply their knowledge in new situations or think about the material conceptually. If not, change it.

- Incorporate opportunities for student reflection. Students' understanding of course concepts will improve if they participate in a reflection process that emphasizes writing and communication.

### Help Students Acquire Metacognition and Self-Regulation Strategies

- At the conclusion of a challenging class, ask students, "What confused you most about the material we discussed today?" This will help students improve their metacognitive processing while also establishing that confusion is a normal part of the learning process.
- Build in opportunities to reflect on material. Consider prompts such as, "How has your thinking changed due to what you just learned?" so that students learn to recognize their own cognitive growth.
- Ask students to monitor their own learning progress and thinking skills through personal journals. Assign questions that encourage students to reflect on how they're learning rather than what they're learning, such as "What study strategies worked well for me as I prepared for this week's test?" or "What study habits have been successful for me? Which should I try next week?"
- Consider CAT 20: Lecture Wrapper, in which students self-monitor behavior as they identify key points from a lecture and then compare their points to your list of points.

## CONCLUSION

Learning requires students to integrate new information or ideas into what they already know so that they develop new (or modify existing) knowledge, attitudes, values, skills, or behavior. The process of learning has been studied for centuries. Theories on learning, learning philosophies, and findings from neuroscience provide us with frameworks for understanding how learning occurs. Engaged teachers develop their knowledge of the learning process and are familiar with the learning challenges that are common to college classrooms and then do their best to mitigate them. As you learn more about learning, we encourage you to clarify your own beliefs. With this knowledge, you will be able to make better instructional choices and help more students succeed.

## FOCUS ON ONLINE TEACHING

The information we share in the main body of this chapter applies to both onsite and online teaching, but here we provide additional insights focused specifically on teaching online, hybrid, and blended courses.

### What: Learning Online

When we teach online, we necessarily reconsider our views of learning when making decisions about how to teach (Major, 2015). A group of learning theorists, who refer to themselves as connectivists, have recently turned their attention toward the interactions between and among individuals and technologies online. That is, they believe that knowledge resides within technological objects and tools as well as individuals. Learning is mediated by technology. Learners interact with each other and with technology; they engage in joint activities and have shared tools. Learners use their objects and tools, and they think and learn with them. They construct a common language and a shared understanding while they simultaneously are engaged in the pursuit of individual and collective objectives. Technology enables and constrains their actions and interactions. From these perspectives, then, learning is the set of connections between people, tools, and the environment. Learning is something beyond an individual act; it is groups of individuals tapping into and building a networked intelligence, which may become even more explicit in an online learning situation. As such, these theories, typically branching from constructivism, portray a socio-technological view of learning (Major, 2015).

### Why: Research on Learning Online

We are developing a well-documented body of evidence that suggests that online learning is an effective method of helping students achieve learning outcomes. Between 1998 and 2021, more than 4,000 research or evaluation studies on the effectiveness of online learning at the higher education level were published in peer-reviewed journals. Taken together, these studies suggest that online and onsite courses often have similar outcomes in the area of knowledge gain. Some results have shown that online courses are slightly better, and others that onsite ones have a modest edge. Such findings, sometimes referred to as the "no significant difference" phenomenon, have gained the attention of many educators. In particular, researchers have compiled a bibliography of hundreds of studies that compare online courses (or other form of distance education) with onsite ones (see *nosignificantdifference.org*).

As the name of the phenomenon suggests, in many cases the mode of instruction does not lead to a significant difference in the amount of content students learn. Some researchers have done meta-analyses of such studies, reanalyzing the published data to determine an effect size (a statistical measurement of how robust a particular factor is), and in general have confirmed the "no significant difference" indication. One of the most recent meta-analyses of these studies (Means et al., 2010) was conducted by the U.S. Department of Education, where researchers found that "*on average, students in online learning conditions performed better than those receiving face to face instruction*" (emphasis in the original, p. ix). This difference was slight but statistically significant.

The researchers also found that "*the effectiveness of online learning approaches appears quite broad across different content and learner types*" (emphasis in the original, p. xv). In other words, online learning was effective for undergraduates, graduates, academics, and professionals. Several scholars claim that research aiming at a comparison between online and onsite courses has been largely exhausted (see Bernard et al. 2009; Clark, 2000; Gunawardena & McIsaac, 2004; Lockee et al., 2001). These scholars suggest that we turn attention instead to what can make learning online better.

## How: Managing Learning Challenges Online

The same challenges that are inherent to learning in an onsite classroom also attend learning online and indeed may even be exacerbated by learning online. These challenges are a good place for instructors to focus their attention to improve learning online. Consider the following potential extensions of the challenges identified above.

- **Misconceptions.** These may be more difficult to identify when you are separated in time and physical distance. To address, consider a technique, such as CAT 31: Background Knowledge Probe, to collect information.

- **Unhelpful mindsets.** Some students may feel particularly concerned about their ability to be successful in online courses. Consider ways in which students can work together to support each other, such as through collaborative learning techniques.

- **Ineffective learning strategies.** Students may not know how to self-regulate and self-monitor their learning online because they don't have to be in the same time and place with the instructor and with other learners. Consider using techniques to support them, such as CAT 11: Active Reading Documents, or to promote metacognition, CAT 21: Post-Test Analysis.

- **Attention limits.** Students may have significant challenges keeping focused on reading on the computer screen or watching information-dense, non-engaging videos. Consider activities that can help them focus, such as CAT 16: Guided Notes.

- **Cognitive Load Issues.** Students may have greater extraneous load issues, such as distractions from computer activities not related to coursework (for example, online shopping or social media) or interruptions (such as from family members, pets, or chores). Consider techniques to help make these issues more apparent to students, such as CAT 17: Lecture Engagement Log.

PART 2

# Planning

*Learning, properly understood, is transformational rather than additive.*

**—K. PATRICIA CROSS**

CHAPTER 4

# Identifying Significant Learning Goals, Objectives, and Outcomes

"If you don't know where you are going, how will you know when you get there?" This folksy adage contains elements of truth for teaching and learning just as it does for travel and life. While the most rewarding experiences are sometimes those that surprise us, in general, when we want to go somewhere, we want to know *what* the where is. The goal of teaching is learning, but if you are not clear on what you want students to learn, you can waste a lot of time and energy, or worse, find that students didn't learn what you wanted them to learn after all. If you are creating a new course or even adapting existing curricula, you will find it useful to begin by outlining what takeaways students should have upon course completion. Defining desired results may aid with selecting materials, choosing teaching strategies, and designing assessments that determine whether learning goals are met.

## KNOWING WHAT: ABOUT GOALS, OBJECTIVES, AND OUTCOMES

The importance of identifying learning outcomes has its roots in Pavlov's famous conditioning of dogs in the 1890s. Building on Pavlov's work, the American "behavioral school" of psychology emerged through the research of psychologists J. B. Watson (1858–1958) and B. F. Skinner (1904–1990). Behaviorism stressed the need for carefully designed, well-defined learning processes that generate observable, measurable results. Setting aside some of the excess in Skinner's ideas about mass conditioning and programmed instruction, the two psychologists had a profound impact on American teaching. Their influence was particularly potent in training conducted in the armed forces, business, and industry. The importance of learning outcomes then grew to encompass all educational contexts, including higher education. Educators championed the importance of measurable behaviors, arguing that learning couldn't be improved without first defining improvement.

## Bloom's Taxonomy

During this time, Bloom's *Taxonomy of the Cognitive Domain* (Bloom et al., 1956) offered a new method for designing measurable learning objectives with specificity and clarity. The text was the synthesis of an effort, beginning in the late 1940s, by a group of educators who hoped to develop a system classifying three domains: cognitive (which involved knowledge or mental skills), affective (which included emotional skills, feelings, or attitudes), and psychomotor (which included physical or manual skills).

The key tenet of Bloom's taxonomy is that educational objectives can be considered to be in a hierarchy, one that moves from less complex to more complicated tiers of knowledge and skills. Each level is successive, and each level must be achieved before moving on to the next. The initial levels offered by Bloom et al. (1956) were ordered as follows: Knowledge, Comprehension, Application, Analysis, Synthesis, and Evaluation. Forty years later, in 2001, Anderson and Krathwohl published a revised edition of Bloom's taxonomy that included updated research from the decades that followed initial publication. The revised levels are as follows: Remembering, Understanding, Applying, Analyzing, Evaluating, and Creating. The changes between the two editions reflected modern education's more outcome-focused objectives. Figure 4.1: A Comparison of Bloom's and Anderson and Krathwohl's Taxonomies shows the differences between the original and the revised taxonomy. Notice that the levels were renamed as active verbs rather than nouns and that the highest two levels were altered, with the peak now being Creating.

New terms and expressions have been added to the common vernacular of instructional development and curriculum planning. Phrases such as *essential questions* and *enduring understandings* have entered the dialogue. These were spurred, in part, by the influence of *Understanding by Design*, a text by Wiggins and McTighe (1998) that offered a framework for designing courses and modules called *backward design*. This framework proposed that teachers should start with identifying goals, then move to assessments, and finish with instructional methods (Barkley & Major, 2016).

Figure 4.1. A Comparison of Bloom's and Anderson and Krathwohl's Taxonomies

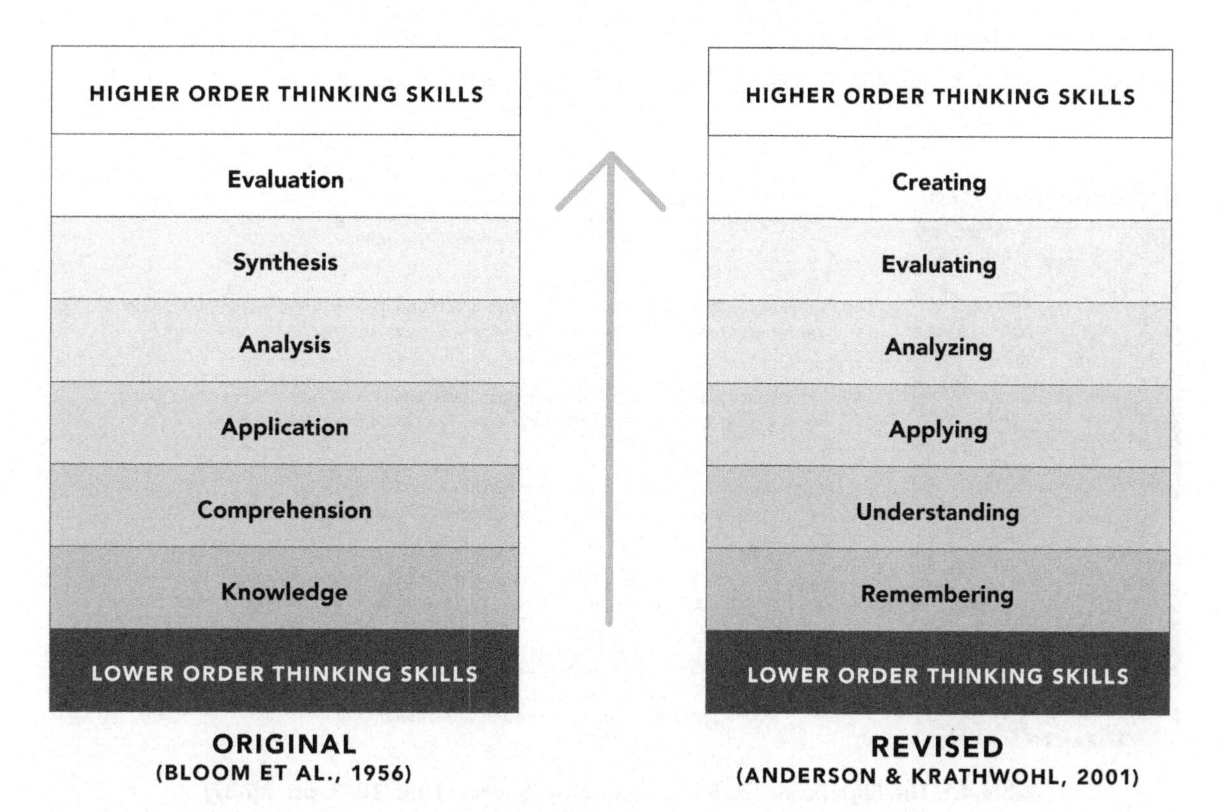


## Fink's Significant Learning Taxonomy

In developing the significant learning taxonomy, Fink (2003) built upon the backward design framework. He also believed that higher education was expressing a need for new kinds of learning that went beyond just thinking and the acquisition of knowledge to include leadership and interpersonal skills, ethics, communication skills, character, tolerance, and the ability to adapt to change (p. 29). Rather than talking with professors, as Bloom did, Fink spoke with students to determine what they believed were truly significant learning experiences, ones that changed them in ways that extended beyond a single course. The central idea in Fink's (2013) concept of significant learning is that "teaching should result in something others can look at and say, 'That learning experience resulted in something that is truly significant in terms of the students' lives'" (p. 7). Thus, Fink argued in favor of meaningful and lasting learning that is worthy of the effort given by students and teachers alike.

The significant learning taxonomy extends beyond the cognitive domain and includes deeper, more nuanced views on learning. The taxonomy reflects modern beliefs and values in that it is not hierarchical but rather relational and interactive. Fink (2013) presented a taxonomy designed to encourage teachers to focus on deeper, more lasting learning and not just information gathering. Fink offered the following categories: Foundational Knowledge, Application, Integration, Human Dimension, Caring, and Learning How to Learn. These categories are described in Table 4.1: The Significant Learning Taxonomy.

| | |
|---|---|
| **FOUNDATIONAL KNOWLEDGE** | Understanding and remembering the information, ideas, and perspectives that form the basis for other kinds of learning in the subject |
| **APPLICATION** | Applying knowledge to real situations through critical and creative thinking, problem solving, performance, and skill attainment so that foundational knowledge becomes useful |
| **INTEGRATION** | Making connections between ideas, learning experiences, and different realms of life so that everything is put into context and learning is more powerful |
| **HUMAN DIMENSION** | Learning about the personal and social implications of what one is learning, thus giving the learning significance as learners learn about themselves and others |
| **CARING** | Developing new feelings, interests, and values that help learners care about what they are learning, which gives them the energy they need for learning more about it and making it part of their lives |
| **LEARNING HOW TO LEARN** | Learning about the process of learning, including a particular kind of inquiry (such as the scientific method) as well as how to become a better, more self-directed learner, which enables learners to continue learning and do so with greater effectiveness |

**Table 4.1. The Significant Learning Taxonomy. Source: Fink (2013, pp. 35-37)**

## Understanding Key Terms

If you hope to report students' learning in formal contexts, you will need to articulate what you want students to learn in specific terminology that facilitates measurement, comparison, and the sharing of results in methods that others in the field will accept as evidentiary. In much of the literature discussing learning assessment in higher education, the terms goals, outcomes and objectives are used. Often the terms are used interchangeably, with distinctions being overlooked because, though their definitions differ, they each require more transparency and specificity to planning in the teaching and learning process. (Barkley & Major, 2016). Commonly used definitions for each are as follows:

- **Learning goals:** General statements about the desired skills, knowledge, and abilities a student needs to successfully perform after completing a course
- **Learning objectives:** Specific statements describing what students are intended to be able to do after taking a course

- **Learning outcomes:** Explicit statements describing the learning that students will have achieved and be able to demonstrate after completing a course

Thus, the language of assessment typically flows from the general to the more specific. Figure 4.2: Differentiating Among Learning Goals, Objectives, and Outcomes uses a metaphor of target practice to illustrate the differences among the three terms. When using this metaphor, we begin by describing what we intend students to learn (goals). We next identify steps students should take to reach that goal (objectives). And then we assess how well students achieved the goal based on measurable evidence of learning (outcomes). Table 4.2: An Example of a Learning Goal, Objective, and Outcome shows the way this might apply in a Survey of International Relations course.

No matter the terms used, engaged instructors design courses and content units based on what they want students to learn. We recommend that you fully consider learning goals, objectives, and outcomes and use these to drive your instructional decisions.

## KNOWING WHY: RESEARCH ON LEARNING GOALS, OBJECTIVES, AND OUTCOMES

It is helpful for engaged teachers to understand why learning goals, objectives, and outcomes are important. Angelo and Cross (1993) published one of the most influential works examining course-level assessment. In their book, they argued, "[w]hat you teach has a good deal to do with how you teach — or at least what your teaching priorities are and how you perceive your primary role as a teacher" (p. 369).

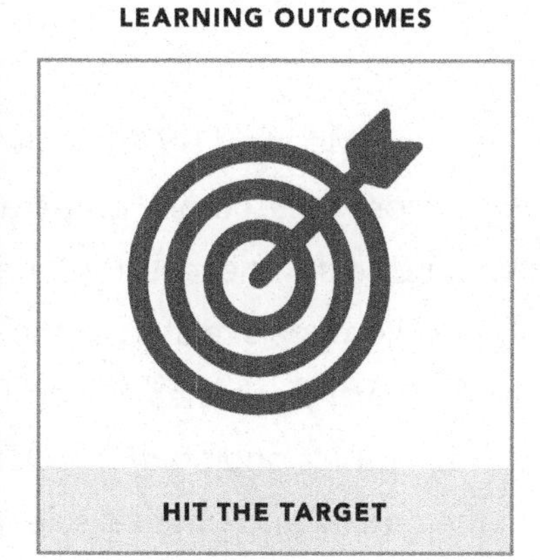


**Figure 4.2. Differentiating Among Learning Goals, Objectives, and Outcomes**

| SURVEY OF INTERNATIONAL RELATIONS | GOAL | OBJECTIVE | OUTCOME |
|---|---|---|---|
| | Students will develop knowledge of key international relations terms and concepts. | Students will be able to demonstrate understanding and appropriate use of key international relations terms and concepts. | In a written essay of their term project, 80% of the students will synthesize and apply key international relations terms and concepts appropriately with supporting citations and evidence. |

**Table 4.2. An Example of a Learning Goal, Objective, and Outcome**

They proposed that academic discipline is the primary factor in determining how we differ as college teachers, writing,

> Faculty teaching priorities are related more to academic discipline than to any other factor. Teachers of a given discipline — whether male or female, full-time or part-time, experienced or inexperienced, teaching in a public community college or a private four-year college — share a value system with respect to teaching goals that is distinctly discipline-related and significantly different from that of colleagues in different disciplines. (p. 366)

Several researchers have confirmed the significance of academic disciplines' influence on teacher attitudes and behaviors (Alpert, 1985; Becher, 1987; Clark, 1980; Ladd & Lipsett, 1975; Lee, 2004; Smart et al., 2000).

Stark and Morstain (1978) wrote that faculty in natural sciences and professional disciplines were more focused on "preparation for life and work" than their counterparts in the humanities and social sciences. By contrast, faculty in the humanities and social sciences were more focused on goals related to the pursuit of ideas than their peers in the natural sciences and professional disciplines. In additional studies, Braxton and Nordvall (1985), Gaff and Wilson (1971), Lattuca and Stark (1994), and Smart and Ethington (1995) determined that instructors in the natural and physical sciences more often required memorization and application than faculty in social sciences, humanities, and behavioral sciences, who more often addressed critical thinking skills.

Additional studies have examined teachers' priorities regarding instructional goals. Most studies indicate that faculty's chief concern is student intellectual growth and development (Jervis & Congdon, 1958; Lawrence et al., 1990; Liebert & Bayer, 1975; Platt et al., 1976; Royal, 2010; Royal et al., 2010; Wilson et al., 1975). Lawrence et al. (1990) determined that the main focus on students' intellectual growth was consistent across institutional types. Leverenz and Lewis (1981) determined that an instructor's learning goals were influenced by their instructors' educational backgrounds. The researchers concluded that teachers with educational backgrounds consistent to their current roles were chiefly focused on discipline-oriented goals, while faculty with backgrounds inconsistent from their current roles were more focused on teaching students life skills.

But is writing objectives related to improved student learning? According to research, the answer is yes, at least when students know what the objectives are. As Richmond et al. (2015), noted, in the 1970s, several researchers found that students learned more when they knew the learning objectives than when they did not (Duchastel & Brown, 1974; Duell, 1974; Gagne & Rothkopf, 1975; Kaplan, 1976; Royer, 1977). In the 1980s, Locke et al. (1981) found that providing people with specific and challenging goals led to improved performance, when compared to no goals or easy goals. More recently, as Fulmer (2017) noted, researchers have made similar findings, drawing on student perceptions and self-reports of their learning (Armbruster et al., 2009, Rust et al., 2003; Winkelmes et al., 2016) or, alternatively, drawing from data demonstrating improvements in student learning within specific domains in courses redesigned around Fink's Significant Learning Taxonomy (Levine et al., 2008). While some researchers have not found a relationship between objectives and increased outcomes (e.g., Mitchell & Manzo, 2018), when considered as a whole, the evidence supports developing and sharing learning objectives for the improvement of student learning.

## KNOWING HOW: AN ENGAGED APPROACH TO WRITING GOALS, OBJECTIVES, AND OUTCOMES

Most faculty recognize the importance of identifying learning goals, but some find determining objectives and outcomes difficult both in concept and in practice. Some of the issues identified below may be relevant to you.

- You may be genuinely offended at the prospect of reducing the complex, personal, and process-driven experience of learning into a one-size-fits-all, narrowly defined outcome.
- You may be concerned that objectives and outcomes written to satisfy third parties tend to represent the learning goals of idealized, abstract students.

These desired outcomes may not align with the real-world abilities, interests, and engagement of the students who actually take your course.

- You certainly recognize that some students will learn better than their peers. The conventional grading system enables you to assess achievement along a continuum, but when you teach through objectives or outcomes, it may feel more binary: Individual students either achieve the outcomes or they don't.
- Because you likely want to promote significant learning that lasts long after the course is over, you may feel that developing goals that only capture achievement at the end of a term is short-sighted.
- You may be anxious that being required to report students' learning in measurable outcomes means you will wind up teaching to the test and limit your innovation and engagement.
- You may find it very challenging to shift your instructional priorities from what students should know to identifying things that learners can do.
- Recasting course material into an organizational framework of learning objectives and outcomes requires a lot of time and work, and you may wonder if it is worth the effort.

We understand and share these concerns; after all, we are college teachers ourselves. That said, we think it is possible to overcome these hurdles. There are many examples of college faculty who have successfully negotiated these challenges. It is tough work, but it is not insurmountable and may be best completed by collaborating with peers in the field.

The underlying principle is that if material can be learned, then there is always a way to demonstrate whether it has been learned. If that is the case, then the learning can be measured. We encourage you to spend time establishing objectives and outcomes that reflect your commitment to deep and transformative learning. Also, the reality of today's education landscape is that stakeholders increasingly mandate that faculty identify learning outcomes and offer reasonable evidence of student achievement. We therefore provide guidance so that your process will be more effective, efficient, and also feel less cumbersome. We hope you will find the following tips helpful regardless of your field or discipline.

## Identify Course-Level Learning Goals

Most faculty have a general sense of what students should learn from their courses. Indeed, the descriptions listed in a university course catalog or class schedule typically identify the learning goals in expansive terms. For example, a catalog description for Principles of Cell Biology might read:

> An introduction to cellular structure, cellular function, the cell cycle, cell communication and signaling, biological molecules, bioenergetics, the genetics of prokaryotic as well as eukaryotic organisms, and an overview of molecular biology.

The description presents in broad strokes what students should learn by the end of the course. To be useful in assessment, however, you need to state your learning goals in more specific terms.

## Use the Learning Goals Inventory

The Learning Goal Inventory (LGI; Barkley & Major, 2016) was created to help college teachers state specific learning goals. It was inspired by the Teaching Goals Inventory developed by Angelo and Cross in 1993 to help teachers determine what students should learn in their courses. The LGI offers 50 learning goals that could apply to most college level courses, grouped so that they correlate with the Significant Learning Taxonomy. The LGI can be found online at: *https://bit.ly/3JrYBfU*

## Consider Students' Learning Goals

Both teachers and students find value in being partners in the learning process. Weimer (2002) pointed to teachers sharing power with students as a necessary change for learning-centered teaching. Weimer (2002) also noted that this shift won't necessarily come naturally: "[T]eacher authority is so taken for granted that most of us are no longer aware of the extent to which we direct student learning" (p. 23). Sharing power with students requires us to make a small but decisive shift in focus away from what we are teaching to what and how students are learning. Considering students' learning goals is an essential first step. In any given course, students' learning goals likely vary, and many students may struggle to articulate them. To ease the process of helping students identify their individual learning goals, you may want to have students complete and self-evaluate the LGI, and possibly discuss their results in groups afterward.

## Attend to Externally Mandated or Recommended Learning Goals

At the national, state, institution, program, and even department levels, learning goals and competencies are often mandated or recommended. Large stakeholder groups typically hope to achieve broad goals, while professional accrediting agencies or university departments or programs aim for discipline-specific goals. Table 4.3: Examples of Externally Recommended or Mandated Learning Goals (adapted from Barkley & Major, 2016) offers examples of various external goals.

| CONTEXT | SAMPLE GOAL |
|---|---|
| INSTITUTIONAL CORE COMPETENCIES | A course that supports the communication core competency goal helps students develop analytical reading and writing skills, including evaluation, synthesis, and research; deliver focused and coherent presentations; and acquire active, discerning listening and speaking skills in lectures and discussions. |
| GENERAL EDUCATION: HUMANITIES | A course meeting the Humanities General Education Area I Requirement must help students to acquire knowledge and understanding of significant artistic, literary, and philosophical works and the historical and cultural context in which the works were created and interpreted. |
| COLLEGE OF AGRICULTURE | Graduates of the College of Agriculture will be able to make sound, responsible judgments on the ethical policy issues involved in the production of food and fiber. |
| PROGRAM/ DEPARTMENT LEVEL | A course in the Biology sequence must prepare students to use the scientific method to formulate questions, design experiments to test hypotheses, interpret experimental results to draw conclusions, communicate results both orally and in writing, and critically evaluate the use of the scientific method from published sources. |

**Table 4.3. Examples of Externally Recommended or Mandated Learning Goals**

Because faculty are tasked with demonstrating how successfully their students have achieved these externally identified goals, it is probably in your best interest to adapt these goals for specific application to your classroom. In Figure 4.3: Drilling Down from Institutional Core Competency to Course-Level Learning Goal, we outline how one of these broad institutional goals might inform a course-level goal.

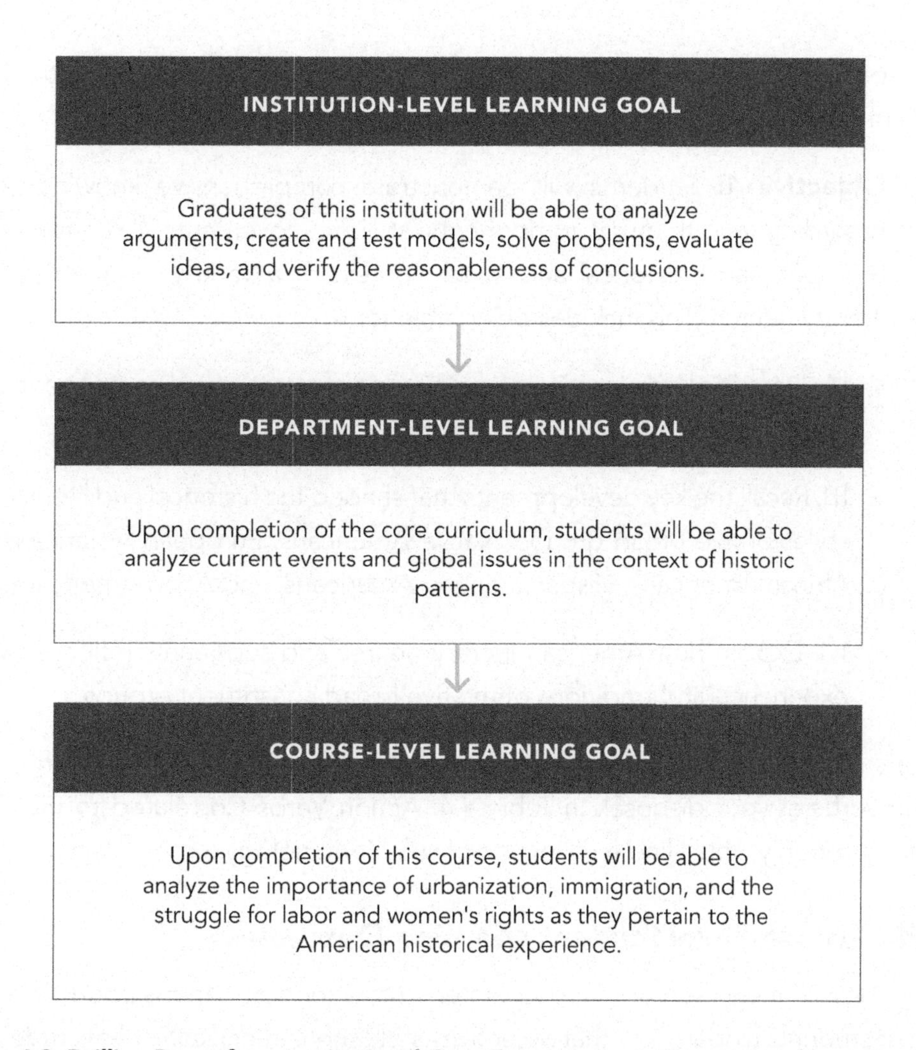


**Figure 4.3. Drilling Down from Institutional Core Competency to Course-Level Learning Goal**

## Determine Course-Level Learning Objectives

Though course learning goals may outline in broad terms what students should learn, objectives lay out the framework for helping students achieve those goals in visible ways. As an example, a teacher's goal may be that their students understand or appreciate some aspect of foundational information, but the words we use may be vague and lead to misunderstandings or a variety of interpretations. Objectives are built by turning goals into statements of tangible things that students can do, such as *solve* or *write* or *create*. These offer teachers something that can be observed, assessed, and used as a point of comparison. You may find it helpful to list your objectives as subcomponents, providing detail and comprehensive coverage. Here is an example of what that looks like in practice (adapted from Barkley & Major, 2016).

- **Goal:** Students will develop foundational knowledge of multicultural American literature from the 20th century.
  - » **Objective 1:** Students will demonstrate comprehensive knowledge regarding the structural components, stylistic movements, key authors and texts, and historical and social context of a variety of American literary genres. This includes being able to:
    - » 1A. Describe American literature in terms of its structural components, stylist movements, and key authors and texts.
    - » 1B. Recall the key developments that shaped the historical and literary styles of five broad groups: Native Americans, European Americans, African Americans, Hispanic/Latino Americans, and Asian Americans.
    - » 1C. Explain how American literary genres and subgenres reflect the experience and traditions of the five broad constituent groups.

As you are converting goals into objectives, you may find it useful to have a large collection of action verbs at your disposal. In Table 4.4: Action Verbs Correlated to the Significant Learning Taxonomy, you'll find a collection of such terminology.

## Identify Course-Level Student Learning Outcomes

You now know that course learning goal statements offer broad terms about what teachers want their students to learn and that objectives state more specifically what students should be able to do to reach those goals. Student learning outcomes (SLOs) are even more explicit as they list what the achievement of those goals looks like in actions that can be observed and assessed. Similar to learning objectives statements, SLOs provide detailed operational terms; however, in this instance, the statements don't reflect what we hope will happen but rather the proof of what actually did happen. SLOs are precise statements articulating the information, skills, attitudes, and knowledge students will to be able to showcase at the conclusion of a course, demonstrating that they have achieved the learning goals.

| FOUNDATIONAL KNOWLEDGE | APPLICATION | INTEGRATION | HUMAN DIMENSION | CARING | LEARNING HOW TO LEARN |
|---|---|---|---|---|---|
| Articulate | Act | Formulate | Arrange | Adapt | Appraise |
| Assemble | Adapt | Generalize | Assemble | Analyze | Assess |
| Choose | Administer | Generate | Break down | Collaborate | Challenge |
| Cite | Analyze | Give examples | Classify | Communicate | Collaborate |
| Define | Apply | Illustrate | Collaborate | Conclude | Communicate |
| Describe | Appraise | Implement | Combine | Criticize | Conclude |
| Duplicate | Arrange | Infer | Compare | Estimate | Convince |
| Examine | Assess | Inspect | Consolidate | Evaluate | Criticize |
| Explain | Calculate | Interpret | Contrast | Help | Debate |
| Identify | Categorize | Manage | Discuss | Identify | Defend |
| Indicate | Change | Manipulate | Distinguish | Illustrate | Dispute |
| Label | Collect | Measure | Evaluate | Infer | Estimate |
| List | Compose | Modify | Facilitate | Intervene | Evaluate |
| Locate | Compute | Operate | Incorporate | Judge | Illustrate |
| Match | Construct | Organize | Infer | Justify | Intervene |
| Name | Convert | Perform | Integrate | Manage | Judge |
| Order | Control | Plan | Judge | Measure | Justify |
| Outline | Create | Practice | Measure | Praise | Measure |
| Paraphrase | Debate | Predict | Organize | Propose | Modify |
| Quote | Deduce | Prepare | Question | Question | Propose |
| Recall | Defend | Present | Rate | Rate | Question |
| Recognize | Demonstrate | Produce | Recognize | Recognize | Rate |
| Record | Derive | Propose | Reconsider | Recommend | Recognize |
| Relate | Design | Provide | Relate | Reconsider | Reconsider |
| Rephrase | Detect | Question | Revise | Reflect | Reflect |
| Report | Develop | Rate | Synthesize | Relate | Relate |
| Reproduce | Diagram | Regulate | | Revise | Revise |
| Restate | Differentiate | Revise | | Support | |
| Select | Discover | Schedule | | Test | |
| Show | Discriminate | Share | | Validate | |
| State | Employ | Show | | | |
| Summarize | Establish | Solve | | | |
| Tabulate | Estimate | Synthesize | | | |
| Tell | Extend | Use | | | |
| | Evaluate | Verify | | | |
| | Extrapolate | | | | |

**Table 4.4. Action Verbs Correlated to the Significant Learning Taxonomy**

Student learning outcome statements can be as straightforward as:

> After completing this course, a successful student will be able to describe the five major theories or perspectives in psychiatry.

However, when crafting learning outcome statements for courses, we think it is helpful to break them down into two components: (1) conditions and (2) performance. To put it another way, we phrase it "when given x," or "through product x" (conditions) "a student will be able to do y" (performance). This formula is illustrated in Table 4.5: Two Recommended Components of a Course-Level Learning Outcome Statement.

| CONDITIONS | PERFORMANCE |
|---|---|
| When given an exam consisting of listening examples of representative music that have not been studied, | students will be able to identify the genre and style. |
| When given a case study, | students will be able to analyze and explain why a particular intervention was or was not effective. |

**Table 4.5. Two Recommended Components of a Course Level Learning Outcome Statement**

## Determine Performance Standards for Learning Outcomes

### ASSESSING ACHIEVEMENTS OF INDIVIDUALS

We start each semester knowing that in the course we are teaching, individual students will attain each learning outcome at some point on a continuum between "did not achieve the objective at all" to "mastered the objective." Therefore, after you have established how each student should be able to demonstrate an achievement, it can be useful to determine the standard that represents the minimum acceptable result. For instance, you may decide that a student should be able to correctly answer at least 70% of questions on a course exam in order to be considered having achieved the learning outcome.

### ASSESSING ACHIEVEMENT AT THE COURSE LEVEL

It is also necessary to set standards for analyzing and reporting aggregate data at a course level. So, in addition to identifying the standard for individual achievement of a learning outcome, you may want to also establish a fair overall minimum achievement standard for the entire class. As an example, perhaps you feel that if 70% of the class demonstrates learning outcome achievement, then it is reasonable to conclude that the course assignments and sessions are helping students reach the desired outcome. Your target class outcome is the performance standard. If, after analyzing the results, you learn that 80% of the class achieved the desired outcome, you may find reason to celebrate; however, if you learn that just 30% of students met the standards, you may find yourself disappointed. Table 4.6: Learning Outcome Statements With Performance Standards offers examples of learning outcome statements including individual and aggregate performance standards.

| AURAL EXAM | CASE STUDY |
| --- | --- |
| When given an aural exam consisting of novel listening examples of representative music, students will be able to determine the genre and style.<br><br>**Individual Minimum Performance Standard:**<br>70% accuracy required for passing the test and to be considered having met the learning outcome.<br><br>**Target Class Performance Standard:**<br>80% of students will receive a passing grade, thus showing achievement of the desired learning outcome. | When provided with a case study, students will be able to analyze and describe why a specific intervention did vor did not succeed.<br><br>**Individual Minimum Performance Standard:**<br>A minimum of Level 3 on each component in the assignment's testing rubric is necessary to be considered as having successfully demonstrated the learning outcome.<br><br>**Target Class Performance Standard:**<br>65% of students will be able to successfully demonstrate their achievement of the learning outcome by being ranked at a minimum of Level 2 on each component in the assignment's testing rubric. |

**Table 4.6. Learning Outcome Statements With Performance Standards**

## CONCLUSION

The goal in assessing learning is to render the invisible visible (Barkley & Major, 2016). To accomplish this, we try to ensure that the learning taking place inside a student's brain is in a format that we and others can see. This is a major conceptual shift. It requires transitioning from organizing instruction around the content we wish to cover to determining how students can showcase their learning.

Designing learning goals, objectives, and outcomes takes time and effort, and given all the competing pressures that faculty face, is it worth it? Honestly, for some, it may not be. But there are many benefits to going through the process for you and students (Barkley & Major, 2016). Stating what you hope students in your class will learn in assessment language deepens the shared responsibility for learning between you and students. This benefits students in several ways. Students may have reduced anxiety because of clear direction, increased understanding of their learning priorities, and greater confidence that assessment will be fair. They may also develop a better understanding for how your course pertains to other courses and to the institution's broader learning goals. This may motivate students to spend more time and effort learning well, because they will see the value of your course.

The time you spend clarifying what you want students to learn is beneficial to you as the teacher, too. Pragmatically, the early time and effort spent designing learning goals, objectives, and outcomes saves time and anxiety in the later grading process. Indeed, you can ask students to participate in self- or peer-evaluation because students have clarity on class expectations. Furthermore, stating what students should learn in assessment language eases the process of measuring what you do to more effectively provide evidence of learning to key stakeholders. What may be most satisfying, however, is knowing that participation in an evidence-based cycle of assessment and reflection demonstrates your commitment to deep, transformative learning and also leads to improved student learning. We hope that knowing this will leave you with the positive feeling that you have made meaningful contributions to the teaching profession.

## FOCUS ON ONLINE TEACHING

The information we share in the main body of this chapter applies to both onsite and online teaching, but here we provide additional insights focused specifically on teaching online, hybrid, and blended courses.

### What: Online Learning Goals

Few individuals can be successful without goals and plans for achieving them. This principle holds true in education, whether onsite or online. One of the major challenges of teaching online, however, is that you often have to be even more explicit than in an onsite course because the typical communication options, including tone of voice, multiple verbal reminders, and informal conversations before and after class, are absent. When you share your learning goals online, you are expressing your hopes and expectations to students, and you have to be sure to do so clearly.

### Why: Online Learning Goals

Research on the relationship between having and sharing learning goals in online courses is sparse, but there is some evidence that a student's own goals for learning can promote or inhibit student achievement online. For example, Adesope et al. (2015) investigated whether student achievement motivations influenced their learning strategies and behaviors. They found that mastery and performance goals positively predicted task value while work avoidance goals negatively predicted effort regulation and task value. The fact that student goals influence behaviors and outcomes, coupled with data gathered in onsite courses that document a positive relationship between having and sharing clear goals and learning outcomes, suggests the likelihood that having clearly articulated learning goals could influence student goals and therefore strategies, behaviors, and outcomes in online courses as well. More research is needed in this area, but good educational practice suggests sharing clear goals with students online is important (Boettcher & Conrad, 2010).

### How: Online Learning Goals

Due to the increased challenges to learning inherent in most online courses (see the "Focus on Online Teaching" breakout in Chapter 3) and the evidence we have cited that supports how goals influence student learning, it may be even more important to identify clear learning goals when teaching online. As we noted earlier in this chapter, the significant learning taxonomy offers a useful framework for identifying learning goals that move beyond information gathering to a focus on deep, lasting learning. For guidance on identifying online teaching strategies that support specific learning goals related to this taxonomy, check out our companion site, the K. Patricia Cross Academy (*kpcrossacademy.org*). On this site, you can search our videos and see our recommendations for techniques correlated with each level of the taxonomy. Below are examples that we feel are well suited for the online environment.

**FOUNDATIONAL KNOWLEDGE**

**CAT 11: Active Reading Documents:** You provide students with carefully prepared forms that guide them through the process of critical and careful reading.

**APPLICATION (ANALYSIS AND CRITICAL THINKING)**

**CAT 25: Triple Jump:** Students participate in a three-step technique that requires them to think through and attempt to solve a real-world problem.

**APPLICATION (CREATIVE THINKING)**

**CAT 27: Variations:** Students create an altered version of the original, such as rewriting the ending of a story or imagining the consequences of a changed event in history.

**APPLICATION (PROBLEM SOLVING)**

**CAT 6: Analytic Teams:** Each team member assumes a different role with specific responsibilities to perform while reading or viewing an online lecture.

**INTEGRATION AND SYNTHESIS**

**CAT 13: Sketch Notes:** Students use handwritten words and visual elements such as drawings, boxes, lines, and arrows to illustrate the main concepts from an online lecture or assigned reading, as well as their interrelations.

**HUMAN DIMENSION**

**CAT 28: Dyadic Interviews:** Student pairs take turns asking each other questions that tap into values, attitudes, beliefs, and prior experiences that are relevant to course content or learning goals.

**CARING**

**CAT 1: Digital Story:** Students use computer-based tools, such as video, audio, graphics, and web publishing, to tell personal or academic stories about life experiences relevant to course themes.

**LEARNING HOW TO LEARN**

**CAT 21: Post-Test Analysis:** This two-stage process that is divided into several steps designed to help students develop greater awareness of their test-preparation and test-taking skills.

*The encouragement to monitor learning and to study it through classroom assessment provides an intellectual challenge to teachers grown tired and bored with the repetition of doing the same old things in the same old ways.*

**—K. PATRICIA CROSS**

CHAPTER 5

# Assessing and Grading Learning

Our primary purpose as teachers is to produce learning, which may be why the two words *teaching* and *learning* are typically paired. Yet, as K. Patricia Cross observed, "Learning can and often does take place without the benefit of teaching — and sometimes in spite of it — but there is no such thing as effective teaching in the absence of learning. Teaching without learning is just talking" (Angelo & Cross, 1993, p. 3). Or, as a colleague once put it, "Saying 'I taught students that; they just didn't learn it' is like saying, 'I sold them the car; they just didn't buy it.'" If our foremost function as teachers is to facilitate student learning, how will we know when students have learned what we taught? How can we evaluate learning, identify areas for improvement, and share the results? These answers can be found in assessment and grading, the means by which teachers gauge for themselves, for students, and for external stakeholders whether and how effectively student learning has occurred.

## KNOWING WHAT: ABOUT ASSESSING AND GRADING LEARNING

College teachers have been evaluating student learning for centuries, while grading and course-level assessment are relatively recent developments. Today, many of us find it difficult to see how grades and learning assessment differ, thus we often conflate the two. Some educators believe the two are completely unrelated, while others believe they are one and the same. Engaged teachers benefit from knowing the distinctions between the two.

## What is Grading?

Grading in the context of education is a system used to evaluate a learner's educational performance. Educational institutions in the United States began using letter grades in the early 20th century. While grades can be a useful, reliable source of data, debates continue about grade inflation as well as the accuracy of grades for representing student learning.

## Types of Grading

The two most common types of grading at a college or university level are norm-referenced and criterion-referenced grading, but standards-based grading (sometimes referred to as *contract grading*) is also gaining popularity.

- **Norm-referenced grading** involves evaluating students in relationship to one another and typically then assigning a letter grade (for example, the top 7% of students receive an A, the next 24% a B, and so forth). This grading system assumes that the level of student performance does not vary much from class to class and that some students in every class will fail.

- **Criterion-referenced grading** consists of evaluating student performance against a pre-established level. Students are evaluated against an absolute scale (e.g., 90–100 = A, 80–89 = B, and so forth). Normally the criteria are a set number of points or a percentage of the total. Since the criterion is absolute, it is possible that all students could get As or all students could get Ds.

- **Standards-based grading** entails assigning a grade based on a student's completion of a contracted number of assignments at a specified quality. Instructors who are looking for ways to promote equity and inclusion sometimes point to this system's advantages of reducing grade competition.

Most instructors teaching today have grown up in an educational system that relied on grading and have adopted a grading system for their own courses, although some professors have begun to adopt an approach called *ungrading*. Ungrading relies on extensive feedback rather than formal grades throughout the term and involves students in determining their final recorded grade. Instructors often are less experienced with and knowledgeable about assessment than they are about grading.

## What is Assessment?

The assessment movement in higher education began in the mid-1980s, when intense reexamination of the quality of teaching and learning at all levels of education revealed that there were gaps — sometimes considerable ones — between what was thought to have been taught and what was actually learned. The ensuing decades were filled with attempts to close that gap. Public and political entities insisted that colleges and universities prove the value of a college education by demonstrating their effectiveness in enabling learning. The increased focus on high quality teaching in hiring, tenure, and promotion policies, the proliferation of campus teaching and learning centers, the attention to monitoring learning through a 'culture of evidence,' and the establishment of a new research discipline called the *Scholarship of Teaching and Learning* (SoTL) are a few of the indicators of the academy's efforts to improve teaching and learning (Barkley & Major, 2016, p. xi).

K. Patricia Cross was one of the first to recognize the mounting pressures on institutions of higher education to provide evidence of student learning. While the assessment movement was being driven primarily as a response to external demands (assessment as accountability), Cross saw its greater purpose as fostering an internal feedback loop to advance the quality of instruction and curriculum (assessment as improvement). She believed that assessment should be built into the teaching and learning process, and that it should be teacher-designed and teacher-driven. But she also recognized that most teachers were not prepared for such work. Nevertheless, she urged college teachers to ask questions about teaching and learning and to seek to answer them. These beliefs seeded her work in classroom assessment and research. She proposed that college teachers use their classrooms as laboratories for the study of learning and make the results of their research public. Her work with her then research assistant, Tom Angelo, produced *Classroom Assessment Techniques* (1st edition, 1988), which consisted of practical advice on how instructors could assess the quality of teaching and learning in their own classrooms.

Higher education has changed dramatically since the first edition of that book. One of the most significant shifts is that college courses are no longer confined to a traditional classroom. Online teaching, for example, is now mainstream and challenges the basic concept of what a classroom is. Yet, although there have been momentous changes in the academic landscape, pressure on institutions to provide proof that students are learning at a level worth the investment persists. Kuh et al. (2015), for example, observed that there is a "palpable sense of urgency for the need to document how college affects students" and advise "a clearer focus on the use of evidence of student learning in more productive and targeted ways" (p. ix, pp. 1-2). Ensuring and demonstrating student learning seems to be the academy's best strategy for confronting criticisms and adapting constructively to change. As institutions strive to meet the demands for evidence of student learning, many educational leaders propose that the most important step is to embed assessment in the classroom at the course level through the regular tasks and processes of teaching and learning (Suskie, 2018).

In our book on assessment (Barkley & Major, 2016), we focused on assessing student learning that occurs at the course level, and used the term *learning assessment* to refer to the actions that teachers and students take to determine how much learning has taken place in a specific class session, module, or course. There are several different types of learning assessment. Indeed, if you were to examine the expansive body of research on learning assessment, you would find a variety of differing terms, resulting in a confusing muddle of terminology. Adding to the confusion, different researchers intend different meanings when referring to these types. Some refer to the purpose of the assessment, others to the timing of data collection, still others to the method of measurement or the mode of appraisal. Our working definition of learning assessment is not based on any of these specific types, but instead is a broader conceptualization of how teachers can assess learning at the course level. In this chapter, we start by providing a concise review of the varying types of course-level assessment to aid your understanding of what learning assessment is and how to implement it in your courses. The definitions also clarify and specify our meaning when using each of the terms.

## Types of Assessment

Below are types of assessment organized according to their key features: purpose, timing, measure, and method of appraisal.

### ASSESSMENT BASED ON PURPOSE

**Diagnostic assessment** is generally done with the intent of determining students' current levels of knowledge. These assessments can help you identify students' misunderstandings and misconceptions before they are asked to learn new material.

**Formative assessment** is intended to improve course-level teaching and learning. A key tenet of the formative assessment approach is that data collection will help you identify adjustments to improve student learning, not just to provide you with evidence for evaluating or grading students. Some teachers refer to this type of assessment as non-graded or low-stakes graded assessment.

**Summative assessment** is designed to gauge students' level of learning at the conclusion of a learning module, unit, or course. These assessments are generally more comprehensive and are best implemented when the data collection is reliable, valid, and free of bias.

Most teachers are not particularly concerned with the theoretical distinctions and mix and match assessment purposes to best suit their needs. For instance, you may assign an essay to examine what students understood at the conclusion of a module, but then offer students comments that are intended to help them better succeed in the next module. Also, we find it rare that teachers collect assessment data from their students without also providing some form of grade, even just assigning a few points through a system as straightforward as a + / ✓ / –.

### ASSESSMENT BASED ON TIMING

**Pre-assessment** occurs prior to instruction to determine students' existing knowledge, preferences, strengths, weaknesses, and skills. For instance, you may want to assess what students understand as they begin your course so that you can better anticipate what their learning needs will be, or so that you can better determine a baseline to assess the knowledge they acquire.

**Interim and benchmark assessments** are conducted periodically throughout the course. Benchmark assessments are similar to interim assessments in that they are gathered in periodic intervals, but they are then compared to standards to measure students' progress.

**Outcomes assessment** is conducted to determine students' acquisition of knowledge and skills at the conclusion of a course or program. This type of assessment has been compared to high-stakes grading and to summative assessments.

Once again, we believe that though these types are distinct in theory, in practice they often overlap. Indeed, some teachers may use a specific assessment instrument or activity before the course, during the course, and then at the end of the course. They may then compare students' results on pre- and post-tests. Some may decide that an interim assessment activity should be weighted with a significant grading component (for instance, a topic proposal for a final paper). Therefore, instructional activities may be used with a variety of assessment purposes in mind and also implemented at various times over the course of a term.

### ASSESSMENT BASED ON MEASURE

**Direct assessment** entails directly observing students demonstrating their knowledge or skills. It often includes examining samples of student work developed during the course. For example, students may write an essay in response to a question, providing teachers with a direct assessment of whether students possess the knowledge necessary to answer the initial prompt. Other examples of direct assessment in action include tests, portfolios, and presentations.

**Indirect assessment** provides teachers with indicators of student learning beyond actual work samples, such as students' perception of their own acquisition of knowledge or skills. For instance, a teacher may have students complete a survey indicating how well they thought they had learned, or participate in a self-assessment or exit interview.

These terms and approaches are useful when dealing with external stakeholders like accrediting agencies that might require direct rather than indirect assessment to maintain validity and reliability. Nevertheless, one assessment may contain both. For instance, a student portfolio may provide direct measurement of a given learning outcome, but also include a final reflection assignment that offers indirect evidence of the student's accomplishment of the learning outcome.

## What is the Difference Between Grading and Assessment?

Assessment specialists propose that the essential difference between grading and assessment lies in their purpose. Grades are symbols of individual achievement in a class section and may be based on more than just learning outcomes, while assessment aims to determine how effective a course's assignments and tests are in helping students to achieve learning outcomes. Some teachers' grading criteria, for example, include activities or behaviors that do not measure learning outcomes directly, such as attendance, effort, improvement, or participation. While these actions may correlate with learning outcomes, and are certainly important for student success, they generally are not measures of learning outcomes in their own right. That said, we believe that course-level learning assessment can and, in fact, should relate to grading.

The Eberly Center (2020) at Carnegie Mellon University argued that to be used for learning assessment, grades need to be deconstructed into their components to determine which aspects indicate learning outcomes and which ones indicate other actions. Moreover, grades need to be established by data that are clearly described and consistently applied. For instance, even if 25% of a class receives a grade of B, that whole group may have shown a high level of aptitude in one area but just moderate aptitude in another. Or the group may be comprised of students who have shown aptitude on a continuum with considerable variety at the individual level. Finding this out can allow professors to adjust their teaching to highlight topics and skills the majority of students need additional support to master as well as offer useful feedback to individual students that can help them focus their efforts.

As the Eberly Center (2020) suggested, this method of analysis is different from producing sub-scores for various course activities, like a score for exams, one for projects, and another for homework. Instead, these are different types of assessment, which may assess multiple abilities and skills and overlap in terms of what they assess. To accurately gauge learning outcomes, each mode of assessment (i.e., homework, projects, exams) needs to be analyzed in terms of the various skills it addresses. Then scores across all the assessment activities need to be compiled and assigned for each skill. Table 5.1: Integrating Assessment and Grading Example (adapted from Carnegie Mellon Eberly Center) illustrates this process.

| LEARNING OUTCOME (LO) | LO 1: IDENTIFY SOLUTION STRATEGY | | LO 2: IMPLEMENT SOLUTION STRATEGY | | |
|---|---|---|---|---|---|
| **Learning Assessment Activity/Points** | **Homework 1** | **Exam 1** | **Homework 2** | **Exam 1** | **Total Score & Grade** |
| POSSIBLE POINTS | 20 | 15 | 10 | 10 | 55 |
| STUDENT 1 | 15 | 10 | 9 | 6 | 40 = C |
| STUDENT 2 | 18 | 14 | 8 | 10 | 50 = B |
| STUDENT 3 | 17 | 14 | 5 | 5 | 41 = C |
| CLASS AVERAGE | 16.67 | 12.67 | 7.33 | 7 | |

**Table 5.1. Integrated Assessment and Grading Example**

In our example, achievement of the two learning outcomes (ability to identify solution strategy and ability to implement solution strategy) have each been scored across three separate assessments: Homework 1, Homework 2, and Exam 1. Looking only at the letter grade assignment, Student 1 and Student 3 both received a C, but when examining their learning outcomes, the two students have quite different results. Student 1 demonstrated weakness in both LO 1: Identification and LO 2: Implementation.

On the other hand, Student 3 showed strength in LO 1: Identification but serious weakness in LO 2: Implementation. Student 2 received the higher grade but showed some weakness in LO 2 on the homework assignment. Therefore, each student's grade by itself does not indicate which skills have been mastered. Additionally, overall letter grades would not indicate to a teacher the skills the class as a whole needs additional instruction to master.

Plenty of teachers already have some form of this information but typically disregard it when formulating overall grades. Because questions on tests and homework are already individually scored, teachers can adapt these scores into student learning assessment by classifying each problem according to which learning outcome it corresponds to and then formulating different totals for each category. Using the example in Table 5.1, however, teachers could gather class level data to understand overall strengths and weaknesses. This type of analysis could then be used by the teacher to make changes in their instruction. By regularly monitoring student learning outcomes, the teacher could also gauge the impact of those instructional or curricular changes on individual learning outcomes. A review of the differences between the two are identified in Table 5.2: Differences Between Grades and Assessment.

| GRADES... | COURSE-LEVEL STRATEGIES... |
|---|---|
| Focus on an individual student | Focus on a group of students |
| Use letters as indirect, symbolic representations of accomplishment | Attempt to pinpoint more precisely what was learned |
| May reflect class management goals related to student behavior that are separate from learning, such as attendance, participation, and on-time submission of assignments | Emphasize only achievement of specified learning goals |
| May not reflect standards | Are matched to standards |
| Reflect student performance in individual courses or course assignments | May measure learning from ungraded co-curricular activities or look for skill development beyond course content, such as critical thinking |

**Table 5.2. Differences Between Grades and Assessment. Source: Suskie (2009)**

## KNOWING WHY: RESEARCH ON GRADING AND ASSESSMENT

Why should we care about grading and learning assessment? The simplest answer is that a combination of both are probably the most effective tool instructors have to understand and document student learning. The research on grading suggests that it often removes students' intrinsic motivation for learning and can increase fear and anxiety (Schinske & Tanner, 2014). However, Swinton (2010) found that a grading system that explicitly rewarded effort in addition to rewarding knowledge stimulated student interest in improvement, which suggests that there are ways to use grades to improve learning.

While the evidence suggesting that grading improves learning is murky at best, research indicates that assessment can improve student learning. For example, Holbeck et al. (2014) had 39 students across four sections of an online university course complete misconception/preconception checks to determine whether this specific technique would affect student learning outcomes. Study results indicated that the technique positively affected student success, and researchers also found that students who participated in the assessment had significantly higher GPAs than those who did not. Similarly, Wininger (2005) examined a group of 71 undergraduate students in an educational psychology course to determine the effect of formative assessment on the second implementation of an exam. The students in the experimental group received feedback from their professor and peers on their performance in the formative assessment while the control group did not. The students in the experimental group performed significantly better on the second administration of the exam, with a 9-point gain compared to the control group's 2-point gain.

Other studies have shown similar results. Buchanan (2000), for example, focused on 148 undergraduate students in an introductory psychology course. The students were given access to an online formative assessment program, with the number of times each student accessed the program recorded. Students who used the program scored significantly higher on their final exam than students who did not. In 2003, Henley published findings from a study conducted in Australia that examined undergraduate student performance on formative assessments in a basic science course. Students in the top 10% of the class used the formative assessment tools twice as often as students in the bottom 10%. Velan et al. (2002) also examined students in Australia, studying the influence of online self-assessment for 44 undergraduate medical students in a pathology course. The researchers found that students showed significant improvement in their performance between their first and third attempts of an online self-assessment.

Meanwhile, Leber et al. (2018) determined that students will adjust their learning strategies to match an announced assessment (called the *backwash effect*). The authors studied 81 university students to determine whether "downward misalignment," like announcing and implementing a fact-oriented test when actually aiming to teach for understanding, would reduce student use of high-quality learning strategies, their learning motivation, and their learning outcomes related to understanding. The researchers determined that students who had correctly aligned assessments performed more sophisticated strategies and had better learning outcomes for understanding, as well as higher self-perceptions of confidence, confirming the backwash effect. Thus, teachers should consider this issue when determining an assessment method to encourage students to engage in relevant learning strategies.

Taken as a whole, the research suggests that teachers should provide students with the option for formative assessment throughout a unit or course and also check to see that their teaching goals and assessment models are aligned with their plans for grading and assessment.

## KNOWING HOW: CRAFTING A LEARNING ASSESSMENT STRATEGY

Engaged teachers are curious about whether and how well students are learning, and they conceptualize grading and assessment as a critical component of teaching. To help you take this stance, we offer the following suggestions. Where appropriate, we identify a Cross Academy Technique (CAT) from our companion site, the K. Patricia Cross Academy (*kpcrossacademy.org*), where you can access both a video and a downloadable template that provide specific guidance on how to implement the technique.

### Ensure Explicit and Engaging Assessment

#### CONSIDER THE OUTCOMES

Effective teachers focus on what students will get out of the course, not on their own needs as teachers (Bain, 2004). Maybe that seems obvious, but it is a struggle for many teachers. Instead of focusing on student achievement they focus on the material itself and how they present themselves in the classroom. When preparing to teach a class, start with these two basic questions: What do I want students to learn as a result of taking this class? What do I need to do to get them there?

#### HOLD STUDENTS TO HIGH EXPECTATIONS

The strongest teachers believe their entire class can succeed. Students thrive with high expectations from teachers who believe in their abilities. Indeed, expectations of higher student performance becomes a self-fulfilling prophecy when faculty, colleges, and universities increase effort and hold themselves to high standards (Chickering & Gamson, 1987). Engaged teachers aim to demand a great deal from their students. However, effective teachers don't just push their students to do their best; they also show students how to believe in themselves and improve their confidence. In addition, they encourage students to try, to fail if necessary, but then try again. To foster constructive learning environments that set high expectations, teachers can pinpoint the most essential lessons that students should learn throughout the course, outline high expectations, and ensure students know they are expected to meet them. Here are some suggestions.

- **Set goals with students.** Identifying clear course learning goals is essential, but this can be supplemented with helping individual students set personal goals. This engages students in their own learning and promotes intrinsic motivation and independence.
- **Provide the class with a clear framework for learning.** Demonstrate trust in student ability to oversee their own learning by outlining learning goals correlated to success criteria.
- **Offer formative assessment and feedback.** Provide students with rich, personalized feedback so that students are better able to make the changes required to improve their learning.
- **Ask open-ended questions.** Create an environment where students feel empowered to offer their own ideas instead of always posing questions with right/wrong answers.
- **Allow students to choose from a range of learning activities.** Some students falter when they are not motivated. Don't mistake a lack of motivation or engagement for a lack of ability. Provide students with multiple ways to learn the material.
- **Correct incorrect answers.** It is essential for the education of the entire class to solicit correct responses, so if you find that you've received multiple incorrect answers, correct misunderstandings with the whole class. In discussion, restate your question and nudge students in the right direction.
- **Be fair.** Every student should have an opportunity to succeed and be confident that their assignments will be judged fairly and honestly (Bain, 2004).

## Aim for Clarity, Organization, and Efficiency

Design your courses to benefit all students. The strongest teachers take their subject matter and present it in a way that engages students and supports long-term retention. Consider the following recommendations.

- **Clarity:** Designing a successful course hinges on understanding your goals at the course, module, and unit level. Establishing a clear foundation stabilizes the whole course as well as each course session.

- **Organization:** Begin by brainstorming ideas for each session and jotting down anything that pops into your mind. Then, organize those ideas, considering your actions as well as students' actions and reactions.
- **Efficiency:** Use all of your available class time in a manner that maximizes student work. Write out a plan, but then also build in some flexibility such as including extension activities if parts of your plan take less time than anticipated.

## Consider Key Instructional Elements

There are multiple factors to consider when choosing an assessment strategy.

- **How would you like your students to access the material that starts their learning process?** The CATs on our companion site offer a wide range of direct and indirect methods for students to engage with information. Indeed, you can sort the instructional videos by activity type, such as discussion, group work, or reading.
- **What type of product do you want students to create?** Choose a strategy that produces the type of product you think will best showcase student learning. Most CATs connect a learning activity to the creation of a learning artifact, such as a presentation, a product, or a written assignment, and many provide additional guidance in the corresponding download on how to assess it.
- **What is your intent for assessing your students' learning?** It is worthwhile to think about why you are collecting your data and for whom it is intended. For instance, if you are performing a formative assessment to give you and your students an understanding of their progress, you should choose an assessment technique that aligns with this purpose. If, on the other hand, you are examining student achievement of desired learning outcomes for your university's assessment efforts, your institution may have certain types of data they consider acceptable evidence and you should choose an approach that produces the requisite data.
- **How complicated of an activity do you want to assign?** Learning assessment strategies vary. They can be simple assignments that require little advance preparation or effort to implement as well as complex methods that demand substantial effort to use effectively. Choose a technique with the complexity level appropriate to your needs.

- **How might students be more invested in the assessment process?** Being active participants in assessment can help students learn. Consider having students make Crib Cards (CAT 40) to think through what is the most important information or consider involving them in creating rubrics.

## Consider Teaching Context

College faculty teach in many different educational environments. Some teach in onsite classrooms while others teach online. Some teach small, seminar-type classes while others teach hundreds of students. Some organize their courses around lecture presentation, while others structure theirs around collaborative learning. All of the CATs on the K. Patricia Cross Academy site are appropriate for most contexts, but here are recommendations of CATs that we feel are particularly effective for assessing learning in a specific teaching environment.

### COLLABORATIVE CLASSROOMS

Most teachers think of learning as something that occurs in the mind of an individual student. Additionally, when we think of learning assessment, we generally start with evidence of individual learning. Now, however, there are many scholars who think of learning as something that extends beyond the individual; instead, it is groups of individuals developing and harnessing a networked intelligence (Major, 2015). Collaborative learning encourages this understanding of learning and is a pedagogy that we champion (for example, see Barkley et al., 2014). Because student learning takes place both individually and collaboratively, the chief question becomes, "Which learning activities are best performed collaboratively and which individually?" Here are three recommendations for CATs that are particularly effective in collaborative learning (Barkley & Major, 2016; Barkley et al., 2014).

- **CAT 37: Think-Pair-Share:** In this simple technique, the instructor poses a question, gives students a few minutes to think about a response, and then asks students to share their ideas with a partner. Hence, think-pair-share.

- **CAT 48: Think-Aloud Pair Problem Solving:** Pairs of students are asked to solve a set of problems and are given specific roles: problem solver and listener. Students switch roles for alternating problems.

- **CAT 23: Role Play:** During a role-play scenario, students perform or assume the perspective of characters or roles they typically would not assume in order to achieve learning goals. Often, students will research the roles on their own, but teachers may choose to offer specific assigned readings as source material.

## FLIPPED CLASSROOM

This is an instructional design in which the common order of components for courses is reversed. Instead of reading or completing activities outside the classroom and then attending class for content-intensive lectures, in flipped classes, students will typically watch a brief video lecture or do other content-rich work outside the classroom and then participate in exercises, projects, or discussions in the classroom. Below we recommend CATs for use in flipped classrooms.

- **CAT 24: Case Studies:** With case studies, students review a real-life problem scenario in depth. This can be done as an assignment prior to the class meeting. Then, students in groups apply course concepts to identify and evaluate alternative approaches to solving the problem.
- **CAT 25: Triple Jump:** This three-step technique requires students to think through and attempt to solve a real-world problem. The first two steps can be done outside of class in preparation for collaborative work or presentation in the onsite class. The three basic steps are:
    1. Students individually review the case or problem and write a preliminary assessment (for example, what I know, what I need to know, how I can find it out).
    2. Students individually conduct research to find the information they need to offer a solution.
    3. Students present a final analysis (for example, "Here are the key issues of the case and here is how I would solve it or here is the answer").
- **CAT 45: Individual Readiness Assurance Tests (IRATs):** Students complete these closed-book quizzes after an out-of-class reading, video, or other homework assignment to document their preparation for onsite class work.

## LARGE CLASSES

Typically taught in auditoriums, large classes frequently have several hundred students enrolled with the primary instructor generally lecturing. These courses present a challenge for engaging students, managing them, and assessing their learning in meaningful ways. Below we recommend CATs that can be used effectively in large classes.

- **CAT 21: Post-Test Analysis (PTA):** This technique is a two-stage process that is divided into several steps designed to help students develop greater awareness of their test-preparing and test-taking skills.
- **CAT 39: Comprehensive Factors List:** After completing a lecture, assignment, or other course experience, students write down as many relevant components related to the topic as they can recall.
- **CAT 10: Quick Write:** In a quick write, students are given a brief amount of time to respond in writing to an open-ended prompt.

## Consider Clustering Multiple Learning Assessment Techniques Together

Though each CAT may be implemented separately, they may also be effectively joined together in instructional sequences. Establishing foundational knowledge may be necessary before applying that knowledge, and application may be essential before integrating that knowledge into what students have already learned.. Therefore, you may opt for linking CATs together. For instance, you may begin with CAT 16: Guided Reading Notes for an individual reading assignment. Then, you may implement a CAT 30: Insights-Resources-Application writing assignment asking students to draw connections between their experiences and

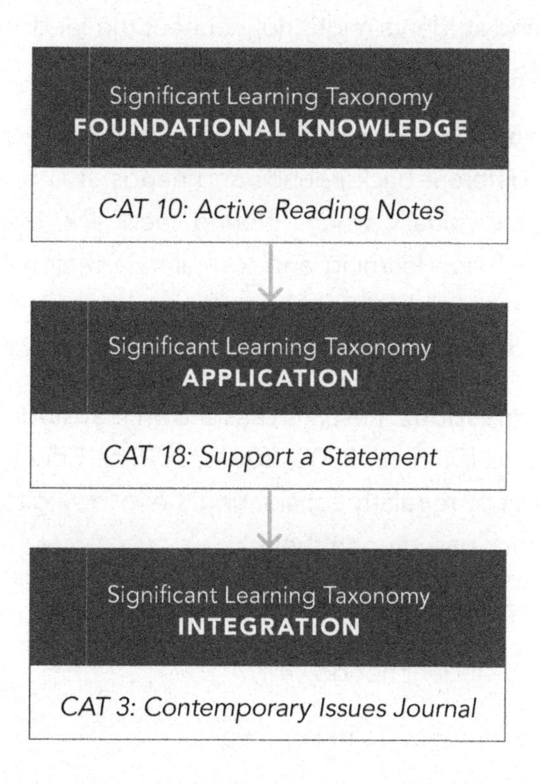


**Figure 5.1. Clustering Cross Academy Techniques (CATs) in an Instructional Sequence**

the reading. In this way, CATs can be used together, as seen in Figure 5.1: Clustering Cross Academy Techniques (CATs) in an Instructional Sequence, in which three CATs aligned with three learning dimensions of the Significant Learning Taxonomy are sequenced.

## Consider How You Will Offer Feedback

Effective teachers understand that the greatest value they can contribute to a student's learning process may be the careful observation, analysis, and feedback that enables the learner to improve. Students who recognize what they do and do not know are better able to focus their learning. Throughout the course, students need consistent opportunities to receive feedback. Here are some suggestions to ensure feedback is constructive.

- **Give feedback that offers teaching points.** Good feedback offers students guidance on what they are doing correctly and incorrectly. The most productive feedback offers students an explanation and specific examples about accuracies and inaccuracies in their work, rather than broad compliments or criticism.

- **Give feedback in a timely manner.** Students respond positively to feedback given immediately, and they tend to remember the experience and be more confident in their learning. When we wait too long, we lose the moment, and students might not connect the feedback to the activity or their learning.

- **Be sensitive to each student's individual needs.** Classrooms are full of students with different backgrounds and needs. It is optimal to consider each student individually when offering feedback. Some need gentle nudges to encourage learning and to maintain their self-esteem; others may need to be pushed to perform at a higher level. Find the right balance between offering encouragement and avoiding hurt feelings.

- **Ask the four questions.** Research has shown that students want to know where they stand (Dinham, 2002, 2007a, 2007b). Effective teachers offer quality feedback by regularly considering the following four questions and offering feedback based upon them:

  1. What can the student do?

  2. What can the student not do yet?

  3. What can the student do to improve?

  4. How does the student's work compare to others in the class?

- **Consider using a rubric.** Rubrics clearly and effectively communicate expectations for coursework as well as the range of standards.
- **Teach students how to offer feedback to one another.** Demonstrate to students what constructive feedback looks and sounds like. Model feedback that is positive and helpful and consider encouraging students to give similar feedback to their peers.
- **Use "I noticed..."** Show students that you recognize their effort. One way to demonstrate that you care is to say something like, "I noticed how you shared new ideas with the class this week." Positive reinforcement can make a big difference in student performance.
- **Provide models or examples.** When assigning coursework, offer an example of what success looks like. "An A+ paper will..." while "a B paper will..." The examples should provide clear contrasts.

## CONCLUSION

Teaching to produce learning is our primary instructional role. Indeed, college teachers today are experiencing increased pressure to teach effectively and to provide evidence of what and how well students are learning. Assessment and grading are the means by which you can gauge and communicate how well students are learning as a result of your teaching. Robust assessment and grading systems will offer students clear guidance on what they should learn and how well they are learning it. Such systems also provide you feedback about your effectiveness as a teacher, give external stakeholders reliable measures of students' progress, and involve both you and students in the continuous monitoring and improvement of student learning. That is engaged teaching at its best.

## FOCUS ON ONLINE TEACHING

The information we share in the main body of this chapter applies to both onsite and online teaching, but here we provide additional insights focused specifically on teaching online, hybrid, and blended courses.

### What: Learning Assessment Online

Engaged teachers gather information from multiple and diverse sources in order to better understand what students know, understand, and can do as a result of their experience in the class. Yet many online teachers rely heavily — if not solely — on the automatically graded quiz tool in their learning management systems (LMS). While using this tool may be an efficient way to determine students' knowledge of basic facts, concepts, and information, there are other assessment strategies students will likely find more engaging and that offer you deeper, more nuanced insights regarding their learning. Learning assessment online means adopting a wide variety of approaches to promote, evaluate, measure, and document the academic readiness, learning progress, skill acquisition, or educational needs of students in the online environment.

### Why: Learning Assessment Online

As we noted in the chapter, research shows that assessment can promote gains in student learning outcomes. While there is not yet as much research on the relationship between assessment and learning gains in an online environment, the available evidence suggests that a positive relationship exists in this environment as well. In a meta-analysis of 58 studies, Li et al. (2020), for example, found that using peer evaluation to promote learning showed even greater gains in a computer-mediated environment than a paper-based one. Smaller studies have supported the findings for the benefits of formative assessment, in particular in the online environment (Chanpet et al., 2020; Chen et al., 2021). Assessing learning online simply provides an opportunity to promote and deepen student learning.

### How: Learning Assessment Online

What learning assessment techniques work well in an online environment? Below we recommend CATs that provide substantial guidance on assessment that we feel work well in the online environment. You can access an online implementation video for these techniques as well as a downloadable template on our companion site, The K. Patricia Cross Academy (*kpcrossacademy.org*).

**CAT 1: DIGITAL STORY**

In this learning assessment technique, students use computer-based tools, such as video, audio, graphics, and web publishing to tell stories. The stories may be personal or academic, but for either focus, students share relevant life experiences as they attempt to connect to an audience about a given issue. Students often tell about their lives through their interactions with others, thus providing them with an opportunity for self-authorship as they curate their lived experiences.

**CAT 3: CONTEMPORARY ISSUES JOURNAL**

To create their journal, students look for recent events or developments in the real world that are related to their coursework, then analyze these current affairs to identify the connections to course material in entries that they write in a journal. This activity helps students understand themselves in relation to the course content, making coursework more relevant to them, which can stimulate their motivation to learn it.

**CAT 9: THREE-MINUTE MESSAGE**

This activity is modeled on the Three-Minute Thesis (3MT) academic competition, in which students have three minutes to present a compelling argument and to support it with convincing details and examples. The limited time frame forces students to choose what is the most essential part of their message and then deliver their information in a clear and concise way using language that is accessible to a non-specialist audience.

**CAT 49: BRIEFING PAPER**

In this assessment activity, students research a current problem of their choice, summarize the main issues, and present solutions to a specific audience, such as a government agency. The audience should be an entity that needs information about the problem and that can potentially help to achieve resolution of it. A briefing paper provides rich assessment information that allows teachers to see students' logic as well as their ability to communicate their thought process.

*Good communication is more than carefully chosen words.*

**—K. PATRICIA CROSS**

CHAPTER 6

# Attending to Visual Elements in Teaching

One of our colleagues in the visual arts begins his course with a projected image of a cellphone's home screen. He then polls students with the prompt: "When you are looking for a specific app, do you look for the app's icon or the app's text title?" Students invariably say they first identify the app by its icon. In this simple exercise, he underscores the power of visual design. Indeed, images have supplanted text as the dominant communication medium in contemporary culture. Good visual design can be a potent, effective tool for increasing student engagement. Most instructors dedicate substantial time to fostering student engagement. They identify worthwhile goals and objectives, develop interesting activities, and craft compelling lectures, but spend little time thinking about the visual design of their instructional materials. Students then give no more than a passing glance to important documents like the syllabus, or they click rapidly through text-based learning modules. It may be easy to dismiss this as a problem with students' focus and attention, but student disengagement can also be a response to poor visual design.

Great material that is poorly presented may not reach your students because students can't or won't process it as intended. The inverse is also true. Bad content dressed up in a beautiful package will also not help students accomplish the learning goals. The challenge is to find ways to present good information in a manner that engages students in the content. Well-designed materials support student learning because they provide clarity, promote positive associations, and emphasize the relevance of course materials. Striving for high quality visual design is therefore an important aspect of engaged teaching.

## KNOWING WHAT: ABOUT VISUAL DESIGN

Visual design is the use of color, shapes, form, imagery, and typography to improve the user's experience with material. When it comes to education, visual design is the process of determining how these various elements can best be incorporated into learning materials to improve learning outcomes. Good visual design isn't just the addition of decorative elements or choice of fancy typefaces. Indeed, too many elements actually distract or confuse students, a sign of failed visual design. The goal is for text and images to work in tandem to guide learners through course materials and activities efficiently and effectively. Visual design determines how your instructional materials look. When elements such as typeface, layout, color palettes, buttons, and site navigation are put together in an aesthetically pleasing manner, students are more motivated to invest the time and energy to learn the content.

### Visual Design Tools

Some of the tools at your disposal to incorporate into the visual design of your materials include typeface/font, photos, graphic elements, and interactive graphics.

#### TYPEFACE/FONT

Good design starts with typography. An appropriate typeface (which is commonly called a font) can spark positive emotional reactions to content. The text or website suddenly has a little more personality. It may look traditional or modern, casual or elegant, simple or artistic. In contrast, a poorly chosen typeface or combination of typefaces can lead users to think the text looks chaotic, difficult to read, or outdated. Visual design thinking challenges you to find the right typeface to further the message of the text and content. For many instructors, this is just a matter of determining a typographic style that may consist of one or two typefaces and sticking with them. Other teachers may vary font style from project to project, depending on the tone of the lesson. There are thousands of fonts available with new ones being created daily, but Table 6.1: Sample Categories of Typeface, describes a few of the standard groups of typefaces.

In addition to selecting the font, there are three ways to improve the design of text in your instructional materials: kerning, tracking, and leading.

| GROUP | EXAMPLE | SAMPLE TEXT |
|---|---|---|
| OLDSTYLE | Palatino<br>Times | This category is based on the handwriting of scribes who used wedge-tipped pens that produced serifs (a small vertical or horizontal stroke on the letter) and thick/thin strokes. This type of font is frequently the best choice for large bodies of text. |
| SLAB SERIF | American Typewriter<br>Courier<br>Rockwell | The concept of advertising emerged with the industrial revolution. To create posters that could be seen from a distance, new fonts with thick, dark lines and blocky serifs were created. These fonts are often best used sparingly for impact. |
| MODERN | Avenir<br>Arial<br>Calibri | As mechanical devices and more sophisticated printing replaced human pen strokes, new typefaces developed that produced a clean, crisp, modern look, partially because they are without serifs. In addition to giving a contemporary appearance, these fonts can be very effective on presentations and web pages because of their clarity. |
| SCRIPT | Lucida Calligraphy<br>Brush Script MT<br>Edwardian Script | Fonts that imitate cursive handwriting and use flowing strokes are called script. These fonts can add elegance, but should never be used for long blocks of text. |
| DECORATIVE | Mistral<br>Tratatello<br>DESDEMONA | These fonts are fun and distinctive, and because of their idiosyncratic nature, should be used sparingly and for special effects. |

**Table 6.1. Sample Categories of Typeface**

**Kerning.** This is the process by which you selectively adjust the amount of space between two letters, characters, or numbers. Adjustments in kerning are applied to the space between a pair of letters. For example, the letters "AV" are typically kerned to be closer to one another in order to avoid an awkward space between them, as demonstrated in *Figure 6.1: Example of Kerning.* While most fonts today automatically adjust for kerning, there may be occasions where you want to increase or decrease the space in ways that increase impact or improve legibility.

**Figure 6.1. Example of Kerning**

**Tracking.** Similar to kerning, tracking also adjusts the space between letters, but it does so for larger amounts of copy. You therefore apply tracking adjustments to entire blocks of text or the whole document to increase the white space so that if feels more open or to make your text more visually balanced. See Figure 6.2: Example of Tracking for an illustration of this principle.

**Figure 6.2. Example of Tracking**

**Leading.** This is the space between lines of text rather than individual characters. The term is pronounced "led ding" because it is derived from the use of strips of lead to separate lines of text in handset printing presses. A simple example of leading is double-spacing, but adjustments can be made on a continuum to change the overall aesthetics of typographical design. See Figure 6.3: Example of Leading.

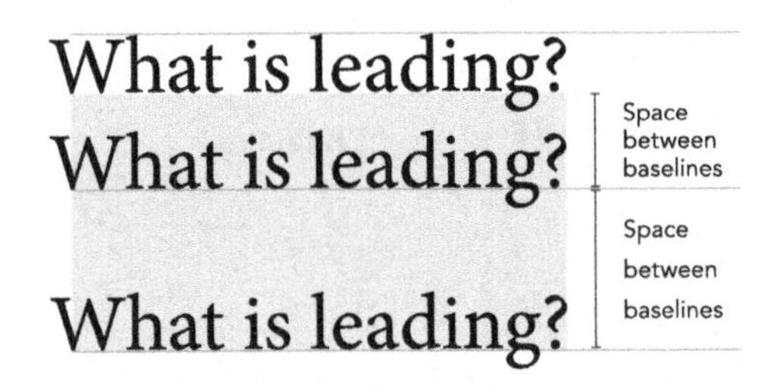


**Figure 6.3. Example of Leading**

### PHOTOS AND GRAPHIC ELEMENTS

Good photos and graphics can enliven course materials. There are many sites that provide cost-free images, but check the copyright stipulations for each so that you can be sure to use them appropriately. Some of these sites include Creative Commons, Pexels, Pixabay, StockSnap.io, and Unsplash. If you cannot find what you're looking for using any of these sites, Google Image Search offers lots of options and is also a useful tool that allows you to sort your searches by copyright. Or you can consider purchasing images through sites such as Shutterstock or Getty Images.

Another option is to create your own images. For example, you can take photos using your smartphone or camera and insert those into course materials. Alternatively, you can illustrate needed visual elements by hand and scan your drawings to add into course material. You can also create visual elements using software like Adobe Photoshop, Canva, Google Drawings, or Microsoft SmartArt and then export those designs as PNG or JPEG files. Many of these programs offer templates or tutorials that make them accessible for instructors without formal design experience.

### INTERACTIVE IMAGERY

Instead of presenting a fixed frame or image, interactive graphics allow the user to interact with the image, creating a personalized experience. For example, a hotspot image allows students to access text, links, or other images when clicking on an icon overlaid on the image. Interactive graphics are engaging and can help you guide students to understand how details fit in a larger context. A clickable map of the universe, for instance, may be more compelling than reading numbers on a page to help astronomy students understand the vastness of the cosmos. You can build hotspot images in tools like Prezi or PowerPoint. There are also programs such as Ion Interactive and Infogram that, while not always free, can provide you with the support needed to create effective interactive imagery.

These tools can be used to create a variety of visually appealing instructional materials that communicate essential ideas in a compelling format, including:

- the course syllabus;
- slide and video presentations;
- content-rich handouts;
- infographics;
- instructions for learning activities;

- tests, grading rubrics, and other assessments; and
- course websites and social pages.

Programs such as Adobe Illustrator, Pages, Canva, Keynote, PowerPoint, Prezi, and Google Slides also offer templates, tools, and tutorials that can guide you through the process of good design.

## KNOWING WHY: RESEARCH ON VISUAL DESIGN FOR INSTRUCTION

Creating well-designed instructional materials takes time and effort. From choosing the right photos or building the right graphics to picking the perfect font, you may wonder if it is worth the effort. In brief, yes. Research has indicated that effective use of visual design in instructional activities improves student motivation, helps students manage cognitive load, and leads to improved student learning outcomes (Carney & Levin, 2002). Studies have identified key aspects of design that can either improve or reduce student learning.

### Typeface/Font

Based on what we understand about universal design for learning, it may not surprise you to learn that typeface choice can affect student learning. While it is essential for students with disabilities, all students can benefit from a font that is easy to read. Researchers have determined that if students struggle to read a typeface, they are more likely to believe the entire assignment will be difficult or frustrating and are less willing to do the task itself. By contrast, a well-chosen font leads students to believe an assignment will be more manageable, and hence they are more likely to attempt it (Song & Schwarz, 2008).

### Photos and Graphic Elements

Graphics and images serve many purposes, including conveying information directly to the student or helping students better understand accompanying textual information in the materials. They can also help students manage intrinsic cognitive load and reduce their extraneous cognitive load by directing their mental energies appropriately through the instructional materials (Sweller et al., 2019). Different types of graphics serve different purposes for education. Some studies indicate that photos and graphics are only effective tools if they enable students to integrate information with little cognitive processing. In other words, mentally taxing graphics may not improve learning. Students' characteristics, including their visuospatial abilities and existing knowledge of material, as well as teaching strategies, can influence graphic processing (Vekiri, 2002).

Other research suggests the importance of pairing visual material, such as graphics, with either spoken or recorded audio. Indeed, the capacity of effective working memory increases with the use of both auditory and visual working memory rather than the use of either processor individually. For instance, Mousavi et al. (1995) presented subjects with a diagram that was either integrated with written text (i.e., visual) or with spoken text (i.e., auditory) and found that the combination of written and oral was the most effective. Their research indicates that it may be equally, or perhaps more, effective to speak textual information aloud rather than just physically integrating it into diagrams. Also, Leahy and Sweller (2011; 2016) indicated that short forms of audio-visual information were more effective than just visual material; however, longer forms were less effective than just the visual material alone.

### Infographics and Slide Decks

Poorly designed, cluttered infographics and slide decks can negatively affect student learning in multiple ways, including limiting a learner's ability to determine which details are important. Designs that are random, messy, or poorly planned can lead students to find the information less credible. For instance, research indicates that slide decks containing irrelevant material can result in poorer performance (Bartsch & Cobern, 2003), which furthers Harp and Maslich's (2005) argument that distracting details inhibit learning.

### Interactive Imagery

The efficacy of interactive graphics has been the subject of more limited research, but initial reports indicate their potential. For instance, Pani et al. (2014) looked at graphic representation in a neuroanatomy course and determined that students rated interactive graphics as an improvement when compared to traditional instructional materials. In addition, variations in learning outcomes corresponded to how differing individuals used the software. This, in turn, reflected students' individual work habits, such as how much time they committed to testing.

In sum, the existing research indicates that good visual design in instruction materials, including the careful selection of fonts, images, graphics, and interactives, can improve student learning.

## KNOWING HOW: TIPS FOR VISUAL DESIGN FOR INSTRUCTION

Building well-designed materials can be fun and exciting. But with so many options for colors, graphics, fonts, and photos available to you, it may be daunting to know where to begin. Here are a few tips and strategies to help you get started in visual design. Where appropriate, we identify a Cross Academy Technique (CAT) from our companion site, the K. Patricia Cross Academy (*kpcrossacademy.org*), where you can access both a video and a downloadable template that provide specific guidance on how to implement the technique.

## Consider Your Purpose and the Content

Especially when you are starting out, it can be easy to get swept up in the creation of visually interesting designs. But it is important to make sure that your designs always adhere to your instructional goals. You also want to make sure that materials are appropriate and accessible for your students. Here are a few questions to consider:

**What aspects do you want to emphasize or make more memorable?** You know the essential lessons that you hope to convey in a course or an individual assignment. Think about these important teaching goals and consider how they can best be illustrated. For example, the use of a compelling photo or illustration can help your students draw connections and relate to the material better than text alone. By focusing on your goals, you will be more likely to ensure the images are not simply decorative, but are relevant and support student learning.

**What is your key idea?** Once you have determined the aspects related to your teaching goals that you want to illustrate, determine your key idea. Students can become overwhelmed or confused if you include too much text, data, or imagery, especially if all of the material is important. Start by developing your key idea or message and then craft your materials to convey that idea to your students.

**What types of materials and mediums best convey your key idea?** After you have identified the key idea, consider how visual elements might help you more effectively convey that information in your instructional materials. Peeck (1993) argued that the effectiveness of imagery used in instructional materials depends on how they spur the student to process the material that they convey. For instance, CAT 29: Advance Organizers can provide students with a visual way to organize information and take notes. In addition, visual diagrams can be a useful tool in anatomy instruction for showing where organs and systems are in relation to each other. When paired with a section of text explaining the role of each organ as it relates to the body, they can help students draw upon and build their knowledge of the subject. Students will benefit from the easy visual reference to understand the spatial relationships of physical anatomy, rather than trying to create in their mind their own visual for it.

Alternatively, illustrations can also be used to convey abstract ideas that are discussed textually in the material. Students can use the graphics to bolster their understanding of the subject or to affirm their understanding of the text by comparing it to the accompanying illustrations. You can also use graphics and visual cues in your materials to encourage your students to pay close attention to a specific idea or to process a section of text more deeply.

**What is the best way to structure your graphic elements to improve student understanding?** The structure of your graphic elements affects how students process them. Sweller et al. (2019) suggested that you structure visual elements to help students manage the intrinsic load related to the material as well as the extraneous cognitive load associated with the instruction. They recommended the following:

- Combine textual and graphic information into a single element, reducing the likelihood that you'll divide student attention. One example is to list out procedural steps in a graphic overlay, illustrating via diagram how each step is performed.
- Omit extraneous textual information. If your visual element can convey an idea on its own without any explanatory text, you reduce mental effort. Therefore, avoid creating multiple stand-alone elements of textual and graphical material that convey redundant ideas.
- Introduce new concepts to students gradually through visual elements using a simple-to-complex approach. This will help students avoid being overloaded with more information than they are able to process.
- Illustrate ideas through increasingly realistic visualizations. Start out with low-fidelity visuals and then work toward high-fidelity visuals. As you do so, students should improve their understanding of the ideas rather than get bogged down in contextual details.

## Focus on the Students

**Who are the learners? What are they interested in?** Student tastes can vary based on their educational level, their fields of study, their ages, and so forth. Thus, not every visual element will be equally engaging to every student. When creating your materials, you will want to consider what images will resonate for your students. For instance, students in a theater class may respond differently to illustrated diagrams than students in a chemistry course. Consider the needs and aesthetics of your students when choosing your elements. What colors and graphics will they respond to? Does the material call for more modern or classic design? Get to know your students and design elements that will best serve them.

**How might learners be involved in creating visual elements?** Students often have great artistic skills or abilities that go unnoticed. Consider having students create visual elements that you display. CAT 13: Sketch Notes, for example, asks students to create visual notes that they can share in the course LMS. In addition, CAT 1: Digital Story can be a great way to have students use many digital tools to create an audio-visual project they can share with the class.

**What are the areas that generally give your students trouble? What are commonly missed answers on tests?** Consider CAT 31, Background Knowledge Probe to identify potential areas in which students lack knowledge. If there are key concepts that your students typically struggle with, you may want to focus on designing graphics that illustrate those ideas. By helping students to visualize the concept as well understand differences between similar ideas, you can help correct any existing student biases or misinformation.

**What pictures and graphics best suit your personal teaching style?** It is not only students' preferences that you need to consider. Your instructional materials are a good way to convey your personality to students and establish the rhythms of your classroom. Do you want to come across as formal or casual? Serious or funny? Adopting a professional style with well-chosen graphics and typography that reinforce it will help you establish those expectations early on. In truth, most teachers alternate between different modes over the course of the semester and selecting the right images to complement either can help students understand how to approach a particular course element.

## Understand the Principles of Visual Design

While the most important idea to remember while creating documents is that everything must serve your key points and message, it is also useful to familiarize yourself with the basics of visual design.

**Strive for unity in design.** Endeavor to establish a sense of narrative harmony and visual consistency in your designs. For teaching and learning, unity offers a cohesive learning experience, weaving a common thread of metaphor, visual themes, or recurring images throughout the materials. Another way to think about unity is consistency. Maintain similar colors, graphic styles, and fonts throughout your documents. Each of the visual pieces you work into your materials should complement each other and form unity. A common error is to use too many disparate elements, which can create distraction rather than convey a coherent idea. Maintaining visual consistently will keep students focused on the key ideas rather than getting bogged down in separate parts of your message. And the need for unity extends beyond visual design; it also applies to the overall learning experience. Ensure documents match the tone, style, and language of your instruction throughout.

**Organize your material with visual hierarchy.** Students will pick up on visual clues like size, scale, and arrangement on the page to understand what's most important. You are establishing a visual hierarchy even if you do not realize it, so it is important to be mindful and emphasize your most important elements. Look at the page you are building. Notice how your eyes are naturally drawn to the biggest elements. By designing your materials so that key ideas are the easiest to recognize and grasp, you will better retain students' interest. For students skimming through a text, the largest graphic may be the only thing they read or retain.

Therefore, you want to make sure the most important takeaways are not buried in smaller fonts or dwarfed by larger graphics. Here are some questions to consider:

- Should you arrange your text by paragraph or by bullet point?
- What photos or phrases help stress the importance of your ideas?
- Should you highlight key ideas or use another approach to visually emphasize them?
- Are you making proper use of white space so that each component stands on its own?

Just remember that students' eyes will naturally gravitate toward the items you give the most prominence, so be conscious that those elements are worth the most attention.

**Use dominance to signal importance.** Examine any two visual elements side by side in a design. If the two elements are not equal in every distinguishable way, then naturally one will attract your attention because it establishes dominance over the other. Because they will stand out on the page, make sure that the dominant elements of your design are signaling the most important material. Dominance helps students understand what to focus on rather than being distracted or overwhelmed by all of the elements on the page or presentation slide. Figure 6.4: Visual Representation of Dominance illustrates this concept.

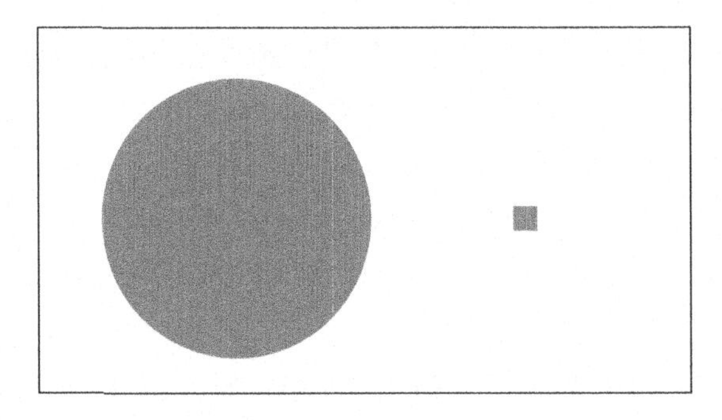

**Figure 6.4. Visual Representation of Dominance**

**Establish balance.** Good balance helps maintain visual stability and ensures you emphasize the most important material. Balance doesn't necessarily mean everything looks uniform. With symmetrical balance, you're basically creating a mirror image on both sides of the page. Symmetrical balance establishes a strong sense of structure. With asymmetrical balance, by contrast, you're balancing smaller visual elements with larger ones on the opposite side of the page. Holistically, the page still looks balanced even if each object is not reflected by a mirroring element. Figure 6.5: Symmetrical and Asymmetrical Balance offers an example of what that looks like.

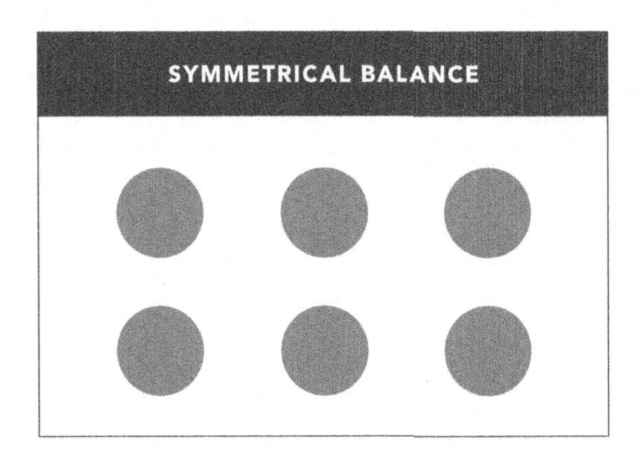


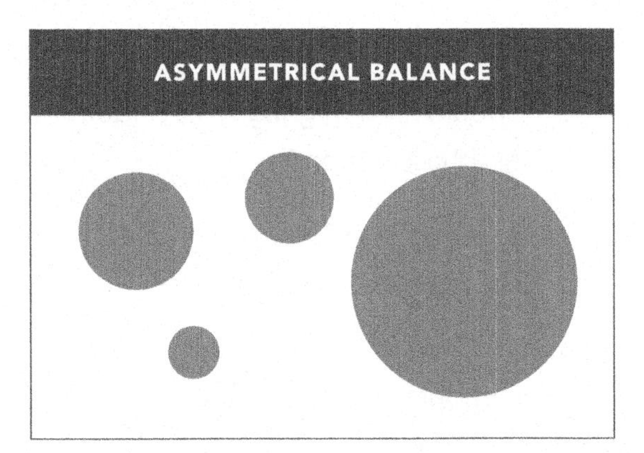


**Figure 6.5. Symmetrical and Asymmetrical Balance**

**Highlight key ideas through contrast.** Design features like contrast can help you distinguish key ideas by drawing students' eyes to specific elements within other materials. One common example to establish contrast is to bold a key word or phrase in a paragraph. Notice how your eyes are immediately drawn to the bolded text. Italicization and underlining can serve a similar purpose, as can varying your font size, shape, or color.

In addition to providing contrast, colors are also connected with viewers' emotions and can alter how students feel about various course materials. Think about the difference between red text and blue text, for example. How might the differing hues affect students' perception of the content? Visual contrast can help you stress essential pieces of information, establish points of interest, draw reader attention to specific graphic elements, and keep students engaged. Also remember that some color pairings do not provide sufficient contrast, such as yellow on white or blue or purple on black. This can make it difficult for learners to read and process information. When using contrast, remember to consider your key objectives. If you use contrast appropriately, you'll draw attention to the most essential elements.

**Use proximity to signal relationships.** Our brains assume that objects arranged near each other go together. Proximity also helps us remember the relationship between two objects, rather than presenting them as a disconnection.

**Establish proportion or scale.** Scale is the design principle that refers to the size relationship between objects. As we established earlier, the size of objects on a page can signal importance. However, if you change font size or object size or move interactive buttons around the screen frequently in order to fit all your ideas on one page, you may overwhelm your students. Establish a set of rules for font sizes and visual elements early on and adhere to it in order to keep from inhibiting your students' progress through needless distraction.

**Ensure sufficient white space.** In page layout, white space is sometimes called negative space. It is the portion of the page that remains empty, without pictures or text. It is the area between type, margins, and graphics. When you are designing a page, using appropriate white space increases the clarity and overall look of your work by balancing out the busier parts and reducing crowding.

**Keep it consistent and repetitive.** Repetition is a key tenet of design. Repeating themes and elements through a presentation help make it feel cohesive, thus improving the entire look and feel of the design. Repetition also reduces cognitive load by providing students with a familiar design. All of the elements should look like they belong together, which will make presentations and assignments flow easily and in ways that students can process.

One easy example is to consider the pages of this book. It would be a less useful reference tool for you if pages were numbered inconsistently or if the font and design changed from page to page or chapter to chapter. You would likely get frustrated and might opt to find another book. Students will approach your content the same way. When you use recurring elements throughout your entire class, the material will be quickly recognizable and identified as belonging to the larger instructional context.

**Divide your design into thirds.** This basic principle suggests that presenting information in thirds is the best approach. This is because a three-part structure combines the brevity that helps viewers keep information within the confines of working memory while also offering a sufficient amount of variety to create an interesting and identifiable pattern. To implement this approach, divide your designs into three rows and three columns. This provides you with a quick guide to positioning your various elements and gives your design more motion and interest. Instead of having your design always centered, make your focal points at or close to the intersections of the vertical and horizontal lines. Many layout programs such as Canva and Pages provide grid tools to guide you in your alignment. See Figure 6.6: The Rule of Thirds for examples.

**Figure 6.6. The Rule of Thirds. Photo Credit: Unsplash.com**

**Ensure accessibility.** Accessibility refers to the ability for all users to access and benefit from devices, services, environments, or products. While it originated as a way to assist people with disabilities, research has demonstrated that accessibility benefits everyone. In education, the concept of accessibility is strongly related to universal design. Applying the concepts of accessibility to visual design means that you try to create your instructional materials so that they are usable by people with the widest range of abilities and within the widest range of contexts. Basic principles to be mindful of in the visual design of instructional materials, especially text-based materials, are:

- Use fonts that have sufficient weight and are at least 12 pt.
- Create bulleted or numbered lists using built-in styles so that they can be read by a screen reader.
- When creating tables, ensure that they don't contain split cells, merged cells, or nested tables and that you specify column header information.

- Check to make sure the order of headings is logical, and then use built-in heading styles so that this hierarchy is read by screen readers.
- Use formatting functions (e.g., paragraph styles) to adjust the amount of space before or after a paragraph rather than inserting repeated blank characters or lines.
- Don't use color alone to convey meaning.
- Ensure type and background provides sufficient contrast.
- Provide text alternatives that screen readers can read that offer specific and instructive information for images and figures.

Your intent should be to design your materials so that they are approachable and accessible to all.

## CONCLUSION

In today's classroom, there are so many opportunities for distraction, and we seem to be constantly competing for students' attention. This challenge can become even greater in online courses, where students have only their self-control to discourage them from scrolling through social media, shopping, or gaming. Instructional materials with good visual design motivate students to put in the time and effort to understand your content. Well-designed materials support student learning by providing clarity, emphasizing the relevance of course materials, and encouraging engagement.

Developing a visual sensibility that complements your teaching style isn't easy, but it can be fun. Yet, it is not just a matter of choosing pictures that are related to the topic. You also have to consider how to arrange every element to facilitate learning. The end result may look simple to students, but, as Apple's Steve Jobs said, "Simple can be harder than complex: you have to work hard to get your thinking clean to make it simple." Adopting some of the visual design strategies outlined in this chapter will help you create instructional materials that help your students better process their cognitive load and have better experiences in the classroom. In this way, striving for high-quality visual design is an important aspect of engaged teaching.

## FOCUS ON ONLINE TEACHING

The information we share in the main body of this chapter applies to both onsite and online teaching, but here we provide additional insights focused specifically on teaching online, hybrid, and blended courses.

### What: Visual Design Online

Visual design for online courses is the process of improving the learning environment through visual elements, such as colors, typography, illustrations, and white space. Visual design is an important element of online courses. Most instructors and online course developers, however, lack a background in design, and so good visual design for online courses can be a challenge.

### Why: Visual Design Online

Creating an online course that has a strong visual design is important in theory because it can help to eliminate confusion and frustration. It is likely that strong visual design can help hold students' attention and make their learning more efficient, effective, and successful. The research in this area is not yet well developed; however, the existing research appears to support these claims.

In one useful study, Szabo and Kanuka (1999) conducted an experimental research study to determine whether artistic screens (those that employ accepted principles of visual design) influenced student learning. Fifty-two learners participated in their study. While they found no difference in achievement scores between the two groups, they found that students who participated in the lesson with good design principles completed the lesson in less time (21% less) and had a higher completion rate (74% vs. 45%) than those who used the lesson with poor design principles.

In another useful study, Nusbaum et al. (2021) conducted an experiment with 488 student participants to determine whether using a more visual syllabus design or more welcoming syllabus language would affect students' perceptions of their instructors or knowledge of the syllabus content. Overall, neither visual formatting nor language had a significant impact on perceptions of the syllabus or quiz scores. However, participants who viewed the visual syllabus rated the hypothetical professor as kinder, more creative, and more approachable than those who viewed the less visual one.

## How: Visual Design Online

Following are suggestions for visual design specific to online courses:

### TYPOGRAPHY

Good typography enhances readability, encourages information processing, and may even help engage online reader emotions. When choosing fonts for an online course, consider the following recommendations:

- Set a limited font palette.
- Choose a legible font size such as 14- to 16- point font for the body copy.
- Keep it simple. Sans-serif typefaces are a good choice.

### COLOR

The color palette should enhance the course site. When choosing colors for your online course, consider the following:

- **Choose just a few colors for your design.** Three is sufficient to create variation while remaining understated.
- **Follow the 60-30-10 rule.** Rather than featuring colors in equal amounts, use a dominant color approximately 60% of the time, the next color 30%, and the last color 10%.
- **Use background color sparingly.** Since background colors can interfere with readability, use them sparingly. If you do use background color, choose fonts with a high level of contrast, such as black on white or yellow.

### WHITE SPACE

Allow for white space in your online course. This will provide you with a clean look and feel that can help students maintain attention. To build in white space, consider the following suggestions:

- Use bullet points.
- Use white space between paragraphs and graphics.
- Allow the body of text to occupy only 25%-40% of the screen.

### VISUALS/GRAPHICS

Beautiful graphics can draw learner attention and offer them a different perspective on the message. Consider the following when choosing visuals:

- All images should serve a purpose. If an image doesn't have a clear purpose, leave it out.
- Images should relate to the content.
- Images should be high quality.
- Images should be clear and prominent.

PART 3

# Climate

*The heart is as important as the head in learning.*

**—K. PATRICIA CROSS**

CHAPTER 7

# Engaging Students

Most of us chose our academic discipline because at some point in our lives we discovered a passion for it. For many of us, academia's allure is sharing this enthusiasm with others and perhaps even recruiting new devotees to our field. It is disappointing, therefore, to be confronted with students who make little effort to disguise their apathy regarding our subject matter. In our onsite classrooms, these students may stare at us with vacant expressions, distract themselves with their cell phones, or respond resentfully when we try to draw them into discussion. They then dart for the door like freed prisoners the moment class ends. In our online classes, disengaged students may be practically invisible. It can be equally distressing to confront students who obsess about their grades, seemingly indifferent to the learning that those grades are supposed to represent. Why do students bother signing up for our courses if they're so disinterested in learning what we are teaching? What makes it so tough to get some students to care...to think...to engage? In this chapter, we offer our model of what student engagement is, why it is important, and how you can best promote it.

## KNOWING WHAT: ABOUT STUDENT ENGAGEMENT

The term *student engagement* has become ubiquitous in higher education, but what does the term actually mean? As we discussed in our book on this topic (Barkley & Major, 2020), student engagement means different things to different people. Bowen (2005) observed that despite higher education's emphasis on creating engaged learning, "an explicit consensus about what we actually mean by engagement or why it is important is lacking" (p. 3). Swaner (2007) noted, "Rather than being concretely defined in the literature, the concept of engaged learning emerges from multiple frameworks and educational practices" (para. 2). Because there are many different lenses through which one can view the concept of student engagement, some scholars have criticized the term for vagueness.

We, however, celebrate its useful ambiguity: it is a multifaceted, multidimensional meta-concept that gets at something deep and central to teaching and learning. Indeed, the former president of the Carnegie Foundation for the Advancement of Teaching, Lee Shulman (2002) argued, "learning begins with student engagement" (p. 37). Therefore, we suggest that engaged teachers necessarily seek to foster engaged students. Through our model of student engagement, we aim to capture this complexity in a way that helps teachers identify practical strategies to promote engagement in today's college classroom.

## Our Model of Student Engagement

As it applies to college classrooms, we offer this definition of student engagement: the mental state students are in while they are learning, at the intersection of feeling and thinking.

### THE FEELING ASPECT OF ENGAGEMENT: MOTIVATION

At its fundamental level, the feeling component of engagement can be distilled to whether students are motivated to learn (Barkley & Major, 2020). Motivation is a theoretical construct that offers the rationale for why we engage in any given behavior. Brophy (2004) defined classroom motivation as the "level of enthusiasm and the degree to which students invest attention and effort in learning" (p. 4). The literature indicates that students acquire the motivation to learn through their cumulative educational experiences. This acquired competence is an intermingling of connected skills, insights, dispositions, and values that build over their total experience in education (Brophy, 2004).

### THE THINKING ASPECT OF STUDENT ENGAGEMENT: ACTIVE LEARNING

In research, the thinking component of student engagement is described as "the student's psychological investment in and effort directed toward learning, understanding, or mastering the knowledge, skills, or crafts that academic work is intended to promote" (Newmann et al., 1992, p. 12). In literature, this thinking characteristic centers on a student's intellectual engagement in the material, assignment, or lesson (Appleton et al., 2008; Barkley & Major, 2020; Fredricks et al., 2004; Marks, 2000; Reschly et al., 2008; Skinner et al., 2009). Intellectual effort and engagement in learning is what teachers aim to achieve when they design their instructional activities to promote active learning.

### THE DOUBLE HELIX MODEL OF STUDENT ENGAGEMENT: THE INTERSECTION OF MOTIVATION AND ACTIVE LEARNING

Whether teachers think of student engagement as primarily associated with feeling/motivation or thinking/active learning, most quickly agree that both are required. A classroom filled with enthusiastic students is great, but it is educationally meaningless if it does not result in learning. Conversely, students who are learning but doing so reluctantly and resentfully are not engaged. Thus, student engagement does not result from motivation or active learning alone, but rather is generated when these two components work together synergistically (Barkley & Major, 2020, p. 9). Engagement may be described as a double helix in which active learning and motivation are spirals working together, building in intensity, and creating a fluid and dynamic phenomenon that is greater than the sum of their individual effects, as indicated in Figure 7.1: Double Helix Model of Student Engagement.

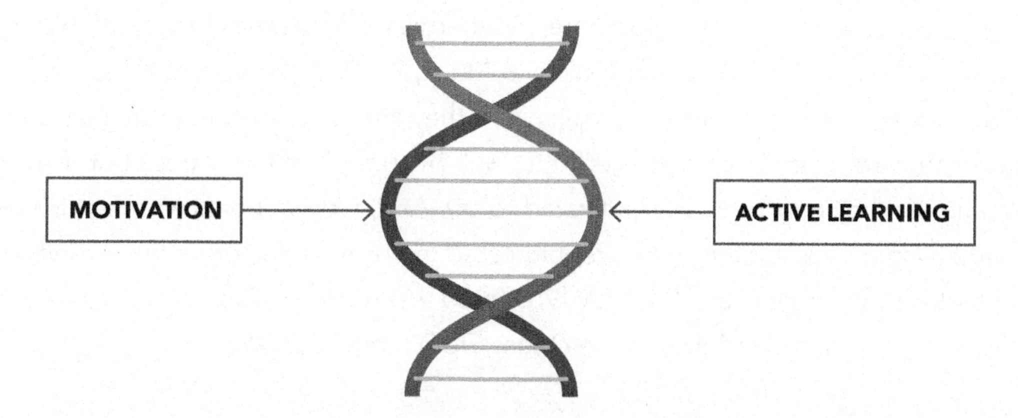


**Figure 7.1. Double Helix Model of Student Engagement**

## About Motivation as an Aspect of Student Engagement

Motivation means striving to optimize well-being, maximize pleasure, and minimize pain. Some motivations may be biological factors such as hunger and thirst; these are often called drives. Other motivations are social and psychological constructs. Motivation driven by social and psychological forces comes in two forms: intrinsic motivation and extrinsic motivation. Intrinsic motivation emerges from internal forces like interest, enjoyment, or personal satisfaction. In college, students who are intrinsically motivated to learn are driven by feelings of autonomy, purpose, and distinction. Extrinsic motivation emerges from external factors, such as students who want to succeed because of a desire for good grades or high paying jobs, or even because they want to please their parents (Barkley & Major, 2020).

While some scholars have found that implementing strategies that promote extrinsic motivation could decrease intrinsic motivation (e.g., Deci, 1971; Kohn, 1993/1999), these findings have been challenged (e.g., Cameron, 2001). Thus, we have yet to fully determine the relationship between extrinsic and intrinsic motivation. What we can say is that most students seem motivated by a mix of intrinsic and extrinsic factors, and that the mix can change over time. Furthermore, despite a student's general disposition, motivation is also activated or suppressed in specific situations. Even students who want to learn may be less eager to do so in a course they feel coerced to take because it is a required element of the general education curriculum. Conversely, students who seem generally unmotivated to learn may become quite enthusiastic about learning the concepts or skills in a specific course.

Motivation has been studied extensively, which has given rise to multiple theories and schools of thought, including goal theory, expectancy–value theory, self-determination theory, and a host of others. In aggregate, the theories indicate that a student's willingness to learn is influenced by perception (Barkley & Major, 2020). If students feel desperate, their motivation decreases; if students are optimistic, they are more likely to engage. If students believe they are being micromanaged, they will become less motivated, but if they feel autonomous, they may be more motivated to try. And, last, students who feel bored will be unmotivated, but students who are interested in the material, or learning itself, will be more motivated to participate. Pugh (2019) offered a valuable outline of key ideas regarding motivation, summarized in Table 7.1: Key Ideas From Motivation Theories.

| | CONTINUA OF FEELINGS | | |
|---|---|---|---|
| | HELPLESS ⟷ CONFIDENT | CONTROLLED ⟷ SELF-DIRECTED | BORED ⟷ INTERESTED |
| RELATED THEORIES | • Attribution theory<br>• Self-efficacy theory<br>• Self-worth theory | Self-determination theory | Expectancy–Value theory |

**Table 7.1. Key Ideas From Motivation Theories**

Motivation is the gateway to student engagement. An unmotivated student has no emotional investment in learning, while motivated students will actively pursue new learning. Just as it can be teaching heaven to face a class filled with students who are genuinely motivated to learn, it can be teaching hell trying to work with students who are apathetic or compulsively obsessed only with grades. Developing awareness of the root motivational cause of a student's lack of engagement may help you select a strategy to re-engage the student. Exploring the underlying complexities of motivation can help engaged teachers establish classrooms that foster an eagerness to learn among as many students as possible.

## About Active Learning as an Aspect of Student Engagement

The concept of active learning has a long history in education, going back to the 18th and 19th centuries as found in the work of Rousseau, Newman, Pestalozzi, Dewey, Kilpatrick, and Piaget. For example, John Henry Newman (1873, p. 97) proposed that true learning consists "not merely in the passive reception into the mind of a number of ideas" but rather "in the mind's energetic and simultaneous action upon and towards those new ideas … and making the objects of our knowledge subjectively our own." Historically, four common themes are associated with active learning: (1) rejection of traditional teaching methods, (2) belief in cognitivism, (3) faith in student ability, and (4) belief in the importance of the relationship of school to society. Although its roots run deep, the term *active learning* was not popularized until the late 20th century with the publication of Bonwell and Eison's (1991) ASHE-ERIC report titled *Active Learning: Creating Excitement in the Classroom.* But what exactly is active learning?

Definitions of active learning are often general and wide-ranging, which we explain in our book on the topic of student engagement (Barkley & Major, 2020, pp. 39-40). Furthermore, the term active learning is frequently conflated with instructional approaches, activities, or techniques (Barkley & Major, 2018). We suggest that active learning occurs when students are dynamic participants in their own education in ways that require that they integrate new information into their existing knowledge and previous experience (Barkley & Major, 2018). Generally, we offer that students are actively learning when they:

- contribute their personal, individual perspective;
- try to understand peers' viewpoints;
- use higher-order learning strategies;
- employ self-regulatory and metacognitive strategies;
- demonstrate intellectual curiosity, enthusiasm, and interest;
- aspire to deep, conceptual knowledge rather than surface understanding;
- seek personal relevance; and
- pursue additional opportunities for learning.

Though active learning can occur in any given time or place, we suggest that when determining an approach to facilitate active learning in a college setting, faculty should consider two components: (1) the learning task and (2) the learning goal for the level of activity employed. By *level of activity*, we refer to students' mental engagement as well as the strategies they employ to self-reflect and monitor the process of their own learning and their results.

Because any one type of learning task does not necessarily require more intellectual investment than another, level of activity is a discrete component. Indeed, any type of learning task can demand more or less mental activity depending on the content, the student, and how the task is designed. For instance, while some teachers suggest students who listen to lectures are necessarily learning less actively than students who are solving problems, consider the following math problem: $X - 5 = 5$. Most college students could solve such a problem without too much mental activity. By contrast, students who are carefully listening to a lecture on number theory may have heightened levels of mental activity as they strive to comprehend a particularly challenging concept.

Learners can therefore have high or low levels of mental activity for any given learning task, while any given learning task can also demand more or less active engagement from learners. Our model illustrates how students engage at different levels of active learning (high, medium, or low) for many common instructional activities. At high levels, they are truly engaged in active learning. At medium levels, they are somewhat engaged in active learning. And at low levels, they have minimal engagement. We provide our own model of the active learning continuum for a few key learning activities in Table 7.2: Active Learning Continuum for Several Key Learning Tasks (adapted from Barkley & Major, 2018). Engaged teachers help students move across the mental activity continuum from Level 1 (low) to Level 3 (high), no matter the learning task.

To summarize, we suggest that teachers can promote student engagement by designing tasks that strive to increase student motivation and also promote active learning. Students do their part by investing emotional and intellectual effort into their learning. The combined efforts of teachers and students lead to the kind of high-level involvement in learning that we recognize as student engagement.

| | ← LEVELS OF MENTAL ACTIVITY → | | |
|---|---|---|---|
| LEARNING TASK | 3 — HIGH | 2 — MODERATE | 1 — LOW |
| LISTENING | Expresses interest and enthusiasm; attempts to critique and evaluate the message; monitors own attention | Maintains concerted attention while trying to understand the message; formulates questions about the message | Listens for facts and information |
| PROBLEM-SOLVING | Considers the processes for solving the problem; self-monitors efforts and progress | Recognizes the underlying structure of the problem | Solves the problem |
| READING | Seeks meaning and monitors own reading engagement; investigates related readings and resources | Seeks structural understanding | Seeks facts and information |
| DISCUSSING | Shares personal perspectives and seeks to understand others; argues and evaluates concepts; self-monitors participation | Conveys ideas and concepts; encourages others | Relays facts |
| WRITING | Critiques, evaluates, and creates; seeks to express personal perspectives and connect with others' ideas; monitors progress and assesses quality | Explains and applies; expresses personal perspectives; seeks out references | Describes and defines |

**Table 7.2. Active Learning Continuum for Several Key Learning Tasks**

## KNOWING WHY: RESEARCH ON MOTIVATION AND ACTIVE LEARNING

We define student engagement as the mental state students are in while they are learning that constitutes the intersection of feeling/motivation and thinking/active learning. Below we summarize key research in each of these two areas.

### Research on Motivation

Much of the research on motivation in education centers around various theories, such as goal theory, expectancy–value theory, and self-determination theory, that have made their way from the field of motivational psychology to educational research. Many researchers have affirmed the relationship between motivation and learning. In addition, they have shown that an instructor's intentional efforts toward promoting motivation can be effective. In a 2016 meta-analysis, Lazowski and Hulleman reviewed research on intervention studies that were grounded in various types of motivation theory. They examined 74 experimental and quasi-experimental studies with 38,377 participants from all educational levels, including 57 studies at the college/university/postsecondary level and looked specifically at papers that manipulated an independent variable and measured the resulting learning. They found that interventions were generally effective at improving motivation and increasing learning outcomes (Lazowski & Hulleman, 2016). While there are many research studies on motivation in education, Lazowski and Hulleman's meta-analysis provides faculty with reliable documentation that efforts toward enhancing motivation can improve engagement and learning outcomes. See our book titled *Student Engagement Techniques: A Handbook for College Faculty* for an expanded review of the research on motivation and citations of additional studies (Barkley & Major, 2020).

### Research on Active Learning

Like research on motivation, research on active learning has been extensive. Frequently, it examines learning achieved from lecturing as compared to learning from an active learning approach. The research greatly corroborates the idea that regularly taking brief breaks from lectures to engage students in activities such as quick quizzes or group discussions is effective at improving learning gains. It is also clear that lectures supplemented with active learning techniques generate higher learning outcomes than lectures by themselves. A meta-analysis conducted by Freeman et al. (2014) of 225 studies examined student learning outcomes in undergraduate Science, Technology, Engineering, and Mathematics (STEM) courses, comparing lectures to active learning. Freeman and colleagues determined that when faculty incorporated active learning methods, students' exam scores increased significantly and their failure rates decreased significantly compared to faculty who only used the lecture method. Prince (2004) conducted an expansive narrative synthesis looking at the effect of active learning in engineering courses and found wide support for collaborative, cooperative, problem-based, and active learning. A recent meta-analysis determined that teaching methods in undergraduate STEM programs can substantially decrease gaps in performance between both traditionally overrepresented and traditionally underrepresented students (Theobald el al., 2020). See our book *Interactive Lecturing: A Handbook for College Faculty* for a fuller review of the research on specific active learning techniques that support learning in lectures (Barkley & Major, 2018).

## KNOWING HOW: PROMOTING STUDENT ENGAGEMENT

To promote student engagement, we recommend that teachers design tasks that increase student motivation and also promote active learning. We offer guidance for accomplishing this in the section below. Where appropriate, we identify a Cross Academy Technique (CAT) from our companion site, the K. Patricia Cross Academy (*kpcrossacademy.org*), where you can access both a video and a downloadable template that provide specific guidance on how to implement the technique.

### Tips and Strategies for Increasing Motivation

Students who are motivated to learn are more inclined to do what is required in order to learn. Many teachers have shared with us that if a student is highly motivated, typical teaching and learning challenges seem to disappear. Below we offer tips and strategies for creating classroom conditions that enhance student motivation.

#### EXPECT STUDENT ENGAGEMENT

Set expectations early on that students should be engaged in their learning, and do not settle for less (Barkley & Major, 2020). While instructors who are noticeably disengaged can hurt classroom motivation, an instructor's enthusiasm can be contagious. To convey that you expect students to be engaged, consider a "no opt out" approach (Lemov, 2010). If a student cannot initially answer a question, build a pathway for success by walking them through the answer, giving them the option to seek help from classmates, or offering them the chance to research and come back with a response. Make it clear that disengagement is not allowed in the course and, if it makes sense to do so, provide them with alternate activities to meet learning goals that they may find more engaging.

### DEVELOP AND DEMONSTRATE QUALITIES OF ENGAGING TEACHERS

Your personality and actions can have a profound influence on student motivation. Students who like and admire a teacher will engage even without intrinsic motivation. By contrast, students are likely to become disengaged if they dislike their teacher (Brophy, 2004, pp. 27-28). We recommend these methods for demonstrating the qualities of engaging teachers (Barkley & Major, 2020):

- Be prepared. Great teachers have a comprehensive plan for their course and strong lesson plans.
- Always show up for class and be there on time.
- Be your best self. Students value authenticity and will sense if you're offering a false persona. That said, be your best self in the classroom: highlight your personal attributes that align with well-liked and well-respected teachers, traits like enthusiasm, optimism, fairness, energy, and passion.

### LECTURE IN A COMPELLING MANNER

When lecturing, use basic public speaking guidelines to showcase your passion. These include facing students when speaking rather than looking at the board, creating polished slide presentations, modulating your voice, and using hand gestures appropriately. Refer to our book *Interactive Lecturing* (Barkley & Major, 2018) for other tips.

### REWARD STUDENT LEARNING RATHER THAN BEHAVIOR

To encourage students to do their best work, instructors commonly reward desired behaviors by providing praise, extra credit, or exemptions from assignments. They also typically try to mitigate bad behavior through non-reinforcement or even negative reinforcement like penalty points, poor grades, or admonishing students. While these methods may offer quick solutions, motivational theorists argue such methods control behavior rather than motivate students to learn (Barkley & Major, 2020). Brophy (2004) offered a thoughtful analysis of the topic. His basic criticisms are that (1) these methods are based on extrinsic rewards instead of helping students generate their own intrinsic sense of pleasure from learning; (2) they can turn into bribes for behavior that students should already be performing; and (3) these methods require momentary compliance instead of fostering better attitudes, beliefs, values, and self-regulation that students will need for a lifetime of learning in formal and informal situations (pp. 154-157). Understanding these issues may help you offer rewards and incentives that encourage learning rather than control student behavior. Consider these steps to ensure you are focused on rewarding learning:

- Make it clear to students that learning and what comes from learning, rather than simply checking boxes for completing activities, is what makes the course valuable. To offer an example, many teachers grade participation, which may feel arbitrary to students, potentially opening a door for them to haggle about their grades. Furthermore, some students may believe participation just means talking in class, so they speak without necessarily contributing anything of value. However, if you make it clear that what you're looking for is engagement in the learning community and the act of learning itself, students may provide better contributions. Additionally, it is helpful to provide students with rubrics that make these criteria explicit and transparent.
- Address students' improvement as individuals rather than comparing them to each other. Instead of grading on a curve, take a criterion-referenced or mastery approach with the assumption that each student can succeed. Additionally, you can detail this approach in student feedback and assessments, demonstrating that you care about their individual education.
- When giving grades and feedback, stress the quality of students' accomplishments rather than the quantity of their work. However, you should also recognize when students have put in a lot of time and practice. That said, although teachers must be aware that practice is necessary, for assessment purposes, the focus should be on the quality of the final work product and whether it demonstrates learning.

**PROVIDE PRAISE AND CRITICISM EFFECTIVELY**

When teachers care about their students and want to establish a positive learning environment, it is natural that they would want to offer supportive compliments. However, this praise does not always have the intended effect because some students are embarrassed and others feel patronized. The main objection, though, is that praise can be seen as manipulation of behavior and as a way of reinforcing a hierarchy between faculty and students. If praise is not always useful, the inverse is also true: Criticism is not always harmful (Barkley & Major, 2020). Wlodkowski (2008) explained that constructive criticism is differentiated from general criticism because, while it identifies errors and areas for improvement, it does not indicate rejection or disapproval. Constructive criticism is particularly useful, and even encouraging, if it provides specific information, addresses specific behavior, offers a correction, is given privately and in a timely fashion, and provides the chance for the student to improve (Wlodkowski, 2008, p. 364).

## ATTEND TO STUDENTS' BASIC NEEDS SO THEY CAN FOCUS ON HIGHER LEVEL NEEDS

While Maslow's (1943) hierarchy of needs is currently criticized for some circular logic issues, it continues to be widely read and influential. Maslow's model argues that students' physiological needs (like hunger and sleep), safety needs (like feeling free from danger or anxiety), and love needs (like feeling accepted by peers and instructors) must be met in order for students to address the higher level needs required for engagement in the classroom. Likewise, Bowen and Watkins (2016) argued that students need sleep, water, exercise, eating, and time (SWEET) and suggested these factors can have as much influence on a student's learning as any teaching method. Today, a greater number of students are balancing food insecurity, mental health issues, and competing work/family/educational demands, creating a tough environment to learn (Barkley & Major, 2020). Try to be aware of students who are struggling to have their basic needs met and if possible, guide them to campus- or community-based resources.

## ENCOURAGE STUDENT AUTONOMY

One of our basic human needs is self-determination, or the control over our own lives. The desire for self-determination works in tandem with helping students develop self-efficacy, or the understanding that they have the power to influence their own behavior and thoughts (Barkley & Major, 2020). Hanstedt (2018) pointed out that the manner in which students are taught affects the development of their feelings of autonomy, authority, and authorship. Here are some strategies to encourage student autonomy (Brophy, 2004; Raffini, 1996; Wlodkowski, 2008):

1. Offer students meaningful reasons that encourage their understanding of the rationale and personal importance of assignments.
2. Recognize students' feelings and emotions when it is essential that you ask them to take an action they do not want to take.
3. Encourage students to determine how, when, and where they complete their activities.
4. Push students to manage their own workload as much as possible.
5. Offer students the opportunity to help determine which assignments will be evaluated.
6. Encourage accountability.
7. Emphasize that students should maintain and monitor individualized goals.

8. Suggest students self-assess their progress while also identifying their individual strengths and potential hurdles.

9. Offer students multiple options for assignments that meet the same learning objective, but be clear about how the options relate to the objective.

10. Give students choices for determining how classroom procedures are implemented.

### TEACH THINGS THAT ARE WORTH LEARNING

It will come as no surprise that students will be more motivated if they find the material you're teaching worth learning. One thing to ponder: Who determines what is worth learning? Clearly you, as the teacher, play a role, but should students have a role as well? Trust students to have perspectives about what material is worthwhile in their daily lives. Teachers and students will likely share a belief that the world is shifting rapidly, and they will need broad knowledge to succeed (Barkley & Major, 2020).

### INTEGRATE LEARNING GOALS, ACTIVITIES, AND ASSESSMENT

If you carefully select and integrate your learning goals, assignments, and assessment to help students attain substantive goals that reflect an expansive conceptual structure, students will find it easier to understand why they are being given an assignment. In response, they may become more motivated. Share your framework with students in the class syllabus but repeat and reinforce it throughout the course. For example, post a list of class session goals at the beginning of each onsite or online lecture. You can also consider including the goal and describing how an activity is designed to help students achieve a learning goal at the top of each assignment.

### DEVELOP AUTHENTIC LEARNING ACTIVITIES

Authentic activities provide students with opportunities to apply what they are learning in a complex, real-world situation. We recommend considering authenticity in three areas:

- **Authentic process:** involving students in the process; for example, asking them to undertake research or to work as functioning teams
- **Authentic subject:** focusing on a subject that has relevance for students beyond the classroom, such as something connected to contemporary issues or current news
- **Authentic products:** creating something with substance, such as a professional product like a presentation

## EXPECT STUDENTS TO SUCCEED

Student motivation and success are greatly influenced by an instructor's faith and support. Students are more likely to succeed if you believe in them and believe that they will succeed than if you doubt their abilities and resign yourself to subpar performance. Some options for conveying your confidence in student success include:

- Tell students directly, in class or in the syllabus, that they can all succeed in the course if they put forth the necessary effort.
- Be explicit that you have high expectations. Establish goals built around higher order learning skills like synthesis, evaluation, and analysis. Resist assigning busy work, and develop assignments that require students to engage meaningfully in learning.
- Instead of grading students on a curve, develop an assessment rubric that rewards students for reaching goals or meeting established thresholds of quality.

## HELP STUDENTS EXPECT SUCCESS

In order for students to succeed, they must believe they can succeed. You can encourage students to expect success by ensuring that assignments and assessments are clearly organized, appropriately challenging, well-communicated, and graded fairly. Additionally, complex tasks can be scaffolded. But beyond these fundamental conditions, teachers can help students by encouraging students to connect their own effort and persistence to their success. Some ways to scaffold and help students attribute effort to outcome include the following:

1. Demonstrate the relationship between effort and outcome by talking out loud while thinking through tasks. Model that learning takes time and could involve confusion or making mistakes, but vocalize your confidence that both you and students will succeed by working deliberately, looking for more effective strategies, and absorbing new information.
2. Tell students that even subjects people think of as ability-driven, like math, the arts, and writing, are areas where students can improve if they learn strategies to succeed. Offer them reassurance that gaining experience will involve making mistakes.
3. Help students understand the criteria for success. Include them in developing rubrics or consider having them identify questions they might see on a quiz or exam by implementing CAT 34: Invent the Quiz.

4. When providing feedback and assessment, emphasize the relationship between effort and outcome. Acknowledge students' progress and achievements stemming from their efforts.

5. Invite former students who gained confidence over the semester and wound up successful to speak with your class and provide their tips for success. Or, if that would be logistically difficult to pull off, suggest students write their advice at the end of a course and then provide incoming students with a curated list of the best tips in the syllabus (Brophy, 2004, p. 386; Wlodowski, 2008, p. 195).

In sum, your best strategy for ensuring students succeed is to design the course so that they can, and then remind students throughout the term that if they keep moving forward in the face of obstacles, they will.

## WORK TO RESTORE THE CONFIDENCE OF DISHEARTENED STUDENTS

In spite of your best intentions to set students up for success, there will be students who will fail. When this happens, students may be quick to conclude it is because they lack ability. Brophy (2004) dedicated an entire chapter to encouraging disheartened students, rebuilding their confidence, and renewing their willingness to engage (pp. 119-150). A few of his recommendations include the following:

1. Give students specific directions and clear structure by subdividing tasks into discrete parts with individual deadlines.

2. Stress personal responsibility by encouraging students to develop their own goals, make decisions, and monitor their own progress.

3. Guide students to set realistic goals and then offer them encouragement that focuses on their efforts and successes, helping them concentrate on improving upon their prior wins instead of competing with their peers.

4. Arrange course material into segments that let students proceed at their own pace and master learning principles, but check in with the students often and offer supplementary education as needed.

5. Establish a study buddy policy so that high-achieving students collaborate with lower achievers.

6. Help students identify campus support programs like tutorial groups or writing clinics so they can establish general academic skills to succeed.

7. Guide students toward a better self-awareness of their abilities as learners, such as determining what learning environments they are comfortable in and which cause anxiety (and why) so that they can take the steps needed to seek help when necessary.

8. Emphasize that you are available as a resource who will help them learn.

9. Last, have empathy for students but also confidence that they can meet their goals.

## Tips and Strategies for Promoting Active Learning

To learn well and deeply, learners need to make sense out of new information and connect it to what they already know. They must be active participants in the learning process. This involves doing something with the new information such as thinking, reading, writing, discussing, problem-solving, or reflecting. Below are strategies that can help you promote active learning in your course.

### BE CLEAR ON YOUR LEARNING GOALS

An unknown author said, "In the absence of clearly defined goals, we become strangely loyal to performing daily acts of trivia." In the classroom, both teachers and students can waste lots of time and energy doing things that don't result in much learning. Once you are clear on what you want students to learn, you can make better decisions and choices on the kinds of tasks that will best promote active learning.

### CLARIFY YOUR ROLE

If your goal is to promote active learning, your role in the classroom changes. Yet, what that role should be is debated in the literature. Some educators contend that instructors should play a minimal role in shaping and directing the work of students. Weimer (2002), for example, stressed, "We must move aside, often and regularly" (p. 74). Others, such as Miller and her colleagues (1996), warned that "a common mistake of teachers in adopting an active learning strategy is to relinquish structure along with control, and the common result is for students to feel frustrated and disoriented" (p. 17). How you operate in the classroom is influenced by your personal vision and philosophy about teaching and learning as well as your discipline, course objectives, class size, student experience, and the unique characteristics of a particular class. Regardless of the role you decide to take, clarifying it for yourself helps you to be clear and consistent in your interactions with students.

### ORIENT STUDENTS TO THEIR NEW ROLES

Students have different responsibilities in active learning than they do in traditional education. The primary method for orienting students to these new responsibilities and teaching students active learning skills lies in the learning tasks themselves. Students will develop active learning skills if they are given tasks that ask them to apply concepts, solve problems, discuss issues, or reflect upon the factors that influence their thinking. Some students may not know how to make this shift; others may resist. Consider taking the time early in the academic term to explain why you have organized the course around active learning principles.

### HELP STUDENTS DEVELOP LEARNING STRATEGIES

Help learners become better able to direct and manage their learning by showing them how to use learning strategies. Svinicki (2004) provided students with a table of learning strategies that illustrates the kinds of strategies or tactics that students could use for learning different types of information or skills. As she noted, many students have never been exposed to the idea that there are different ways of studying. Consider using CAT 30: Insights, Resources, or Applications (IRAs), in which students consider where they can learn more and how they can apply information in new situations, or CAT 32: Online Resource Scavenger Hunt, where they learn how to find and access resources.

### TEACH IN WAYS THAT PROMOTE EFFECTIVE TRANSFER

Active learners connect new ideas and information to already known concepts and principles, and they take already known concepts and principles and apply them to new situations. This involves a process known as *transfer,* which describes the effect that past learning has on processing and acquiring of new learning and the degree to which a learner can apply what they have learned to new situations. Transfer is important both within a course as well as across a series of courses in an academic discipline. Research, unfortunately, has demonstrated that students are often not successful either in accurately connecting new material to existing understanding or in recognizing how what they learned can apply to new situations, suggesting that teachers need to be more intentional about helping students make connections between past learning and new learning.

### TEACH FOR RETENTION

Once students have learned material, we want them to remember it. It is because the ability to store, retain, and subsequently retrieve information is so fundamental to learning that "remembering" is now the first level in the revision of Bloom's taxonomy of educational objectives (Anderson et al., 2001). Consider the following suggestions for helping you and your students assess for long-term retention:.

- Implement pop quizzes. If the quizzes are not graded but rather are administered as part of a supportive, formative assessment process to show both students and teachers what is being stored in long-term memory, they can be an effective way to monitor retention.

- Ask students to respond to a single prompt question by writing what they know about a topic for a minute or two, a form of CAT 10: Quick Write.

- Use flashback questions. When you administer a quiz, ask a few questions from previous quizzes to test retention, making quizzes cumulative.

### LIMIT AND CHUNK INFORMATION

Research has determined that the average adult's working memory can handle between five and nine items of information at once. Additionally, the average adult can process an item for 10 to 20 minutes before mental fatigue or boredom occurs and attention drifts (Sousa, 2006, pp. 45-47). The implications for teachers who are presenting new material include the following:

- Consider what is absolutely the most essential information for students to know.

- Limit topics or items to no more than seven.

- Attempt to group like components together.

- Organize these chunks into an identifiable pattern.

- Break the presentation of new information into sections interspersed with other kinds of activities, such as discussion or writing, that give students a chance to apply what they have learned.

### PROVIDE OPPORTUNITIES FOR GUIDED REHEARSAL

Rehearsal reinforces learning and increases retention. There are two types of rehearsal activity:

- **Rote rehearsal** is used to remember and store information in the same form that it entered working memory, such as in memorizing a poem or the precise steps of a procedure. We can help students by teaching them strategies such as mnemonic devices to remember lists, facts, and definitions, helping them to associate abstract ideas with concrete objects, or teaching established memory techniques or link systems (described, for example, in Bautista, 2000).

- **Elaborative rehearsal** helps the learner process the information so that it is more meaningful. Elaboration strategies include forming associations, organizing information into categories, outlining, clustering concepts into taxonomic categories with shared characteristics, paraphrasing, summarizing, creating analogies, and self-quizzing.

### ORGANIZE ONSITE OR ONLINE LECTURES IN WAYS THAT PROMOTE ACTIVE LEARNING

In any given learning episode, learners tend to remember best that which came first, second best that which came last, and least that which was in the middle. This is called the primacy–recency (or serial position) effect. Limited attention spans combined with the primacy–recency effect suggest that it is generally most productive to divide presentation time into short segments of about 20 minutes. After presenting information, consider having students apply what they just heard by participating in small group work or pausing to fill out a worksheet. You can even tell a story or a joke, play some music, allow students to talk off-task with their neighbors, or get up and stretch or walk around the room. This can reenergize students so that they can focus again during the next 20-minute learning segment (Sousa, 2006, pp. 92-93). See our book titled *Interactive Lecturing* for additional ideas to organize class time (such as bookends, interleaves, and overlays) in ways that can significantly reduce the proportion of downtime in a class session. Consider using a CAT for interactive lecturing (e.g., CAT:18 Support a Statement) or structuring notetaking (e.g., CAT: 41 Cued Notes or CAT: 42 Notetaking Pairs).

### USE FLIPPED, REVERSED, OR INVERTED CLASSROOM ORGANIZATION

In a flipped classroom model (also known as *reversed* or *inverted classroom*), teachers organize curriculum such that onsite class meetings are used to follow up on assignments done out of class. One of the early strategies using this approach is Just in Time Teaching (JiTT). In JiTT, students complete an asynchronous online assignment (such as taking a quiz or responding to a prompt based on reading a chapter in the textbook) that is due shortly before class. The instructor checks students' submissions just in time to adjust the onsite session to respond to student needs. The onsite session is designed for active learning through the use of mini-lectures, demos, classroom discussion, worksheet exercises, and even hands-on mini-labs that are informed by the instructor's analysis of student responses. This provides a feedback loop in which students' class preparation fundamentally affects what happens during in-class time.

### USE RUBRICS TO GIVE LEARNERS FREQUENT AND USEFUL FEEDBACK

One of a teacher's most important responsibilities is giving learners feedback. Learners need to know what they are doing right and what they are doing wrong so that they can adjust their efforts and improve. Feedback gives students information about the specific skills they have developed or need to improve to be successful in their course. Students can use feedback to adjust their work on subsequent assignments, thus becoming more independent learners.

Most teachers know this, but giving feedback is labor- and time-intensive, especially in courses with large numbers of students. Rubrics are an effective solution. They can be used to explicate and grade a wide range of learning tasks. It takes time and effort to create an effective rubric, but once done, it saves time and effort (Stevens & Levi, 2005, p. 18). Sample rubrics that you can adapt for your specific purposes can be found easily online. In addition, Rubistar is a free online tool that guides teachers through the process of creating quality rubrics: *http://rubistar.4teachers.org/index.php*

## CONCLUSION

Motivation and active learning are twin helices that work together synergistically. While motivation is the gateway to student engagement, teachers also need to create a course context that promotes active learning. As these two components work together, student engagement can build in intensity. Experiences can even be transformative, representing treasured milestones in one's education. While these kinds of experiences are appealing, they are not sustainable on a constant basis. They would be too exhausting. But as college teachers, we can strive to increase experiences of deep engagement, reduce the incidence of lack of engagement, and attend to the many ways we can adapt our teaching methods to enhance engaged learning throughout the range in between these extremes.

## FOCUS ON ONLINE TEACHING

The information we share in the main body of this chapter applies to both onsite and online teaching, but here we provide additional insights focused specifically on teaching online, hybrid, and blended courses.

### What: Engagement Online

In this chapter, we defined student engagement as "the mental state students are in while they are learning that constitutes the intersection of feeling and thinking." We believe the same definition applies in an online environment. There can be more challenges to student engagement online as well as more distractions, however. For example, research demonstrates that people find faces engaging, but students online often see simply a full screen of text. In addition, it is easy to be distracted online; students can be pulled away from their coursework to check email, scroll social media, and shop online. Thus, while the definition remains the same, instructors may need to lay more groundwork to help students stay engaged when learning online.

### Why: Engagement Online

As we have noted, student engagement is linked to many important learning outcomes. Researchers for the National Survey of Student Engagement (NSSE), for example, have linked student engagement to improvements in student learning outcomes (Hu & McCormick, 2012), student achievement as seen through GPA (Kuh et al., 2007; Pascarella & Terenzini, 2005), self-perception of and satisfaction with learning (Hu & McCormick, 2012; Filak & Sheldon, 2008), and persistence (Hu & McCormick, 2012; Kuh et al., 2008). Researchers also have used NSSE data to compare engagement of online and onsite students (Chen et al., 2009; NSSE, 2013; Rabe-Kemp et al., 2009; Robinson & Hullinger, 2008). The good news is that these researchers have found that compared to onsite learners, online learners report some advantages. The bad news is that they also report disadvantages. A NSSE report (2013), for example, found that online students used effective learning strategies more often and rated their quality of interactions with peers, advisors, and so forth higher than onsite students did. However, they also found that online learners experienced less collaborative learning and interactions with faculty compared to onsite learners and scored the environment as less supportive. Paulsen and McCormick (2020) had similar findings, noting that in online courses, students experienced less collaborative learning and interaction with faculty.

If we want to optimize student learning online, we need to find ways to engage them. Research documents that students understand that their own personal commitment and motivation are important for engagement (Blakey & Major, 2019; Isaias et al., 2017; Ng, 2018;

Papadima-Sochocleous & Giannikas, 2019; Thistoll & Yates, 2016). But research involving surveys or interviews with students also shows there are ways to promote student engagement online. For example, researchers have found that students describe peer-to-peer interaction as engaging (Athens, 2018; Bigatel & Edel-Malizia, 2018; Gonzales & Moore, 2020). They also have discovered that students find video lectures to be engaging (Ahn & Bir, 2018; Choe et al., 2019; Hew et al., 2018; Howard et al., 2017). Additionally, students find active and collaborative activities and learning communities to be engaging (Blakey & Major, 2019; Charbonneau-Gowdy & Chavez, 2018; Shelton et al., 2016; Thistoll & Yates, 2016).

## How: Engagement Online

An online course that merely provides information is not going to engage students. Students need more support and interaction. Approaches that foster motivation and promote active learning in onsite classes are also generally effective in online courses. But here are additional tips that focus on teaching online.

### MOTIVATION

To help engage students, Darby (2019) pushed teachers to "show up" for their online classes and establish strong teacher presence. This addresses the common misconception about online courses that teachers can just "set it and forget it." She offered the following suggestions:

- Join students in online discussions.
- Post an announcement each week previewing the topic of the upcoming week, reviewing the work from the previous week (see CAT 7: *Team Jeopardy*), or both.
- Return students' graded work promptly.
- Set a schedule for virtual office hours, offer them by appointment, or both.
- Respond promptly to questions.
- Use videos to clear up any misconceptions about course work or tasks.

### ACTIVE LEARNING

The basic approach for promoting active learning in an onsite class also applies to online courses. Instructors should identify the learning goal and then choose the task or technique that helps students achieve the learning goal with a high level of mental activity. Thus, we encourage faculty who are teaching online to first consider what their learning goal is. Then consider what technique you can use to best accomplish it. We recommend visiting our free K. Patricia Cross Academy (*kpcrossacademy.org*) to access a video library with downloadable templates of 50 teaching techniques that promote active learning in both onsite and online classes. The library can be searched in multiple ways, including by activity type, teaching problem addressed, and learning taxonomy dimension.

*College graduates frequently report that some of their richest learning experiences in college come from interacting with their fellow students.*

**—K. PATRICIA CROSS**

CHAPTER 8

# Supporting Community

Humans have a basic need to connect socially with others. As teachers, we know that students thrive when they feel they are included, important, and respected members of our classroom community. It is, therefore, deeply satisfying when students in a particular class bond quickly and then work together productively. It is even more rewarding when they encourage each other and appear to genuinely enjoy each other's company. However, there are also classes in which students barely interact, resist working together, and don't offer each other much in the way of support. Engaged teaching means understanding what community means in an educational context and knowing how to promote it in your class so that you and students can more often experience the positive effects of belonging to a vibrant learning community.

## KNOWING WHAT: ABOUT COMMUNITY

The word *community* has Latin roots and basically means to give or to make common among others. Scholarly efforts to define community can be so vague and broad that they offer no real insight into the necessary processes needed to establish it (see Jenkins, 2014a, 2014b). But three interconnected ideas are generally used: (1) a shared space, (2) common values and interests, and (3) a communication process.

The idea of community has recently received more attention in higher education, and increasing emphasis has been focused on creating and supporting learning communities, such as freshmen interest groups and living–learning communities wherein students live together and take the same courses. Such communities provide broad opportunities for students to gather around a common focus area and share ideas and information. But what does community mean in a given course? How do we know it when we see it?

## Definitions of Course Community

The idea of community in a given course has also received scholarly attention. McMillan and Chavis (1986) referred to the classroom learning community as a way to describe the culture of a given course in which each student has mutual involvement and shared understanding of any presented concept. Other scholars describe communal classrooms as environments wherein students feel both "nurtured and supported" (Church, 2015, para. 1), a climate allowing for wide-ranging discussion and academic inquiry (Goos, 2004, p. 259), and a context in which students have an "active role in... constructing meaning" (Bloome, 1986, p. 71).

## Components of Community

McMillan and Chavis (1986) described four key components of community that are useful to our understanding of the student experience: community membership, influence, integration, and shared emotional connection.

### COMMUNITY MEMBERSHIP

Community membership offers boundaries, limiting who does and does not belong to a community. In a classroom, membership is defined fairly quickly and decisively. Membership is bounded by who is in the course; students enrolled in the class have the right to be there. The sense of belonging may be evident in shared styles of clothing such as school colors or mascots. And students may signal their membership through gestures like nodding, waving, or eye contact. Community membership indicates that students have invested themselves in the group and therefore earned the right to participate (McMillan & Chavis, 1986).

### INFLUENCE IN COMMUNITIES

McMillan and Chavis (1986) argued that influence in communities exists in two forms that operate in tandem: member-on-community and community-on-member. Member-on-community means that community members should feel like they have some form of influence in the group; individuals who acknowledge other members' beliefs and contributions often have the most influence in the group. In the second form, community-on-member, the group exerts influence on its members in order to establish cohesion. These forms of influence can be seen in the classroom. For instance, if the instructor stands at the front of the classroom, some students may signal their importance by sitting at the front; others may direct class discussion by raising their hands more frequently. And the class as a whole may influence students. If some students feel their classmates are not participating, they may encourage them to do so. Or if a student is dominating too much of the discussion, other members may signal so through their body language.

### INTEGRATION IN COMMUNITIES

An essential element of community is integration into the group and fulfillment of member needs (McMillan & Chavis, 1986). Individuals should feel rewarded and reinforced by their community participation. Members feel reinforced through factors like membership status, community success, and their peers' competence and skills. In the classroom, members may signal recognition to their classmates through nonverbal actions like nodding if a student offers a good insight. Through that recognition, the student will feel empowered to participate more in the future.

### SHARED EMOTIONAL CONNECTION

McMillan and Chavis (1986) suggested that shared emotional connection, which includes collective history and participation, is the "definitive element for true community" (p. 14). They suggested the following factors contribute to a shared emotional connection:

- **Contact:** As students interact, they become more likely to develop intimacy and become close.
- **Quality of interaction:** Positive experiences and relationships lead to greater bonds.
- **Closure to events:** If tasks feel definite and have a clear sense of closure, groups will have a greater sense of connection, while unresolved tasks lead to less cohesive groups.
- **Shared events:** Important shared events (e.g., working through a crisis together) lead to a stronger community bond.
- **Investment:** If members invest themselves emotionally or financially, they become more involved and connected.
- **Honor or humiliation:** Individuals are greatly affected by the sense of reward or shame they receive in a group.
- **Spiritual bond/community spirit:** If individuals feel a strong spiritual connection to the group or sense of community spirit, they develop more positive feelings about the community.

All these factors can exist in a class and hence contribute to the development of a classroom community. For example, each class session has a natural sense of closure. Depending on the way the instructor structures the class sessions, students may regularly share ideas and materials, interact with each other, and experience shared events. Additionally, students create community through the time and energy they invest in each other both in and out of the classroom.

## KNOWING WHY: RESEARCH ON COMMUNITY IN COLLEGE AND UNIVERSITY COURSES

Why is community essential to engaged teaching? Researchers and instructors generally agree that a mutual sense of community improves student success, both current and future (Shaffer & Anundsen, 1993; Tebben, 1995). Community in a given course may help students better relate to their classmates, in and out of school, which may in turn promote learning. Pascarella and Terenzini (2005) reviewed research on how college affects student learning and found that regular student–faculty and student–student interactions promote learning. Researchers have also found that college students who say they have strong communal ties are more likely to stay enrolled in a course, more likely to consistently attend class, and more likely to graduate (McKinney et al., 2006; see also Rovai, 2001, 2002).

Students are also more likely to contribute during discussion if they have a sense of community, and they are less likely to feel personal anxiety in school (Freeman et al., 2010). Tebben (1995) determined that a shared sense of community not only contributed to student contentment but also improved overall academic performance. Likewise, Harris (2001) concluded that almost 90% of students pointed to a feeling of classroom community as having a significant contribution to their completion of course assignments (p. 22). McMillan and Chavis (1986) stated that the establishment of communities in courses has been demonstrated to improve students' classroom loyalty, participation, and overall satisfaction (pp. 2, 7). These scenarios are particularly evident with undergraduate students, first generation college students, and students from underrepresented communities. This underscores the significance of classroom community in an increasingly diverse world (Akerheilm et al., 1998; Ashar & Skenes, 1993; Terenzini et al., 1996).

Through a survey of more than 500 students at 25 universities and colleges in Southern California, Elliot et al. (2016) developed a list of best practices for developing a feeling of community in college classrooms. Their list aligns with contemporary studies on the topic and offers four specific ways in which students understood higher education communities: (1) shared space, (2) acceptance and openness, (3) shared interests, and (4) a sense of belonging.

From their survey results, Elliot et al. provided four real-world implications for instructors and students who wish to build a sense of community in their own classrooms. They suggested fostering: (1) *third places* (a term introduced by sociologist Roy Oldenber that describes a place where people spend time and build relationships outside of home and work), (2) genuine dialogue, (3) strong ties, and (4) superordinate goal(s).

## KNOWING HOW: PROMOTING AND GAUGING COMMUNITY

Instructors are a key factor for building a sense of community among their students, argued Wong et al. (2013). The authors suggested that faculty contribute to class culture and also create its norms and expectations by "modeling preferred attitudes for community, creating a physical environment conducive to community, and framing the subject of inquiry for the class" (p. 49). By contrast, Greene and Mitcham (2012) stressed the importance of focusing on students creating their own community. Instructors, they argued, should establish a supportive setting for students but not assume the role of classroom overseer. Instead, the teacher should be an active member alongside students. For example, in discussions, the teacher's task is to persuade students to open up about their own views and to advocate for their own learning: "The classroom [is] a community, for both teachers and students, [which] requires a proactive attitude and demands the willingness to support an environment of collegiality and respect" (Green & Mitcham, 2012, p. 107).

Just as there are different ways to describe classroom communities, there are also different methods and techniques recommended for fostering them. Some scholars stress the significance of using high-impact teaching methods (McMillan & Chavis, 1986), other authors highlight the responsibility of the teacher (Wong et al., 2013), some stress the responsibility of the students (Greene & Mitcham, 2012), and others point to macro-level planning in academic programs (Bettez & Hytten, 2013). To drill down further, McMillan and Chavis (1986) stressed the importance of student participation and the use of active learning methods, such as class discussion, role playing activities, or game-based learning (see Rutherford, 2012). They also recommended that students have the opportunity to communicate with each other and address issues that come up during class. To supplement these suggestions, we offer the following strategies for fostering community in college classrooms. Where appropriate, we suggest a Cross Academy Technique (CAT). Visit our companion site — The K. Patricia Cross Academy (*kpcrossacademy.org*) — to find more information about each technique along with guidance on how to implement each technique in both onsite and online classrooms.

## Use Icebreakers

Many students (and instructors) will reflexively recoil or feel anxious about icebreakers. It is a reasonable reaction to activities that may feel awkward or forced, or that distract from time for instruction. However, by spending time early in the course focused on a well-planned and implemented icebreaker, instructors can create a sense of student community that improves course outcomes later in the semester. If the icebreakers connect to the course material, students may also buy in more readily.

- **Goal ranking and matching:** Start with a CAT 37: Think-Pair-Share activity, and ask students to individually list three to five learning goals for the semester and then rank them by importance, with 1 being the most important and 5 being the least important. Then have students share their goals with a partner and examine the ways in which their responses align and differ. Ask the pairs to share their responses on the white board or collect their responses and provide the class with a tallied list.
- **Syllabus review:** Teachers give students a syllabus every term often knowing that students may not actually review it. You can solve this problem by dividing students into groups of four to six, choosing a group recorder, and then asking students to create a list of questions about the course in a round robin format. After students have developed their list, distribute the syllabus and have them review it and determine if their questions have been answered. Also, ask students to list any information in the syllabus that they had not considered to ask about. End the class with a discussion about the syllabus and course based on any remaining unanswered questions or thoughts.
- **Future employer:** Ask students to develop a list of attributes they think a future employer may be interested in (either a generic employer or one reflective of the course discipline). Common answers include "mastery of the subject area," "ability to work in teams," "written and oral communication skills," "problem-solving ability," and "ability to learn on my own." Use these answers to kickstart a conversation about course goals and learning objectives (Miller et al., 1996).

## Encourage Connections Between and Among All Students

Students and teachers enter the classroom with norms and expectations that have been established by their communities and cultures. Engaged teachers can capitalize on these by building on the norms and expectations to establish community. Here are some tips for encouraging connections:

- **Build rapport with and among students.**
  - » **Use students' names and pronounce them correctly.** You may want to take simple steps like having students print their names on name tents. To ensure you are pronouncing an unfamiliar name correctly, ask for a phonetic spelling or recording.
  - » **Maintain a friendly, supportive tone in all communications.** Send an encouraging "Welcome" message to all students prior to each term. Include a statement that expresses your commitment to inclusive teaching. Answer all questions in an encouraging manner that conveys that you value students' courage in reaching out to you.
  - » **Reduce the barriers implicit in teacher–student roles.** Share your personal experiences as you pursued your education. Be open about the difficulties you may face as you continue to learn new material or keep current in your discipline.
  - » **Get to know students as individuals.** Schedule individual or small group instructor–student visits early in the term during regular class time. Encourage students to visit during office hours, or extend synchronous Zoom sessions so that you can interact with students in small groups or one-on-one. Set up a discussion forum online for students to introduce themselves. Encourage uploaded photos or avatars in online classes (but let students opt out if they do not feel comfortable doing this).
- **Help students build rapport among themselves.**
  - » **Build into your course opportunities for students to interact with each other.** These can be icebreakers, interviews, role plays, or group projects. Institute informal, non-graded discussion forums that provide the means for students to help each other as well as share beyond-classroom information with each other. Plan regular group discussions and small group interactions in break-out rooms during Zoom sessions.

» **Encourage students to partner with you to create a productive, inclusive learning community.** Discuss with students how recognizing and valuing others' perspectives is critical to the development of a true learning community as well as preparing them to be citizens of a complex contemporary world. Then create assignments (such as role-playing opportunities) that ask students to assume viewpoints other than their own.

## Create Opportunities for Information and Expertise Sharing

One factor that attracts people to communities is the collection of rich resources provided by individual members. Giving students the chance to share information and resources with each other is a strong way to build community. Some steps could include:

- **Break students into study groups.** Organizing students into smaller groups within the large class offers an obvious method of establishing a sense of community among students. Encourage students to get comfortable with each other and to build a system of friendly faces that they will encounter elsewhere on campus. Consider CAT 22: Test-Taking Teams.
- **Create a shared "Relevant Resource" section for the class.** Invite students to share information (such as blog posts, YouTube clips, TikToks, and so forth) about current events in the world that connect to course material. If students understand why course material is relevant to their everyday lives outside the classroom, they will be more apt to engage with it. Consider CAT 3: Contemporary Issues Journal.
- **Assign a social reading activity.** Social reading (i.e., sharing ideas about what they've read with classmates) is a useful tool for encouraging students to collaborate and develop community.

## Use Collaborative Learning Methods

Students and faculty agree on the importance of interaction with each other, and the research backs this up. As we discuss in Chapter 12: Implementing Collaborative Learning Techniques, this instructional approach requires students to work together, which can decrease the likelihood of individuals feeling isolated. Besides simple recognition that classmates are in similar situations, when group work is done well, students also value the interaction with peers and resulting relationships (Barkley et al., 2014). These relationships can generate more positive student experiences.

## Create Third Places

In class, setting aside some time and space for collaboration can allow for a kind of third place environment wherein students and teachers interact and develop relationships outside of the typical setting. Here are some strategies to foster a third place atmosphere:

- **Town hall meetings:** Modeled after the style of a town hall meeting, students each have the opportunity to voice various viewpoints. It is a good technique for beginning a class period or before starting any formal instruction.
- **Student lounge:** A common tool for online courses, this can also be implemented in onsite courses. A student lounge is generally a chat room or forum within the course website where students can interact with each other about coursework as well as their lives outside of the classroom.
- **Gallery walks:** In this technique, students move in small teams, sharing ideas and responding to various questions, images, documents, texts, and situations that are stationed around the room. This instructional method is a nice break from typical classroom activities because students walk around the classroom, interact with each other, and stay actively engaged.

## CONCLUSION

We know that humans need social interaction and a sense of belonging, so the way students come together and mesh in a course is important. When students feel like they are valued members of the class community, they are more willing to participate and engage. Furthermore, when students relate to each other in a positive and supportive manner, they are more satisfied both in and out of the classroom. But the way these class-based communities form can be ambiguous. In some ways, community is one of those "you know it when you see it" situations. Indeed, communities may look different from class to class.

In the end, building community is a shared effort between students and instructors, but faculty play a key role in developing an environment where communities can flourish. In order to establish opportunities for strong community, provide students with encouragement, have patience, and offer the right tools and activities. Investing the time and effort to foster a strong sense of community will not only help students, but will also be important for your own experience as an engaged teacher.

## FOCUS ON ONLINE TEACHING

The information we share in the main body of this chapter applies to both onsite and online teaching, but here we provide additional insights focused specifically on teaching online, hybrid, and blended courses.

### What: Community Online

Community is particularly important in online courses given the potential for students to feel isolated and alone. When we teach online, community forms and happens differently than when we teach onsite. The social connection is mediated by technology. In short, community happens by text rather than geography, with different markers of who has more or less influence in the group, and in spite of lack of nonverbal cues rather than because of them. Online community is not necessarily worse than onsite community, it is simply different. Indeed, some educators argue that community can be deeper online than onsite. The characteristics that differentiate community in online courses, however, have implications for our roles and responsibilities as teachers.

### Why: Community Online

Much of the research around online learning and community focuses on the community of inquiry (COI) framework (Garrison et al., 2000). The COI model identifies three critical forms of presence in online courses: teacher presence, social presence, and cognitive presence (Anderson et al., 2001). Teacher presence involves course design, instruction, and facilitation of discourse (Shea & Bidjerano, 2009; Shea et al., 2006). Social presence involves the ability to project oneself and establish purposeful relationships (Ryman et al., 2009). Cognitive presence involves the extent to which the participants can construct meaning through sustained communication. Lee and Huang (2018) used the COI framework to consider whether providing additional time and opportunities for interactions would improve social presence and in turn whether the social presence would be related to improved learning outcomes in a five-week intensive online course. They found the intervention improved social presence but did not find a relationship to learning outcomes.

On the other hand, examining a teacher leader program at a small public university, Swan et al. (2012) found that drawing on the COI framework can improve student learning outcomes. We need more research on this framework to know whether it does improve learning outcomes; however, the research suggests that it does influence student engagement (Cobb 2011), student satisfaction (Bulu, 2012; Cobb, 2011; Hostetter & Busch, 2006; Noteboom & Claywell, 2010), student participation and motivation (Richardson et al., 2015), and retention rates in online learning (Boston et al., 2009; Richardson et al., 2015).

## How: Community Online

It can be difficult to achieve community in an online course and to know whether it has developed, in part because it can happen under the radar of the course, through private texting and emailing, for example. If we are not included in the communication loop, we can feel that an online course does not have the same level of community as an onsite class does, even though there may be a vibrant community forming in backchannels.

Community is more than participation; it requires engagement, involvement, and action. Thinking through what appeals to us about other communities, whether onsite or online, can provide us with important clues about how to establish community online. There are several strategies we can use to promote community in an online course.

- **Create a plan for communication:** Communication is essential to community, and before you ask students to put themselves out there, it is a good idea to model effective communication. Create a calendar of when you will contact students, individually or as a group. Communicating at the start of each module with announcements or texts can be beneficial. Touching base prior to high-stakes assignments is also important. Such regular communications encourage community.
- **Create a plan for student communication:** Consider developing guidelines of netiquette to suggest preferred patterns of communication, such as the following:
    - **Identify yourself.** Begin messages with a greeting and close with your name.
    - **Avoid sarcasm.** It can be misinterpreted and cause hurt feelings.
    - **Keep the dialog collegial and professional.** Some discussion topics may be controversial.
    - **Do not flame (i.e., have outbursts of extreme emotion or opinion).** Think twice before you submit a response. You may not be able to edit or delete your posts once they have been submitted.
    - **Do not use offensive language or profanity.**
    - **Use clear subject lines for your posts.**
    - **Do not use all caps.** It is the online equivalent of YELLING!

» **Avoid using abbreviations or acronyms**—like UNESCO—unless the entire class knows them.

» **Use emoticons to clarify your emotions.** They add context to your words that cannot be seen otherwise.

» **Be forgiving.** Anyone can make a mistake.

- **Present a social presence and have students do so as well:** Social presence, or the sense that individuals have that they are connected to other real people, is an important concept for developing community. To promote social presence in an online course, both the teacher and the students need to be in attendance and be seen by everyone involved. There are several related factors that influence social presence, including immediacy, the psychological distance between communicators, interaction, and the notion that individuals will adjust their behaviors to maintain equilibrium. To develop and foster social presence online, try the following:

  » Create an introductory video and have students do the same; these can be simple smart phone videos where everyone introduces themselves and shares two to three facts about themselves.

  » Give students reason to come to the course site often.

  » Let students share work that represents them.

- **Meet in real time:** It is not always possible (or even desirable) to schedule synchronous meetings, but they can have a powerful impact on encouraging community. Students get to know each other, recognize faces and names, share information, and be assured they are participating in a learning community that includes real people. If a class meeting time is not built into the established schedule, make the sessions optional or consider having several synchronous sessions on the same topic at different times of the day and week so everyone can attend one.

*Years ago, the purpose of higher education was to select only the most academically promising young people. The new purpose of higher education is not to select those who will be successful but to make successful those who come.*

**—K. PATRICIA CROSS**

CHAPTER 9

# Promoting Equity and Inclusion

Equitable and inclusive teaching have received increased attention at college and university campuses around the country. A growing number of educators charge that many current educational practices reinforce a dominant paradigm that fails to meet the needs of marginalized groups. While these educators urge institutions to examine the existing structures that may disempower students at every level, they emphasize that creating more positive and supportive course environments is one of the most effective ways to address this challenge. Engaged teachers recognize how the social, emotional, intellectual, and even physical climate they establish in their courses can affect students. They then use this knowledge to create inclusive, equity-promoting environments.

This is not just a matter of being attentive to student preferences. Decades of studies indicate education does not occur in isolation; rather, students experiences within their learning environment, including whether it is supportive or marginalizing, can dramatically affect learning outcomes. How students experience their learning environment also influences student engagement, satisfaction, retention, and persistence to graduation. Additionally, establishing a classroom environment that supports equity and inclusion can benefit all students because many of the strategies that help foster a productive climate for traditionally marginalized students are also effective for all students.

Engaged teachers strive to ensure all students reach their full potential. Yet building a truly equity-minded, inclusive learning environment can be a challenge, largely due to the deeply entrenched marginalization that is manifested in traditional course design and the myriad ways in which inclusion and dis-inclusion can arise. While most instructors acknowledge the importance of equity and inclusion, it is seldom discussed in a practical way, leaving many instructors wondering how and where to begin. In this chapter, we explore specific strategies you can implement to create a classroom environment that promotes equity and inclusion.

## KNOWING WHAT: ABOUT EQUITABLE AND INCLUSIVE TEACHING

The chief responsibility of any teacher is to help students learn. As demographics change in higher education, undergraduates enter our classroom with a wide range of backgrounds, cultures, skills, experiences, personalities, and abilities. Engaged teachers work diligently to ensure that all students, not just some of them, learn — and that they learn as much as they can. Promoting equity and inclusion begins by fully understanding and cognitively grappling with this concept. Because the terms *equity* and *inclusion* are often used interchangeably, let's start with differentiating the two terms.

Equity essentially means being fair and impartial. In the classroom, it means ensuring all students have equal access to opportunities for learning, regardless of who they are. The term equity is often confused with *equality*. But treating students equally — as though they are all the same — does not acknowledge that long-standing forms of marginalization continue to negatively affect students' success and retention. When an instructor designs and teaches their courses to promote equity, they aim to help all students achieve excellence, but they give special attention to those who come from groups traditionally underrepresented in higher education.

Inclusive teaching is a broad term covering a complex network of social behaviors, pedagogical strategies, and norms that ensure people feel welcome. It describes a variety of teaching methods that account for the diverse backgrounds and needs of all students. Inclusive teachers view many forms of diversity — ethnicity, disability, gender, ideology, socioeconomic background, race, personality traits — as strengths. Inclusive teachers recognize that effective teaching is more than simply covering disciplinary content. Instead, they know that the classroom climate they establish has direct correlation with learning outcomes. Students' feelings of belonging predict their achievement, engagement, and motivation (Zumbrunn et al., 2014). Thus, maintaining an inclusive classroom will not just help students with learning differences; it will help all students.

Inclusive teaching is no longer optional but instead is an essential teaching competency when working with racially diverse, first generation, and low income and working-class students (Addy, et al., 2021). Creating an inclusive class environment where all students feel welcome regardless of their race, gender, socioeconomic status, sexuality, and ability is therefore an essential strategy for promoting equity, but by itself it is not sufficient to achieve equity. Teachers who strive for both equity and inclusion also assume an active role in dismantling structural inequities in their pedagogy and course design. Through their deliberate, thoughtful efforts they aim to maximize learning for all students in their courses.

## KNOWING WHY: RESEARCH ON EQUITABLE AND INCLUSIVE TEACHING

How can we be sure that promoting equity and inclusiveness is effective teaching? After examining a large body of extant research and theory that includes critical scholarship focused on teaching and learning, we feel confident suggesting that student learning outcomes improve when teachers:

1. Intentionally create learning environments in which each student is treated equitably, has access to learning, and feels welcomed, supported, and valued in the classroom and

2. Work to eliminate or reduce the ways in which systemic inequalities shape teaching–learning dynamics, affect students' experiences in classrooms, and influence the design of courses and curriculum.

The evidence for the efficacy of this approach to teaching includes the education research that we include in each of the chapters of this book. For example, as we described in Chapter 3: Understanding and Supporting Student Learning, mindsets related to intelligence influence student learning and persistence, and all students need to have positive mindsets about their ability to learn and succeed (e.g., Aronson et al., 2002; Dweck, 2006; Paunesku et al., 2015; Yeager & Dweck, 2012). The research done on climate, which we highlight in Chapter 7: Engaging Students and Chapter 8: Supporting Community, as well as this one, is clear: Students who feel safe and valued learn more. But there have also been research syntheses focused on inclusive teaching specifically that document its benefits (for example, see Hockings, 2010; Lawrie et al., 2017; Wlodkowski & Ginsberg, 1995). Several researchers have examined the relationship between race and learning and the influence that inclusive teaching can have on learning improvement. Gurin et al. (2002), for example, explored the relationship between student experiences with diverse peers and educational outcomes, finding that classroom diversity and informal interaction among African American, Asian American, Latino/a, and White students on learning and democracy outcomes leads to improved learning. In addition, reduction of stereotype threats, which serve as a barrier to student academic success, improves student learning (Steele, 2011). Moreover, reducing identity-based microaggressions and their negative relationship with learning can improve learning outcomes (Solórzano et al., 2000; Sue, 2010; Verschelden, 2017).

Researchers have studied the impact of promoting equity and inclusion on marginalized groups as well. Research on teaching first-generation students, for example, shows that cultural obstacles can impede learning (Stephens et al., 2012). In another study, instructors' use of language in STEM courses that signals inclusion (or exclusion) to students of color affected not only students' experience in the class but also their learning potential (Good et al., 2020). Several researchers have found that the creation of equitable learning environments and supporting historically underserved college students improves learning for students from marginalized groups without disadvantaging others (Eddy & Hogan, 2014; Winkelmes et al., 2016). Researchers have also examined the relationship between social belonging and student learning and persistence, with findings that suggest that belonging is related to improved learning outcomes (e.g., Hausmann et al., 2019; Hurtado & Carter, 1997; Walton & Cohen, 2011). Finally, student development, in particular development of reflective judgment and intercultural maturity, is connected to improved student learning (e.g., King & Baxter Magolda, 2005).

To summarize, ample research addresses and documents how inclusive teaching practices can help all students learn, but these strategies are particularly effective for students from underrepresented backgrounds or who are traditionally underserved in higher education. Teachers can feel confident that focusing their efforts on promoting equity and inclusion can bridge the achievement gap and help all students learn more.

## KNOWING HOW: AN ACTIVE APPROACH FOR PROMOTING EQUITY AND INCLUSION

You may be thinking, "promoting equity and inclusion in my teaching sounds great, but how do I do it?" The reality is there are many ways to go about it. In this chapter, we offer suggestions drawn from a wide range of sources. We found the Georgetown University Inclusive Teaching Toolkit (*https://cndls.georgetown.edu/inclusive-pedagogy/ip-toolkit/introduction/*) and the *Guide for Inclusive Teaching at Columbia* (https://ctl.columbia.edu/resources-and-technology/resources/inclusive-teaching-guide/) particularly useful.

### Reflect on Your Own Social Identity and Beliefs

In the midst of the semester, it is easy to fall back on comfortable teaching strategies, habits, or instincts that mirror our own preferences. No matter how noble our intentions, this reversion can keep us from understanding students' perspectives. To counteract this, it is helpful to reflect on your own identities and belief systems. Pausing to reflect on our attitudes, assumptions, beliefs about teaching and learning, and the habits and affect we demonstrate in the classroom can help us keep students engaged with the course material, our instruction, and each other. By taking time to reflect and reveal, you can pursue opportunities for improved self-awareness as well as new methods to better include all students in their learning (Bennett & Bennett, 2004; Goodman, 2011; Hearn, 2012; Lee et al., 2012). Consider these strategies from multiple sources including the Georgetown University Inclusive Teaching Toolkit:

- **Commit to teaching as an iterative exercise that includes self-reflection.** This commitment should include examining your own personality, demographics and background, self-presentation, biases, and the way you share information with students. As Brookfield (2017) argued, "becoming aware of the implicit assumptions that frame how we think and act is one of the most challenging intellectual puzzles we face in our lives. It is also something we instinctively resist, for fear of what we might discover" (pp. 2-3). Yet if we are truly committed to inclusive teaching, it is essential we maximize our self-awareness. Harvard University's Project Implicit (*https://implicit.harvard.edu/implicit/*) is a website that offers several self-inventory tools that can help you discover your unspoken beliefs about race, gender, sexual orientation, and other topics.

- **Share your own social identities with students.** Explain how your identities may influence your work, your role, and your engagement in the classroom.

- **Search out opportunities to learn more about perspectives that are different than your own.** Look for new perspectives in publications, Ted Talks, websites, and so forth. Attend presentations by scholars from under-represented identities at professional conferences or in webinars. Share these different perspectives with students, explicitly communicating your own perspective.

- **Acknowledge aspects of course content that are or were motivating or challenging to you.** This strategy can be particularly powerful if your reaction to the content is or was influenced by your personal identity.

- **Make space for students to express their own expertise and perspectives rather than always framing the conversation around your own views.** This approach may mean taking time to let students struggle to uncover their own unconscious biases or preconceived expectations of teachers' social identities.

## Consider the Course Content

Course material in which students see people like themselves reflected and valued is a major component in promoting equity and inclusion. As Ambrose et al. (2010) observed,

> For students who are developing their sense of identity, purpose, and competence, some of [the messages conveyed in course content] can be translated into messages about their own power, identity, and agency and can influence engagement and persistence in the field. (p. 179)

But it is not just course readings that should be considered. Students can internalize ideas about who belongs from many different interactions in the classroom. Content is a broad concept that includes the examples, metaphors, and case studies you use as well as the project topics you let students choose. "Just as important as those used are those omitted, because they all send messages about the field and who belongs in it" (Ambrose et al., 2010, p. 179). To establish inclusive course content:

- **Select material that engages multiple perspectives and beliefs.** Work toward creating an inclusive curriculum so students can learn about concepts and views from many different perspectives. Check with colleagues or consult professional organizations for additional sources. Critically examine how material is presented. If a text is problematic or perpetuates stereotypes, address these shortcomings and potentially supplement the content with additional material. Share with students the historical biases of your academic discipline. Encourage students to critique material for an inclusive perspective.
- **Choose material by creators with diverse backgrounds.** Include works created, researched, or written by thinkers from a variety of backgrounds. Taking this step can validate students who hope to see themselves represented in the course and field.
- **Use a variety of examples.** When lecturing or presenting material for class discussion, use a variety of examples that translate across gender, culture, socioeconomic backgrounds, religions, ages, and more. Make sure examples are grounded in specificity, not stereotypes. As needed, discuss the limitations of examples and do not assume every student will pick up on the same cultural, historical, or literary references. Instead, try to pull from resources, humor, stories, and materials that relate to the subject.

- **Bring additional voices into the classroom.** Invite speakers from other departments or from nonprofit or student organizations. Find supplementary material in Ted Talks, documentaries, YouTube videos, websites, and elsewhere.
- **Try to reduce the cost of course materials.** Students should have access to course content regardless of their financial background. You may be able to minimize the use of costly materials and resources by using open educational resources (OERs) or other types of free content. You might also be able to place required texts on reserve in the library, or have the library provide access to digital materials.

## Incorporate Principles of Universal Design for Learning

Universal design for learning (UDL) is an approach to teaching that is focused on the accommodation of the needs and skills of all students and the elimination of unnecessary hurdles to student learning. Designing instruction around UDL principles can aid you in developing learning environments that are flexible enough to accommodate student learning differences by presenting materials in a variety of ways and offering students options to demonstrate their learning. It can help you dismantle obstacles to education or other learning barriers students confront. To adhere to the principles of UDL, consider these steps, recommended by Cornell University's Teaching Center (2012) as well as Rose and Meyer (2002):

- **Ensure your course is accessible.** This requires knowledge of and adherence to accessibility requirements, including potentially providing students with extra time on exams, extended deadlines on assignments, note takers, and so forth.
- **Offer options for how students access information.** Tied to the idea that students may process material differently or have a variety of preferences and abilities, offer students several flexible methods for receiving information. For example, use presentation slides as a complement to a lecture or make material accessible in written and auditory formats.
- **Offer options for student expression.** Stemming from the idea that students have differing abilities to demonstrate learning, offer several flexible methods to demonstrate knowledge or express skills. For example, have students respond to questions through an online poll instead of raising their hands in class. Or offer extra time for students as needed.

- **Offer options for comprehension.** Based on the idea that students have a variety of motivations for learning, offer multiple methods for engaging in learning. For example, identify your learning goal and then provide options such as attending lectures, going on a field trip, or conducting independent research that students could do to achieve that learning goal.

## Engage with Students in a Safe Space

Students who are anxious about feeling chastised by their classmates will not participate in class activities. Create a safe space by helping students understand how to productively communicate with each other. Instill in students the confidence to know they can participate without shame.

- **Establish a set of rules early in the course.** Consider including guidelines such as the following:
  - » **Participate.** Each student is responsible for the success of the community. Your participation will help everyone succeed.
  - » **Keep to the golden rule.** Treat your classmates the way you want to be treated. Sticking to this rule will make sure we are respectful to everyone.
  - » **Don't flame or make personal attacks.** Flaming is when you insult another person online. In this class, no student should make personal attacks. Everyone's communication should be respectful and refrain from condescension, disrespect, or ridicule.
  - » **Stay PG-13.** This is a college setting, and everyone is an adult. Furthermore, inappropriate comments may follow you through your career. Make sure your comments would all be appropriate for younger readers.
- **Model the behavior and interactions you hope to see.** Demonstrate the skills for promoting inclusiveness that you hope students will demonstrate in their interactions, assignments, and assessments. Be an active participant in the learning community by following community agreements and guidelines for discussion.
- **Demonstrate sharing pronouns.** At the beginning of the term, and on your syllabus, list your pronouns. Encourage students to share theirs if they are comfortable and then use students' preferred pronouns, but don't force it as some students may not be comfortable sharing. Students will see you model inclusive behavior, and students who identify as LGBTQIA will appreciate the gesture.

- **Respect students' individuality.** Do your best not to make assumptions about students' membership in any demographic groups. Let students self-identify, and only when they feel comfortable doing so. Support each of their unique abilities and assets, and offer each student the same amount of respect.
- **Demonstrate trustworthiness.** Be consistent when enforcing class policies. Don't play favorites or single out students for correction. If it is necessary to alter your policies, be transparent. Explain why the change is fair and in the best interest of students.
- **Acknowledge students' tough times.** There will be moments external to the classroom that affect your students' lives. Some are national, some local, some personal, and you may be unclear about how to express your concern without alienating other students. Consider something simple like, "I know this may be a difficult time, and I want to make sure you know I am thinking about you."
- **Establish a liberal attendance policy.** This demonstrates you trust students will make good decisions.
- **Keep your focus on teaching rather than policing.** Shifting attention away from cheating or plagiarism demonstrates you trust students' integrity.
- **Be aware of existing stereotypes and avoid perpetuating them.** Refrain from expecting individual students to represent the perspective or experience of an entire group; intervene if students expect this of their peers. Help students avoid being self-critical based on feelings that they believe represent certain groups. Make efforts to neutralize or deliberately discuss moments when stereotyping occurs in material or in student comments.
- **Establish processes to solicit feedback on the classroom environment and directly address tensions as they come up.** As much as possible, turn heated moments into learning opportunities.
- **Allow for anonymous participation.** Some students may be introverted and feel out of place in the classroom, others may have a minority opinion on a topic and look for ways to participate in class without speaking publicly. For example, provide a prompt and then have students write anonymous responses on notecards. Ask your students to swap cards and then swap cards again. Begin a group discussion by asking a few students to read

aloud from the cards they now hold. Or consider a classroom-response system (i.e., online polling) or a message board in which students may be anonymous to each other but not to the teacher.

## Use Learning-Centered Teaching Methods

Effective teachers can foster a learning environment that naturally supports equity and inclusion when they step out of the role of sage on the stage and embrace the responsibility of guide on the side (or possibly, a sage on the side; Bain, 2004). Students should not be spectators in their own learning (Barkley et al., 2014). Learning is better considered as a team sport that involves collaboration and teamwork.

- **Organize your course so that students are dynamic participants in the class.** Provide them with opportunities to discuss what they're learning, connect it to their own lives, write about it, and apply it to their own understandings of the world. You can do this by prompting students to integrate and synthesize their learning (Chickering & Gamson, 1987) and steering students toward important problems that cultivate intellectual curiosity.
- **Nudge students to question their own biases and underlying assumptions.** Effective teaching necessitates that students develop their own perspectives on the leading questions and issues in the field (Bain, 2004). Encouraging students to work together increases their participation in their own learning. And describing their ideas to their peers, while also listening and responding to their ideas, deepens student understanding and improves their critical thinking ability (Chickering & Gamson, 1987).
- **Include opportunities for students to draw upon their diverse backgrounds and lived experience to understand and apply course concepts and information.** Encourage them to reflect upon, write about, and then discuss with each other their individual learning experiences. Consider CATs such as 38: Affinity Grouping, 8: Paper Seminar, and 36: Class Book. These strategies can help students see the diversity of responses and perspectives and to share well-formed ideas with each other.

## Share Responsibility With Students

One factor in building a positive, supportive course climate is giving students more control over their experience. This not only contributes to the overall inclusive tone of the class, but it also empowers students to become competent, self-directed, and lifelong learners. Ginsberg and Wlodkowski (2009) argued that establishing mutual responsibility requires instructors to alter their understanding of their main role: "Rather than knowing what to do to the learner, successful educators seek to understand and strengthen the potential for shared meaning" (p. 29). Consider these strategies:

- **Involve students in shaping the course syllabus.** For example, survey students to learn their specific interests and learning goals related to course content. Ask students to identify the kinds of expertise the course should help them to acquire and invite them to suggest how they think they could best demonstrate their achievements. Give students some control over the dates for assignment deadlines and assessment activities. If you do not feel comfortable with giving students direct say over syllabus content, at least try to develop a syllabus that feels more like a letter to your students than a contract.
- **Give students leadership roles and opportunities.** Have individual or small groups of students critique a reading, lead a discussion, or craft a specific assignment.

## Engage With Individuals

In traditional classrooms, some of those identities, cultures, and backgrounds have received more privilege and power than others. Effective teachers want all students to have an experience that is positive and inclusive rather than "chilly" and marginalizing. Here are some tips to achieve this:

- **Reach out to students individually.** Send congratulatory notes to students who performed well on early assignments. For students who are performing poorly, missing classes, or falling behind, reach out and offer your help and support.
- **Acknowledge self-perceptions that can inhibit student learning.** For example, discuss growth mindsets in the classroom and help students understand that intelligence and ability can be developed with effort. Explain that the "fraud complex/imposter syndrome" is a well-known phenomenon and reassure students that while many students may feel this way, all students belong and can be successful in your course. Tell students that learning can be tough, but it is not impossible. Emphasize the "yet," as in: "I have not learned how to do calculus well **yet**, but I'll get there!"
- **Demonstrate the same level of confidence in the aptitude of all students.** Be mindful of becoming either overly-protective or excessively

strict toward some students. Be equitable in recognizing student accomplishments and areas for student improvement. Stress that you have high standards for everyone and confirm that your goal is to provide support for all students to meet your standards.

- **Discuss with students the barriers to success they face.** Solicit from them their suggested solutions, and then trust them to follow through.
- **Respect students' privacy.** Be mindful when returning graded assignments. If it is necessary to address student conduct or poor performance, speak to students individually, away from their peers.
- **Be sensitive to students' feelings.** Show students that you are on their side, that you're rooting for their success. Listen attentively, respond effectively, and avoid embarrassing them.

## Plan for Civil Behavior

A growing number of instructors are concerned about student incivility in their courses. Behaviors ranging from being inconsiderate to overtly hostile and aggressive can undermine a classroom's sense of community and harm student learning. These strategies may help you prevent or manage student incivility.

- **Develop community agreements.** Create collective agreements about what comprises a supportive learning environment so that students feel a sense of ownership over the class climate. This may also help you reestablish control in tense classroom moments. You can reinforce the importance of inclusion by working with students to establish mutual guidelines for everyone in the classroom and stressing the importance of respecting those agreements.
- **Involve students in designing a policy for classroom civility.** In the policy, outline expectations and consequences for unacceptable actions.
- **Be explicit about your own expectations for student behavior.** Include a statement in your syllabus that outlines expectations for positive student behavior.
- **Hold students accountable for behavior by reducing anonymity.** Learn and use students' names, and help students learn each other's names.

- **Provide opportunities for students to give course climate feedback.** Set up an opportunity for students to share their grievances like selecting a student ombudsman, creating an anonymous feedback survey that is always available, or offering a critical incident questionnaire.

- **Document occurrences of incivility.** If the actions are especially egregious, have students who saw the incident record their observations of what occurred.

- **Understand your institution's policies and procedures for dealing with disruptive behavior.** Consider ensuring students know policies and procedures as well. For example, include links to institutional documents on your syllabus and take time to review them when you are orienting students to your course.

## Assess to Promote Equity and Inclusion

Teachers need to know what and how well students are learning. An equity-promoting, inclusive classroom design acknowledges that students learn differently and therefore avoids a narrow approach to assessment because it may not capture demonstrations of learning by all students. Here are some ways to ensure that you are accurately assessing what students are learning.

- **Clearly share your learning goals.** Provide students with a syllabus that plainly states semester goals as well as daily objectives. Students can use these as a roadmap to guide them in their learning efforts. Encourage students to ask questions if they are unclear about your goals and expectations.

- **Show students what success looks like.** Provide students with examples of excellent work, either hypothetical examples that you create or real ones that you solicit from prior students. By showing students sample work, you can better demonstrate expectations and standards for assessment to a variety of learners.

- **Give multiple low-stakes assessments and quizzes.** Some students may not understand they are struggling until they fail their first exam. By providing multiple assessments throughout class, you and students can make adjustments early so that all students have a better chance for course success.

- **Offer clear guidelines for every assignment.** Be transparent on grading, such as assigning grades based on a carefully constructed rubric before students begin work on the assignment.
- **Give students multiple ways and repeated opportunities to demonstrate their learning.** For example, instead of a traditional paper or exam, create assessment activities such as presentations, podcasts, videos, and projects. Allow students to submit drafts or do dress rehearsals to get formative feedback to improve their work.
- **Scaffold large projects.** Break down complex assignments into smaller, manageable steps and provide feedback along the way.
- **Implement pre- and post-class, low-stakes but required assessments.** These distribute learning over a wider range of time and help students develop study habits that reduce cramming. Some students have already learned to seize each moment they can to practice, but others haven't, which can exacerbate achievement gaps.
- **Lower the stakes of major tests and papers.** Single assignments that carry significant weight can potentially do severe damage to a student's overall grade. Reduce the emphasis of high-stakes work by: (1) letting students drop one or two of their lowest scores on quizzes, exams, or other assignments; (2) allowing students to replace one of their earlier scores with a cumulative final grade; or (3) replacing part of the weight of high-stakes assignments with more frequent, smaller quizzes.
- **Be clear on your deadline policy.** If you believe it is important to have a fixed schedule, then determine deadlines for major assignments and tests at the start of the term and then stick to them as much as possible. If you allow late submissions or are more flexible with deadlines, be transparent about this so that all students know your rules.
- **Consider contract- or labor-based assessment.** Design a grading policy that gives students more control over how they can attain different course grades and that also focus on learning and progress.

## CONCLUSION

Educators at all levels of higher education are striving to create learning environments that promote equity and inclusion. As college teachers, we can help achieve this by structuring our classes so that all students learn and thrive, including those from marginalized backgrounds.

We can conduct ourselves in the classroom in ways that are responsive and which make all students feel like valued members of a learning community. If we teach students the importance of equity and inclusion, we can work toward a more tolerant and accepting society and world. We know that different students have differing needs, but many solutions benefit all students. To emphasize, this approach to teaching creates a space that is safe for learning by all. It will not harm students who do not need additional support (and could even help them), but it will be an important contribution to leveling the playing field, thus ensuring that all students learn to the best of their ability. This is an essential element of the engaged teaching process.

## FOCUS ON ONLINE TEACHING

The information we share in the main body of this chapter applies to both onsite and online teaching, but here we provide additional insights focused specifically on teaching online, hybrid, and blended courses.

### What: Equity and Inclusion Online

Like an equitable and inclusive onsite course, an equitable and inclusive online course is one in which all students can learn and that features content and activities that are diversified and speak to all students. There are differences in how to engage with equitable and inclusive teaching online, as the text heavy medium of the online environment changes how you carry out different strategies. Instructors can draw on principles of inclusive teaching to help online students feel a sense of belonging, ensure they can access course materials, and support them in achieving learning goals.

### Why: Equity and Inclusion Online

Given that it is a relatively new body of work, research on equity and inclusion in online courses is slim, and research that documents improvements in learning by adopting inclusive teaching practices online is even slimmer. But logic suggests that students who feel safe, included, and have trust in their instructor, peers, and the learning process will do better than those who do not. Evidence of the importance of these characteristics for both onsite and online learning is provided throughout this book. In particular, see the Focus on Online Learning in Chapter 7: Engaging Students and Chapter 8: Supporting Community, as well as the Focus on Online Learning in the instructional methods chapters in Part 5.

### How: Equity and Inclusion Online

Online and hybrid teaching can enhance or hinder classroom equity. Equitable teaching means that the outcomes of our teaching are "fair and just" regardless of the differences that the students bring to the classroom. Even though we may have the good intention to treat students equitably, good intentions alone are often not sufficient. Consider the following strategies for implementing Inclusive Teaching online (adapted from University of Iowa Center for Teaching and Learning *https://www.celt.iastate.edu/teaching/creating-an-inclusive-classroom/*).

### ENSURE ACCESSIBILITY

In particular, content needs to be accessible for students with physical impairments that could interfere with reading, seeing, or hearing as well as for students with psychological or learning differences that require certain accommodations, such as extra time to process materials or additional exam time. You should also consider students with limited access to computers or stable internet service. Consider the following tips:

- **Ensure all files, images, videos, and other content are accessible.**
- **Ensure good universal design for all students.** This requires knowledge of and adherence to accessibility requirements, including the proper use of heading structures, ordered and unordered lists, meaningful links, alternative text for images, color contrast, and video closed captioning. Check with your institution for resources to help you on this important comprehensive task.
- **Consider whether content is suitable for accessing on a mobile device, such as a phone.**
- **Consider whether content is accessible without highspeed internet service.**
- **Consider open educational resources (OERs) or other types of free content.** Students should have access to course content, regardless of their financial background.
- **Be aware that not all students will have equal access to technology or internet.** Plan for sharing content and facilitating activities in which all students can engage. This may mean relying on good old standards like the course LMS or even email and text. Ensuring student access will increase all students' comfort and improve their learning.

## Be Identity-Conscious

We know students are not all the same, that they come to us with sometimes vastly different experiences. Those experiences may be tied to their social identities (such as race, gender, sexual orientation, first-generation status, and so forth). Demonstrate that you understand this fact in meaningful ways.

- **Integrate culturally relevant online materials.** These could include images, texts, and videos.

- **Be aware of variation.** Students will have different levels of capacity to manage remote learning.
- **Be mindful.** Recognize how current social, political, or environmental situations may impact different communities.

## BE FLEXIBLE

Strive to be flexible along multiple dimensions. Consider the following tips:

- **Have flexible policies.** Adjust your grading weights, late policies, and other course requirements and procedures to accommodate students who are learning in a different environment.
- **Use flexible activities and assessments.** Try to offer multiple ways for students to learn and to demonstrate their learning. For example, you might post a reading as well as an audio recording and then offer students a choice of demonstrating their learning in a paper or a digital project.

## ESTABLISH RELATIONSHIPS

Forming supportive interpersonal relationships with students is one of the most fundamental tenets of effective teaching. It can be particularly important for students from traditionally underrepresented backgrounds. Consider the following strategies.

- **Hold virtual office hours.** Letting students know when you are available can be helpful to them and encourage them to reach out.
- **Provide opportunities for live synchronous engagement.** Consider making this optional, however.
- **Involve students.** Invite them to create a discussion forum.
- **Have individual or individual group of students adopt leadership roles.** They could critique a reading, lead a discussion, or craft a specific assignment.
- **Provide students with support.** This could include additional resources they could access outside of synchronous sessions.
- **Ask for feedback.** Consider creating an anonymous online survey either through your LMS or a program such as SurveyMonkey to solicit feedback on your online course's classroom environment. You can respond to the feedback in your weekly announcements.

PART 4

# Methods

*Passive learning is an oxymoron; there is no such thing.*

**—K. PATRICIA CROSS**

CHAPTER 10

# Lecturing Effectively

Most of us have experienced that dreaded feeling of being trapped in a room listening to a lecture. The speaker's voice droned on and on, our minds wandered, our bodies fidgeted, and we struggled to devise a discreet escape strategy. Few teaching techniques are more heartily maligned than the lecture. As Albert Camus commented, "Some people talk in their sleep. Lecturers talk while other people sleep." Or as a student lamented, "I was so bored, I feared all the blood had left my head and I would pass out in the aisle" (El-Shamy, 2004, p. 24). Lecturing is criticized for being boring, ineffective, old-fashioned, overused, obsolete, and even unfair. Indeed, many educators today consider lecturing to be so bad that one author imagines a future when universities will be required to issue a warning to students that "lectures may stunt your academic performance and increase risk of failure" (Dawson, 2016).

Yet, in spite of continued complaints, research suggests that most higher education faculty still lecture. For example, when students are surveyed about their classroom experiences (such as those administered by the Mathematics Association of America or the National Survey of Student Engagement) their responses suggest that between 60% and 75% of faculty still lecture. A Higher Education Research Institute faculty survey reported that over 50% of faculty lecture extensively (Eagan et al., 2014). The percentage could actually be higher: Ebert-May et al. (2011) found that in a week-long active learning workshop, 89% of faculty reported they used active learning techniques, but under observation, 75% still depended heavily on lecturing.

Lectures continue to be prevalent for several reasons, and certainly among them is the fact that they serve many educational purposes. Faculty lecture to:

- present essential background knowledge,
- convey material otherwise inaccessible to students,
- clear up misunderstood ideas, principles, or material,
- exhibit enthusiasm for the subject,
- articulate why the material is worth studying,
- offer synthesized information from a variety of sources,
- demonstrate higher order thinking skills and strategies,
- structure information in a logical manner,
- point out differences and similarities, and
- help students consolidate knowledge.

Also, despite those unfortunate experiences many of us have had listening to a dreary lecture, lectures do not need to be dull. Just as we have all experienced bad lectures, most of us have also experienced absorbing, captivating lectures. Those types of lectures can be transformative events. Furthermore, listening to lectures does not have to be a passive activity. We assert in our publication *Interactive Lecturing: A Handbook for College Faculty* (Barkley & Major, 2018) that lecturing can be an active learning pedagogy. To achieve this, engaged teachers strive for stimulating presentations that are punctuated by carefully crafted active learning techniques.

## KNOWING WHAT: ABOUT THE LECTURE

Lecture is derived from the Latin root *lectare*, which roughly translates as "to read aloud" (Barkley & Major, 2018). Among ancient Greeks, the lecture was the main way of conveying knowledge and material (Brown & Atkins, 1988). This laid the foundation for later methods. Around the 6th century CE, scholars often journeyed hundreds of miles to hear monks read aloud in European monasteries. While monks read from lecterns, scholars would hand copy the text verbatim (Exley & Dennick, 2004). Lectures continued through the Middle Ages when universities were established and remained the core pedagogical method in European higher education in the centuries that followed. This tradition was then transplanted to the U.S. colonies. By the middle of the 19th century, lecturing had been solidified as the main tool for instruction in American colleges (Garside, 1996, p. 212). So, what is a lecture?

## What Is a Lecture?

Bligh (1999) offered a working understanding of a lecture as, "a more or less continuous exposition by a speaker who wants the audience to learn something" (p. 4). The literature is filled with comparable definitions, such as:

- A lecture is an educational talk to an audience, especially to students in a university or college (Oxford Dictionary).
- Lecture is a method of teaching in which the instructor gives an oral presentation of facts or principles to learners, who are responsible for note taking (Good & Merkel, 1959).
- [A lecture is when] a teacher is talking and students are listening (Singh, 2006).

These definitions of lecture primarily describe it as a way to transmit information. Lecturing as the means for information transmittal became the predominant pedagogy because it offered a model for disseminating knowledge in the centuries before the invention of the printing press permitted large-scale publication of books. The information transmittal lecture remains the iconic lecture format, but it is not the only form of lecture. Rather, lectures come in all shapes and sizes, as described below.

## Types of Lectures

Lectures differ along five key elements: formality, duration, interactivity, format, and medium (adapted from Barkley & Major, 2018; Major et al., 2021, pp. 3-5):

#### FORMALITY

- **Formal lectures:** Well-planned, tightly-coordinated, and polished presentations
- **Semi-formal lectures:** Less elaborate presentations, similar to formal lectures
- **Informal lectures:** Loosely organized or impromptu presentations

### DURATION

- **Full-Session lectures:.** A continuous transmission of information lasting a full class period
- **Lecturettes:** Roughly 15 to 20 minutes, and may be connected to other lecturettes
- **Mini-lectures:** Tight, focused presentations that offer approximately 5 to 15 minutes of content
- **One-minute lectures:** As you may guess, roughly one minute of focused material; when designed for online distribution, they are called micro-lectures

### INTERACTIVITY

- **One-way, little student interaction:** Questions reserved for the conclusion of a lecture
- **Two-way, limited:** Occasional student interaction, initiated by the teacher
- **Two-way, negotiated:** Occasional interactivity, begun by teachers or students
- **Participatory:** Students involved in a variety of exchanges, sparked by teachers and students

### FORMAT

- **Socratic lectures:** Coordinated sequences of questions challenge one student at a time to use logic and inference combined with their course readings to answer questions
- **Point-by-point lectures:** Presentations with single idea, issue, or question; and generally structured in an outline
- **Lecture-demonstrations:** Presentations demonstrating activities or processes, typically presented in chronological order
- **Storytelling lectures:** Narratives used to illustrate concepts generally involving character development, exposition, rising action and a climax, followed by falling action and resolution

- **Problem-solving lectures:** Demonstrations involving working through problems to arrive at solutions, highlighting the order of steps needed to determine the solution
- **Oral essays:** Arguments with primary theses or assertions and supplemental material and justification, generally listed in order of priority

**MEDIUM**

- **Oral only:** Direct talks to students without the use of any technology
- **Chalk and talk lecture:** Talks given while actively transcribing notes on a medium visible to students like whiteboards or chalkboards
- **Multimedia lecture:** Talks accompanied by audio-visual presentations that illustrate key material
- **Video lecture:** Talks recorded and edited into videos that may be used in online education, blended learning, or flipped classrooms

The factors outlined above can be combined in many ways. One teacher may offer formal, point-by-point, video lecturettes, while another instructor may prefer informal, oral-only, mini-lecture demonstrations. Engaged teaching means understanding the various lecture types and options and then using the format that best serves the pedagogical purpose.

## KNOWING WHY: RESEARCH ON WHAT MAKES LECTURES ENGAGING

For several decades, researchers have examined the effectiveness of lectures primarily by comparing them to other teaching techniques. Bligh (1999) conducted one of the more expansive studies, using a meta-analysis of extant published research. In this synthesis, Bligh compared the results of lectures to other teaching techniques, such as discussion, inquiry projects, and independent learning. By examining the transmission of information to students, he determined that "the lecture is as effective as any other method for transmitting information but not more effective" (p. 4). In recent years, studies have compared the lecture method alone and in combination with other teaching techniques: problem-based learning (Strobel & van Barneveld, 2009), case-based learning (Baeten et al., 2013), and cooperative learning (Johnson et al., 2014), as well as comparisons that are more broadly connected to active learning (Deslauriers et al., 2011; Freeman et al., 2014). Together, the research showed that an instructional approach that consisted of lecture only was not as effective as instruction that combined lecture with additional approaches that involved student activity. The combined lecture–student activity approach showed higher gains in problem-solving, critical thinking, and long-term information retention. Teachers can increase the effectiveness of lectures by (1) making sure their presentations are engaging and (2) integrating active learning techniques (Barkley & Major, 2018).

Some instructors may not feel they have personalities conducive to the vocal variety, animated face, movements, and gesturing typically associated with an engaging presentation, but expressive delivery can result in learning gains. Furthermore, students are more likely to give their attention to lively lecturers. Research investigating differing levels of expression (low, medium, or high) indicated that learners who witnessed highly expressive instructors performed better on multiple choice recall than those who watched less expressive teachers (Murray, 1997). Don't mistake this for a call that instructors need to become entertainers. Instead, instructors should attempt to tie expressive presentation to important content. Students rate class lecturers highly based on both content and the instructor's communication method (Hodgson, 1984). In her study, Hodgson (1984) described various experiences of relevance, in other words, the idea that how students perceive their instructor's love and enthusiasm for the material can bring it to life in ways that affect the student experience. Though it may be challenging for some, instructors who can incorporate expressive cues can help students connect to the lesson in a variety of ways.

Students also need time to digest new material. Our brains use different processing paths for oral and visual information (Baddeley, 1998). Giving students too much information at once can lead to cognitive overload (Mayer & Moreno, 2003). For example, instructors can cause cognitive overload by fostering too many sensations at once. For instance, when an instructor delivers a slide presentation filled with text and then verbally describes the text, students cannot process both the written and spoken text at once, and so must choose which to give their attention. But if an instructor presents just images or a few specific words to highlight the key points of a lecture, coupled with verbal explanations, students are better able to maintain attention. Additionally, performance lectures that may incorporate humor, personal stories, questions posed to the class, and learning activities are not only more appealing to students but also can result in improved learning (Short & Martin, 2011).

## KNOWING HOW: CREATING ENGAGING LECTURE PRESENTATIONS

Engaging presentations are essential components of interactive lectures. Though we recognize some instructors may be naturally gifted at lecturing in a manner that students find inherently engaging, a good many of us who lecture day in and day out are...not. Additionally, some of the material we must convey just lacks panache. However, no matter our personal methods or the hurdles of particular content, we can work to make as much as possible out of lectures. We offer the following recommendations for designing lectures that will engage students. Recommendations are divided into five categories that align with our model of the five elements of engaging presentations: focus, format, supports, climate, and communication (adapted from Barkley & Major, 2018). Where appropriate, we suggest a Cross Academy Technique (CAT). For more information on each CAT, visit our companion site, The K. Patricia Cross Academy, where you will find videos and downloadable templates to guide implementation in both onsite and online classrooms.

## Develop a Clear Focus

Crafting an effective lecture hinges on knowing its true purpose. Clearly stating your general purpose (Big Why) as well as a more specific purpose (Little Why) offers a firm basis for building the content and structure of your lecture. Without this firm base, the organization of your lecture will be less sturdy, and it will have less influence.

Studying student characteristics may aid your ability to understand your audience and refine your message. A student characteristics analysis, which can be in the form of a quick survey in which you ask students questions relevant to the course you are teaching, allows you to examine relevant student attributes as they relate to the material. The data provide a clear description of student characteristics that can allow you to better target your teaching. The Rule of 3 is a foundational communication concept that recommends presenting information in written or oral communication in groups of three. This rule works because a three-part format blends the brevity that helps students use their working memories with the establishment of enough material to reveal an identifiable pattern.

## Choose an Effective Format

Lecturettes are brief, self-contained presentations that last approximately 15 to 20 minutes. Connecting two or three lecturettes together as linked lecturettes in a larger talk gives you more flexibility and offers the chance to be more spontaneous in the classroom. You can break up these lecturettes and reset student attention by weaving in active learning assignments. *Bookends* are activities that appear before or after a lecture to help support the presentation (Smith, 2000; Smith et al., 2005). You may include a bookend before your lecture in the form of something like a preparation guide or an online activity, or you may incorporate it to start the presentation itself, such as a brief prediction activity. By contrast, *overlays* are activities that students complete during a presentation to focus their attention on the material, such as active listening activities or notetaking assignments. *Interleaves* involve an instructor switching between lectures and active learning activities that give students time to digest the material. For example, you could interleave your presentations

| PLAN COMPONENT | BOOKEND | OVERLAY | INTERLEAVE | OVERLAY | INTERLEAVE | OVERLAY | BOOKEND |
|---|---|---|---|---|---|---|---|
| TIME ALLOTTED | 5 MINUTES | 15 MINUTES | 5 MINUTES | 15 MINUTES | 5 MINUTES | 15 MINUTES | 5 MINUTES |
| STUDENT ACTIVITY | Do *CAT 14: Update Your Classmate* | Listen to Lecture Presentation<br>Do *CAT 16: Guided Notes* | Do *CAT 37: Think-Pair-Share* | Listen to Lecture Presentation<br>Do *CAT 16: Guided Notes* | Do *CAT 10: Quick Write* | Listen to Lecture Presentation<br>Do *CAT 16: Guided Notes* | Do *CAT 20: Lecture Wrapper* |

**Table 10.1. Lecture Plan Incorporating Bookends, Overlays, and Interleaves**

with quick small group discussions or brief writing assignments, such as CAT 18: Support a Statement. See Table 10.1: Lecture Plan Incorporating Bookends, Overlays, and Interleaves for an example of how a typical class session might work using such a plan.

## Select Suitable Supports

The most common lecture support currently is a slide deck. But slides need to be well designed to be effective. Less is more, for example, is a reminder to make your slide presentations minimalist, which can make them more effective and compelling. Your slide should not convey your message in full. It should instead contain a key word or phrase to support your message. Consider the effectiveness of the two slides in Figure 10.1: Two Slides Demonstrating Effectiveness of Minimal Text.

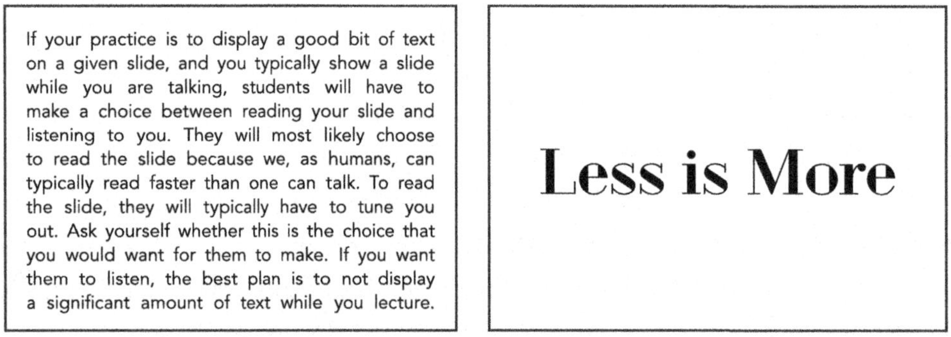

If your practice is to display a good bit of text on a given slide, and you typically show a slide while you are talking, students will have to make a choice between reading your slide and listening to you. They will most likely choose to read the slide because we, as humans, can typically read faster than one can talk. To read the slide, they will typically have to tune you out. Ask yourself whether this is the choice that you would want for them to make. If you want them to listen, the best plan is to not display a significant amount of text while you lecture.

Less is More

**Figure 10.1. Two Slides Demonstrating Effectiveness of Minimal Text**

Graphic elements can be impactful, efficient alternatives to text. Look at the two slides in Figure 10.2: Verbal and Graphic Version of Polygon Description and consider which is the more efficient form of communication. Chapter 6: Designing Visual Elements for Teaching offers additional information and guidance on good visual design. Instead of relying solely on presentation slides, consider varying your approach and use slide replacements. Props, videos, flip charts, signs, and whiteboards can serve as alternatives that reduce presentation boredom.

A polygon is a plane figure in geometry that is described by a finite number of straight line segments connected to form a closed polygonal chain (or polygonal circuit).

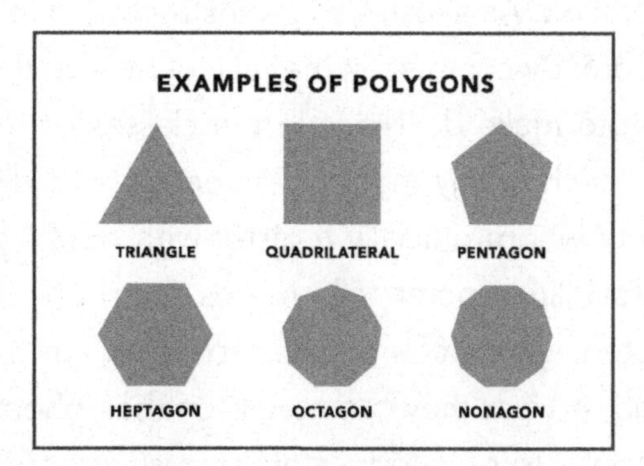


**Figure 10.2. Verbal and Graphic Version of Polygon Description**

Finally, many times students will ask you for copies of your slides. Well done slides are meant to support a talk in real-time rather than serving as a handout. Rather than printing out your slides, posting them online, or emailing them to students, consider creating a content-rich handout that provides a more focused resource. A content-rich handout is a concise document designed to provide explanatory written information related to the lecture topic that may include illustrations, figures, or tables.

## Establish a Supportive Climate

It is critical to get students involved and interested before, during, and after the lecture. Get students intrigued about the material ahead of class with a lecture preview, in which you share some information about the upcoming topic and the presentation's key points. You can do this as closure to the current lecture, or send your preview electronically ahead of time through your course site, social media, or email. Advance notice will also give students time to better prepare.

Grab students' attention by starting your lecture with a hook such as a compelling quotation, a stunning statistic, an engaging story, or any other attention-getting information.

These can be displayed verbally or nonverbally. Express clearly why the lecture is valuable to highlight the reasons students should care about the subject. If students understand the importance of a lecture, they are more likely to put in effort to pay attention and to learn the material.

An increasingly common issue in today's classroom is how to regulate personal technology use. Many instructors are concerned by the potential for distraction and, honestly, it can be discouraging to see students scrolling through social media during an important presentation. As a result, many instructors ban laptops, smartphones, and tablets from the classroom. By contrast, some faculty believe that because students are adults, they should be free to make decisions in the classroom, for better or worse. Furthermore, a blanket ban on technology in the classroom could discriminate against learners with disabilities, not all of whom officially register with disability services. Making exceptions for students with disabilities potentially makes them uncomfortable with their peers. There are also instructors who prefer to use technology in the classroom, for instance, polling students through services they can access on their phone. In order to address these issues, however you choose to proceed, establish a classroom technology policy and make sure students understand what is expected of them.

## Use Good Communication Strategies

Most of your lecture communication strategies will be verbal ones. Thus, high-impact language can be important. High-impact language is comprised of terms and phrases chosen to have a more powerful effect on students. Using clear and concise words will help you present specific messages that students will better understand and remember. Table 10.2: Examples of Low- and High-Impact Language offers high-impact suggestions that can serve as alternatives to the lower impact version.

| LOW IMPACT | HIGH IMPACT |
|---|---|
| At the present time | Now |
| Are in agreement with | Agree |
| Due to the fact that | Because |
| Is fully operational in close proximity to | Works near |
| In the event of | If |
| Each and everyone | Each |
| In the course of | During |
| Never before or since | Never |
| Somnolent (jargon) | Drowsy |
| Awesome (slang) | Impressive |
| No brainer (cliché) | Easy decision |

**Table 10.2. Examples of Low- and High-Impact Language**

In addition to high-impact language, supplement your oral presentation with nonverbal cues that can include adjustments in facial expressions, body positioning, and gesturing. These serve multiple purposes:

- They can underline an instructor's verbal points. For instance, a rap of the knuckles on the lectern, or moving to the front of the classroom, can emphasize a message.
- They can support an instructor's message with intentional irony. For example, if a lecturer wants to convey sarcasm, an obvious role of the eyes or a thumbs down can make it clear a comment is sarcastic. However, keep in mind that non-verbal cues may not be understood by all students, or may be understood differently by students from different cultures, so use them carefully.
- They can be a substitute for language. For instance, if a lecturer is discussing a plane crash, a clap of the hands could replace the word for emphasis.

Your nonverbal cues need not be excessive nor extravagant. If anything, they should feel like natural extensions of the way you speak.

### Craft a Suitable Closing

Occasionally, lectures feel like they sputter to an end, after which students quickly pack up their belongings and shuffle out the door. Instead, end a presentation in a robust manner that drives home the importance of the message. This can keep students engaged and looking forward to the next session. It serves the added purpose of bringing the conversation full circle so that the beginning and ending of the lecture connect, driving home the idea that it is a full, cohesive unit.

## CONCLUSION

Despite criticism that lecturing is an ineffective pedagogical approach that perpetuates passive learning, most college instructors continue to rely on it as their primary teaching technique. They do so largely because lecturing serves many positive purposes, including offering students synthesized information from a variety of sources and clearing up misunderstood ideas, principles, or material. We offer our interactive lecturing model as an effective alternative to the traditional transmission lecture model (Barkley & Major, 2018). Interactive lecturing combines engaging presentations with active learning segments, thus maximizing the benefits and minimizing the obstacles of both lecturing and active learning. Engaged teachers always try to find the best ways to teach students, and for those instructors who choose to lecture, adopting the principles of interactive learning can help them in their ongoing pursuit of improving student engagement and learning.

## FOCUS ON ONLINE TEACHING

The information we share in the main body of this chapter applies to both onsite and online teaching, but here we provide additional insights focused specifically on teaching online, hybrid, and blended courses.

### What: Online Lecturing

Lecturing online is simply what it sounds like: offering lecture presentations via the internet. One of the ways we accomplish this is to create asynchronous video lectures that students can watch anytime, anywhere. Another is to use synchronous videoconferencing, which allows us to lecture when students aren't in the same location as the teacher and when our interactions are mediated by technology.

### Why: Online Lecturing

The research on videos for asynchronous lecturing is more developed than that focused on synchronous videoconference lectures, which is unsurprising since extensive use of videoconferencing for lectures is a relatively recent phenomenon. The existing literature suggests that video lectures may be more effective than many people realize. In a study published in *Review of Educational Research*, a peer-reviewed journal of the American Educational Research Association, Noetel et al. (2021) systematically reviewed 105 prior studies with a combined sample of 7,776 college students. The researchers found promising results for pre-recorded video lectures. When students learned from video instead of existing methods (such as an onsite class or text-based pages), the average grade increased from a B to a B+. When students had video lessons in addition to an existing class, the impact was even greater, with their grade rising from a B to an A. Researchers concluded that videos are unlikely to be detrimental and usually improve student learning. More research is needed on asynchronous video lectures.

### How: Online Lecturing Asynchronously

Videos are not the answer to all remote teaching needs, however, and you should use them judiciously. A few effective ways to use asynchronous videos are as follows:

- a welcome video
- an introduction to a topic or module
- a demonstration
- a description of a difficult concept
- a synthesis of material from the learning module or unit

Once you decide how you will be using videos, you'll want to consider the best form to help you accomplish your goals. Following are a few options for creating videos at home on your phone or laptop:

- **Narrated slide presentation:** In this video format, the slides are the only thing that show in the video. The teacher does a voice-over to accompany the slides. While these can become tiring, particularly when used in long videos, they are useful for presenting complicated material for which visuals will likely enhance students' understanding. PowerPoint has a built-in feature for recording over slides, but it can be clunky to have to click "play" between each slide. Consider exporting your slides and audio to YouTube or Vimeo or use a screencast program such as Screencastomatic or Screencastify, which you can also share to YouTube or Vimeo.
- **Presenter-only lecture:** In this kind of lecture, the instructor appears without other visual supports. If this approach is overdone, it can make the instructor appear as a mere talking head; however, they can be useful in short segments to add teacher presence to the course, helping students feel like you are "there." These can be done in a fairly low-tech way, such as through a smart phone video or a Zoom or Blackboard Collaborate recording done ahead of time.
- **Slide presentation with presenter view:** This approach is a combination of presenter and slide presentation, which allows you to capitalize on the benefits of both approaches. Programs such Panopto and Tegrity provide a professional look, but you can also record in Zoom or other videoconferencing programs ahead of time.

To create the most engaging asynchronous video presentations possible, consider the following suggestions:

1. **Pay attention to your lighting.** Make sure that you have ample lighting and that the light hits your face rather than coming from behind you.
2. **Storyboard your message.** If you are doing the lecture for the first time, consider creating a storyboard, which is simply a plan of what you will say, show, and describe. A good storyboard can provide a roadmap for you.

3. **Develop a script.** Develop a script of what you will say, to ensure that you address the most important content. You can then use the script as the transcript of the video to ensure ADA compliance. If you would like to be more impromptu in your approach but need to create a transcript, consider using a program like Zoom that will allow you to record and change the settings to prepare a transcript, which you can then edit.

4. **Create visually appealing slides.** See our blog post on creating engaging synchronous lectures (*https://kpcrossacademy.org/creating-engaging-asynchronous-lectures/*) for tips on effective slide design for video lectures.

5. **Get permission when necessary.** Because your video will be tangible and long lasting, you need to ensure that you have permission to use all images, video, music, or other content that is not your own. You can find many free images and music through sources such as Creative Commons, Unsplash, or Pixabay, just be sure to give credit and cite appropriately.

6. **Consider the shelf life of your topic.** You may well want to use the video in the future, and you will be better able to do so if you are attentive to the shelf life of your content. While it may feel almost impossible not to mention a current hot topic, try not to do so or at least consider limiting your references so that you are able to edit the information out later.

7. **Break content into manageable chunks.** It is exceedingly difficult to watch long lectures, particularly on video. Try to break your lectures into no more than 10-minute chunks per video. If you simply cannot do this, consider asking students to stop the video to complete a task every 10 minutes.

8. **Use active learning.** While the video will be asynchronous, you can and should still expect students to learn actively while they are watching. Consider the following potential lecture breakers for an asynchronous video lecture. See the corresponding videos and download for each technique on the K. Patricia Cross Academy (*kpcrossacademy.org*).

    » CAT 16: Guided Notes helps students engage cognitively by helping them understand what are the more important concepts of a lecture. In Guided Notes, instructors create a template of their lecture that cuts out key words and concepts that students then fill in during the lecture. This concept also provides a valuable tool for students to reference in the future.

» CAT 10: Quick Write is a learning assessment technique where students respond to an open-ended prompt. You can create points within asynchronous lectures during which students do a quick write to translate a point you just made, respond to a question, or engage in another quick write technique.

## How: Online Lecturing Synchronously

With physical distance separating us, we have an even greater challenge capturing student attention. The good news is that you can deliver compelling lectures by way of videoconferencing that communicate important information while also holding your students' interest. If you choose to lecture via videoconferencing, consider it your job to invite students to engage. There are several ways to go about this.

### USE YOUR VOICE AS A TOOL OF ENGAGEMENT

When you offer a lecture, speak expressively and share your passion for the topic. This goal can be challenging for some of us to achieve, especially those of us who are more introverted, but you can also use emotive words to convey expressions, for example: "I'm happy to see you" or "I'm so glad we have a chance to talk about this important topic."

Vary your speaking rate as well as the volume of your voice to help students pay attention and to motivate them to listen. And you can give verbal signposts to help students follow the structure of your lecture: "Today we will cover three main points. Our first point is...The second main point is. Our third and final main point is..."

### REMEMBER THAT VISUALS MATTER

When you use a videoconferencing tool, students will see you when you talk. Most videoconferencing programs also allow you to share a whiteboard with students so that you can write as you would on a whiteboard in a classroom. It can be a great tool for doing a quick illustration, but you should keep this practice to a minimum, however, as too much time on the whiteboard can become boring.

You can also choose to share your screen with students, which will let you use a slide deck. The same tips that apply to in-person slide presentations apply to videoconferenced ones. Consider the following points.

- **Visual slides can be more effective than text-focused ones.** We tend to process visual information more quickly and efficiently than verbal information. Thus, when possible, choose a visual image over text.

- **Fonts matter.** Some fonts, particularly sans serif fonts, are easier to read on a screen than others. Font size matters as well. Common advice is that you should use at least 24-point font size, but remember that you will be sharing a screen with other things, including images of you, students, and the slides, so the bigger the font, the better.
- **You have options other than slides.** If you use a whiteboard, be sure to write clearly and make sure everything is legible. You can also hold up physical objects or artifacts as effective visuals.

Students often have trouble paying attention while in a physical classroom, and this is only compounded by working from their own environments, which may contain a host of potential distractions, such as snacks, pets, television, or social media. In an online lecture, then, you can lose people and not even know it. We suggest stopping about every 10 to 15 minutes and asking students to do something in order to check for attention or understanding. This could be responding to a question in chat, "raising their hands," signaling whether they are following the talk by choosing an emoticon such as a thumbs up, or answering a poll question. You might also consider the following activities during a synchronous videoconference lecture:

- CAT 15: Translate That! allows you to pause your lecture and call on a student at random to translate the information you just provided into plain English for an imagined audience that you specify.
- CAT 43: Punctuated Lecture asks that students listen to the lecture for approximately 15 to 20 minutes. At the end of the lecture segment, the teacher pauses and asks students to answer a question about what they are doing at that particular moment.

*Class discussion covers a wide range of learning sins and virtues. Class discussions can offer powerful learning experiences, but they can also be deadly, stifling time wasters.*

**—K. PATRICIA CROSS**

CHAPTER 11

# Facilitating Discussion

The open exchange of information, ideas, and perspectives in provocative discussion lies at the core of a quality education. McKeachie (2002) proposed that discussion is the ideal tool for teachers striving to build a course environment centered on active learning (p. 30). As Davis (1993) wrote, "A good give-and-take discussion can produce unmatched learning experiences as students articulate their ideas, respond to their classmates' points, and develop skills in evaluating the evidence of their own and others' positions" (p. 63). College teachers are so aware of the benefits of good classroom discussion that it is now the single most popular type of instruction in higher education classrooms, with a majority of all college teachers using it in all or most of their courses (for example, see Sax, 1996, p. 291).

What is the key to discussion's enduring appeal? Most likely, it is because discussion promotes learning in several different ways. Discussion encourages students to develop their ideas and then practice communicating them clearly. Discussion provides a framework for students to think in the language and habits of the discipline. Discussion exposes students to the varied perspectives and backgrounds of their peers, deepening each student's consciousness of the complexity and ambiguity of their discipline, and directing them to confront their assumptions and biases. Discussion can also help students learn to be attentive, respectful, and active listeners. Finally, discussion helps students make connections between new and prior knowledge, leading to deeper learning and longer term retention.

Yet, generating good classroom discussion is not easy. Students who are accustomed to sitting passively and receiving information may be quite content to let more active students direct the conversation. Good discussion requires students to speak up and be forthcoming with what they truly think, feel, and believe. Many students are reluctant to take this risk out of fear of being wrong, appearing stupid, or getting chastised for expressing an unpopular opinion. The biggest challenge to generating discussion is fostering an environment where students of any background feel empowered to express their thoughts openly and candidly. While this is important for all students, it is imperative for students from historically marginalized groups and students who may not speak English as their primary language. In this chapter, we offer you guidance on how to address the challenges in ways that help ensure the discussions you implement in your classes are successful.

## KNOWING WHAT: ABOUT DISCUSSION

Discussion is one of the oldest forms of instruction, dating back centuries to classical teachers like Socrates (469 - 399 BCE). Socrates rejected the lecture as a method of instruction, instead relying on asking provocative questions to push his pupils to deepen their critical thinking and understanding of the known world. However, a key difference between a Socratic lecture technique and the modern discussion method is that he generated conversation between student and instructor, rather than among students. That approach has its supporters, but his detractors considered it a cleverly disguised form of the banking method of education, with Socrates depositing his information and ideas into his students' minds (Freire, 1970).

In contrast to the Socratic method, the contemporary use of discussion as a teaching methodology refers to an instructional strategy that emphasizes participation, dialogue, and two-way communication. But even under this broader umbrella of discussion methodology, educators offer differing definitions. Nilson's (2010) definition is broad, referring to discussion "as a productive exchange of viewpoints, a collective exploration of issues" (p. 127). Many teachers champion a democratic approach to student discussion (Brookfield & Preskill, 2005). This style of deliberation calls for open-ended, collaborative exchanges of knowledge and viewpoints among students or between a teacher and students (Lowman, 1995). Morrison et al. (2009) also defined discussion instruction as "the most common form of face to face teaching where ideas, opinions, and facts are exchanged" (p. 231).

Other proponents of discussion-based teaching argue students need to engage in discussions that mirror a real setting for conversation and involve an immediate audience (McCann et al., 2006). Through this method, students share ideas among each other in their raw form, not filtered through and retransmitted by the teacher. Instead, students evaluate and respond to their peers' ideas using critical thinking.

However, Nilson (2010) warned:

> [t]o bear fruit and not degenerate into a free-association, free-for-all bull session, you as the instructor must chart its course and steer it in the right direction. It is your responsibility to plan and control the content and conduct, to keep hot air from blowing it off course. (p. 127)

The key to using discussion is to find balance between the extremes.

## Discussion's Role in Improving Learning

The objective at the heart of discussion-based teaching is pushing students to engage in higher order thinking and thoughtful deliberation around key course concepts and ideas, and deepen their thinking skills (Lowman, 1995; Morrison et al., 2009). From this perspective, discussion-based teaching is a critical thinking exercise performed within a group (McCann et al., 2006). Individual critical thinking exercises may involve solving puzzles, quizzes, or riddles, but discussion teaching requires the student to evaluate problems while working with a group, rather than alone. Whereas lectures typically are intended to convey knowledge, discussions are designed to encourage students to process and apply material, thereby generating deep learning (Hedley, 1994; Kember & Gow, 1994).

Brookfield and Preskill (2005) offered several results that discussion can produce for college students, such as

- Students are exposed to a variety of viewpoints.
- Students develop an increased tolerance for ambiguity or complexity.
- Students learn to analyze their biases.
- Students are affirmed contributors to shared knowledge.
- Students learn to clearly communicate their ideas.
- Students acquire collaborative learning skills.
- Students become better connected to a subject.
- Students gain respect for their voices and perspectives.
- Students internalize the habits of democratic discourse.
- Students develop active listening skills.

- Students gain new respect for ongoing differences.
- Students improve their intellectual agility.
- Students develop empathy.
- Students develop skills of synthesis and integration.
- Students are transformed. (pp. 21-22)

In addition to the listed skills, students may improve in the articulation and defense of their viewpoints, learn to evaluate evidence, and learn to develop and enact responses (Brookfield & Preskill, 2005; McGonigal, 2005). As a bonus, discussion-based teaching helps students with active engagement (Svinicki & McKeachie, 2013).

There is also evidence that discussion enhances students' desire for education (Brookfield & Preskill, 2005). Exposing students to a variety of topics and subjects may help students identify their core beliefs and values while also enabling students to recognize and alter some of their attitudes and behaviors (Cashin, 2011). Because students are able to actively engage with the subject, increasing the opportunity to relate the material to their own world, students are more likely to retain the content long term (Eble, 1976; Goldsmid & Wilson, 1980; Hollander, 2002). Or, as Frederick (1994) explained, "the fundamental value of discussions is that through them students develop a sense of ownership and responsibility for their own learning" (p. 100).

## Obstacles to Implementing Discussion Effectively

While classroom discussions are a proven, time-honored teaching strategy, they also have some challenges. Good discussions require more preparation than instructors may expect (Cashin, 2011). Murphy et al. (2009) stressed that "simply putting students into groups and encouraging them to talk is not enough to enhance comprehension and learning; it is but a step in the process" (p. 761). Good discussions also take up significant class time and are not the most efficient way to cover a lot of material (Cashin, 2011).

Discussions can also be an impediment to a teachers' preferred style. Some teachers flourish in the role of sage on the stage, and hence may prefer a classroom that maintains their leadership position. Discussions also require more comprehensive familiarity with a subject than in a controlled lecture, and so some instructors may not feel comfortable enough with the course material to let the class conversation evolve organically. Furthermore, a teacher's predetermined discussion questions may be abandoned as students' interests and questions lead the group into new areas of conversation.

Another challenge for instructors is soliciting student participation in class discussions (Cashin, 2011). If you ask a question and no one answers, how should you respond? Other teachers face the opposite problem, with too much or unbalanced participation: A few students dominate the discussion while others stay quiet and disengaged (Karp & Yoels, 1976). Some students may have better developed speaking and listening skills than others, potentially diluting the quality of shared discussion.

There may also be times where controversial subjects trigger highly emotional discussions (Brookfield & Preskill, 2005). These occurrences can establish an uncomfortable environment for the students experiencing the emotions as well as their peers. Furthermore, discussions can be challenging to assess and hence can pose a grading problem for teachers. Research and good practice literature offer myriad options to address these challenges, and we share this guidance in the "Knowing How" section of this chapter.

## Types of Discussion

There are many ways to categorize types of discussion. For our purposes, we organize discussions in the categories of size, function, level of structure, and environment.

### BY SIZE

One method for describing discussion types is to refer to the grouping of students, such as the common groupings defined below.

- **Whole class discussion** involves instructors leading the discussion and asking questions of the full class. This form allows the teacher to promote participation by most of the students in the classroom. Additionally, students are able to hear all the ideas shared by their peers.
- In **small group discussion**, students are divided into smaller groups of four to six students and then collaboratively discuss a topic. Tables rather than fixed seats may better facilitate small group discussions, but they are not necessary. Many teachers have had success using small groups in fixed-seat environments.
- **Dyads** entail students discussing topics in pairs. Dyads generate the most engagement of the groupings because 50% of the students in the class are speaking at any time. By comparison, in a whole class discussion, just one student speaks at a given moment. Dyads may precede small group or whole class discussions.

### BY FUNCTION

Discussions may also be categorized by their function or purpose. Kurfiss (1988) offered these types of discussion:

- **Informational discussions** consist of teachers challenging students to help each other understand the subject by sharing information. With this type, teachers take on the role of mitigating conflict and creating an environment where students will be challenged, but not personally attacked, when sharing their ideas.
- In **problematical discussions**, the teacher poses a problem to students and then challenges them to consider the data needed to solve it.
- For a **dialectical discussion**, the teacher encourages students to synthesize diverse opinions into a new formulation of the issue. If this is not possible, they are allowed to agree to disagree, but they must state their opponents' viewpoints fairly in order to demonstrate a better understanding of the nature of their differences.
- **Reflexive discussions** involve students sharing what they discussed in their groups with a larger group or the whole class in order to contribute to the learning of all (p. 67).

### BY LEVEL OF STRUCTURE

Discussions can also be sorted based on how and to what extent the components are arranged or planned.

- **Spontaneous discussions** are generally unstructured and are allowed to unfold in a natural manner. For example, the teacher might open by posing a question about a current event and then allow discussion to move unconstrained from one point to another.
- In a **planned discussion**, the teacher develops a list of unified questions to structure the discussion. Planned discussions are typically tightly designed and may be structured so that participation proceeds from student to student, until all students have had the opportunity to contribute.

### BY ENVIRONMENT

Another way to look at discussions is to identify where they occur.

- In **onsite or face-to-face (F2F) discussions**, the teacher and students participate in discussions in the same place at the same time, as in a conventional classroom.

- **Online Discussions** occur in discussion forums, chat rooms, or through social media threads. Students can participate and comment at different times (asynchronous discussion) or collaborate simultaneously in a chat room (synchronous discussion).

**BY ORGANIZATION OF COMPONENTS**

Discussions can also be identified by the way teachers arrange various components, as indicated in the following two methods.

The **Initiation-Response-Evaluation (IRE) method** is the most common strategy for structuring discussions.

- **Initiation.** The teacher asks a lead-off question that prompts students to join in open discussion. Many researchers recommend instructors start by asking questions that do not have a specific correct answer. Students are encouraged to respond to the instructor's question as they engage with their classmates, their teacher, and the material (Kloss, 1996; Lowman, 1995; Svinicki & McKeachie, 2013).
- **Response.** Students listen to each other share viewpoints and personal perspectives about the subject. As students hear their peers disclose knowledge and opinions, they integrate these ideas with their own (Gagne, 1984). It is necessary to center conversation in the tenets of civic dialogue in order for students to develop and voice their ideas openly (Brookfield & Preskill, 2005). Students need room to establish their views and relate them to the subject matter (Gagne, 1984). Teachers have to be attuned to their students' perspectives and be responsive to student voice in order to develop everyone's understanding (Christensen et al., 1991). Heated, personal debates should be avoided. By focusing on what students say, teachers can de-escalate discussions that may fall into unproductive arguments (Johnson & Johnson, 1997). Instructors are required to redirect the conversation and keep it connected to the subject, instead of condoning student attacks.
- **Evaluation.** The instructor offers feedback and constructive criticism of student responses. An important part of the teacher's job is to clear up misunderstandings that linger for students following class discussions. In student-led discussions, there is more opportunity for confusion or misunderstandings (Lowman, 1995). Bringing discussions to a close can facilitate a greater understanding for students and reinforce accurate knowledge of the material (Clarke, 1988).

IRE, as described above, is a simplification of what actually occurs in class discussion, but this minimal explanation makes more transparent the structure and procedure. Facilitating successful class discussion requires ensuring high quality for each of the three phases. If, for example, the opening question is too simplistic, the ensuing discussion will likely also be simplistic. If the opening question is too difficult or not rooted in the course material, participants will be unprepared to respond and there will be little participation. In the response phase, students have to willingly engage and avoid surface-level answers in order to maintain a high-quality discussion. And if the teacher fails to wrap the discussion with feedback and or critique, then the quality of student takeaways will falter.

**Interteaching** is another approach to discussion wherein the instructor steers students through assigned readings using a preparation guide. Students are given several days to finish the assignment before class. Then, in class, students are divided into pairs to discuss the guide. Instructors keep students focused and ask questions. Afterward, the class completes record sheets evaluating their discussions and the guide. The teacher uses this feedback in the next class to clear up any lingering confusion and provide clarity. Students continue working through their preparation guide and the process continues. This method has been demonstrated to enhance education outcomes, especially when compared to more traditional teaching environments such as lecturing (Saville et al., 2011).

## KNOWING WHY: RESEARCH ON DISCUSSIONS

Research provides valuable insights on why discussion is an important teaching approach. In one of the earliest empirical studies of discussions used at the college level, Axelrod et al. (1949) examined the differences in learning between students in predominantly lecture presentation classes and students in predominantly discussion-based classes. The researchers found that students in the discussion-based classes learned more and were generally more satisfied with their classes than those in the presentation-based classes. Other studies have upheld these findings. Garside (1996), for example, compared the effectiveness of lecture to group discussion in improving critical thinking skills among 118 students taking introductory interpersonal communication courses. Although both methods improved critical thinking between pre-test and post-test, the students who participated in group discussion demonstrated significantly improved learning on higher level items. From our analysis of research into the discussion method, we offer the following observations.

### Active Preparation Improves Outcomes

The research indicates students must be well prepared in order to engage in quality discussion. For example, in a graduate-level accounting course, researchers examined the relationships between preparation, participation, and comfort with discussion, as well as student confidence about their future participation and the effect of their participation on their learning. The researchers concluded that deliberate preparation for discussion correlated to a student's report of developing communication skills, both written and oral (Dallimore et al., 2008).

### Discussion in Small Groups Can Increase Participation

Smaller groups may produce greater outcomes than whole class discussions. One study comparing small and whole class discussion in a political science course indicated small group discussions generate higher participation. Smaller groups also elicit more participation from students of different ethnic backgrounds (Pollock et al., 2011). Additionally, students perceive that they're learning more in smaller groups.

### Participation Is Improved by Grading

Some instructors question whether it is necessary to grade student participation in discussions, wondering if it could stifle student involvement. However, research indicates that not evaluating student participation actually leads to less involvement. One study found that in courses where participation was graded, students more actively participated in class discussions and were more engaged (Dallimore et al., 2006). Students can also be induced into participation. One study indicates that using tokens can improve student participation (Boniecki & Moore, 2003). As a reward for participation, students were given tokens that could be used to earn extra credit. As a result, students were more engaged both directly and indirectly and answered faster, even after the token system ended.

### Class Comfort Improves Participation

Students need to be comfortable with the format in order to engage in discussions. Research also indicates that students are more likely to prepare for and participate in discussions if they're comfortable. For example, in a study of 323 sophomore accounting students, researchers studied pre-course and post-course student perception surveys, analyzing class discussion as well as student grades. Their findings indicated a positive correlation between preparation and class participation as well as student comfort (Dallimore et al., 2010). Establishing a sense of community and belonging can increase student comfort as well as student engagement. Discussion can be used to contribute to building class community in many ways. For example, faculty have used Twitter to generate academic discussions (Junco et al., 2011). Using a scale based on the National Survey of Student Engagement (NSSE) to evaluate engagement, the results indicated student and faculty alike were engaged by Twitter discussions.

### Cold Calling Can Improve Learning, Comfort, and Voluntary Participation

A dilemma instructors often face is whether to encourage voluntary participation in discussion or to call on students randomly to answer questions (i.e., cold calling). Research indicates a relationship between the two methods. One study found a positive correlation between cold calling and students' voluntary participation. Indeed, in classes with a high level of cold calling, a significantly higher number of students volunteered to answer questions. Additionally, the study indicated high rates of cold calling increased the number of students who volunteered answers over time, and student comfort with participation increased (Dallimore et al., 2013). Some students experience anxiety from cold calling, however. One way to decrease their anxiety is to give them a moment to write before responding to the question or providing an opportunity to discuss the question in dyads first.

## KNOWING HOW: STRATEGIES FOR IMPLEMENTING AND FACILITATING DISCUSSION

Educators agree that helping students participate in a stimulating discussion is an effective teaching strategy with many benefits. We offer the following tips and strategies below to help guide you in implementing and facilitating discussion. Where appropriate, we suggest a Cross Academy Technique (CAT). For more information on each CAT, visit our companion site, The K. Patricia Cross Academy, where you will find videos and downloadable templates to guide implementation in both onsite and online classrooms.

### Find the Right Question

Good discussion prompts are generally thought-provoking and open-ended, requiring students to understand subject matter and use this knowledge appropriately. To achieve this, questions should be open-ended with more than one correct answer. This helps generate discussions with multiple perspectives, prevents a simple yes or no response, leads to richer learning, and eases student anxiety about giving the wrong answer. Questions should also be relevant to students. Some questions may seem tangentially related to the topic, but they are valuable because they push students to apply the subject to their personal lives. Different questions solicit different responses, so be sure to ask yourself what you hope to accomplish with your question and then ask it when it will be most effective. Davis (2009) offered the following suggestions for types of discussion questions.

- **Expand the discussion through expansion questions.** "How does your answer tie back into this earlier comment?"

- **Pose an alternate scenario through hypothetical questions.** "Imagine that Terry had grown up in the country instead of the city; what would be different?"
- **Identify key issues using priority questions.** "After everything we have covered, what is the predominant cause of Brexit?"
- **Probe motives through diagnostic questions.** "Why did Winnie move to a new state?"
- **Solicit conclusions through action questions.** "How should the university president respond to mass protests?"
- **Determine relationships through cause and effect questions.** "If a patient is unable to get medical appointments in a timely manner, what is the impact on the health care system?"
- **Tie together information through summary questions.** "What are your big takeaways from today's discussion?"
- **Determine basic knowledge through exploratory questions.** "What evidence is there for climate change?"
- **Examine student assumptions through challenge questions.** "How else could you determine the outcome?"
- **Solicit comparisons of ideas through relational questions.** "What premises of the Voting Rights Act did the Supreme Court throw out in its ruling on Shelby v. Holder?" (pp. 119-120)

## Set the Stage

To generate good discussion, it is important to invest time not only in crafting the right set of questions, but also preparing the context in which the discussion will take place. To set the stage, consider doing the following:

- **Use students' names and learn the strengths and viewpoints they can offer to class discussions.** Early in the course, be sure to consistently call on students by name. Frequent use of student names will increase students' sense of being seen as valued individuals, deepening their trust and interest in the course. Students will also learn their classmates' names. Additionally, understand their strengths and knowledge and look for specific ways to challenge each student.

- **Establish a welcoming classroom.** Position the chairs in a setting that will encourage students to listen to one another. Also consider sharing your personal interest in the subject.
- **Outline your expectations before the start of class discussions.** Make sure students know what a successful discussion looks like before it begins. Does it mean everyone speaks or offers a variety of perspectives? No one veers off topic? Multiple subjects are discussed with depth? Students need clarity of expectations as well as the understanding that their participation is essential to a good discussion.
- **Ensure students understand the relationship between a successful discussion and their performance in the course.** If you plan to use discussions regularly, evaluate students based on participation and inform them of the criteria used before discussions begin. Will students be judged on the depth of their contribution or its frequency? Are they expected to listen and respond to each other's statements? Is the grading based purely on in-room discussion or also on contributions to online discussions or group projects? Create a clear rubric for grading participation in discussion and share this with students at the beginning of the term. Providing students with preliminary grades as the term unfolds can help them understand where they need to improve.

## Plan Ahead

As with so many aspects in teaching, planning ahead is essential for ensuring effective discussions. Murphy et al. (2009) stressed that "simply putting students into groups and encouraging them to talk is not enough to enhance comprehension and learning; it is but a step in the process" (p. 761).

- **Train students on how to be effective discussion participants.** Most students would like to participate effectively but some may simply not know how. Consider preparing students by providing guidance on how to both speak and listen in a discussion.
- **Plan class discussions in advance.** Have specific outcomes in mind and plans for each discussion and make sure your questions are carefully constructed to guide students toward achieving those goals.

- **Give students structure.** Provide the class with an outline or guided questions. Post them in the class or online before discussions begin, dividing each session into a beginning, middle and end.

## Engage Students

As noted earlier, soliciting student participation in class discussions can be a significant challenge. Here are some suggestions to keep all students engaged in the discussion.

- **Give students time to think before responding.** All students will benefit from having time to compose their thoughts before responding to a prompt in front of a large group. CAT 10: Quick Write will allow them to write for a minute on a prompt before sharing their ideas. You could also give a longer assignment that they complete before class, such as CAT 33: Frames, CAT 35: Letters, or CAT 46: Quotation Summaries.
- **Establish wait time before students are allowed to answer questions.** After asking an opening question, provide students with at least five to 10 seconds to consider their responses. You may ask them to write their answers before speaking aloud, often improving the quality of responses. Don't be afraid of silence or fill it by answering your own question. If you are patient, you may solicit more thoughtful and complex responses.
- **Encourage students to talk with each other.** Students may default to speaking to you, so work to get them to engage with each other's ideas. Small groups offer one method to get students more familiar with each other and more likely to communicate both within their group and later in the whole class.
- **Increase student involvement in discussions through both verbal and nonverbal cues.** Eye contact, cold-calling, and moving freely around the classroom can keep students attentive, establishing expectations that they will need to participate.
- **Use established, well-researched discussion techniques.** Popular discussion formats, like CAT 37: Think-Pair-Share, CAT 44: Fishbowl, or CAT 4: Jigsaw, each offers a unique, tried-and-true structure for cultivating different types of discussion.

## Facilitate Discussion

- **Show students respect.** One key to establishing respect is to take students' ideas seriously and help them clarify and develop their arguments. For all questions or answers, listen to students and thank them for contributing. Elevate the student's response by repeating it for the class to hear. Then outline the core of their arguments and guide students who offer incorrect or irrelevant answers to better responses. Provide corrections as needed so that students don't leave the discussion having stored incorrect information. For example, "I understand why you think that, however..." is one way to redirect the conversation.

- **Establish balance between maintaining the group dynamic and allowing individual members to speak.** Students will look to you as a subject matter expert, but it is important to develop moments for students to critically engage with each other's viewpoints and develop their own knowledge of the subject. Solicit answers from as many people as possible while also kindly discouraging over-contribution. Over-contributing students may need gentle reminders of the importance of other viewpoints, while students who under-contribute may need additional time to think through their responses.

- **Ask follow-up questions.** If students provide answers that are too brief, draw out additional thoughts with a follow-up question like, "what else can you tell me about that?"

## Deal Effectively With Hot Moments

Even with your best intentions and planning, students will sometimes be incivil during a discussion, and it can be difficult to address. But when dealing with these challenges, stay calm and avoid letting students provoke you. The University of Michigan Center for Research on Learning and Teaching (CRLT) suggests the following steps for dealing with hot moments in the classroom:

- **Wait before reacting.** Take a moment to determine whether to confront the incident immediately, address it separately and only with involved students, or address it in the next class. Consider silently counting to 10 before reacting or speaking. If you do not feel prepared to address a question, comment, or issue immediately, make a note of it as something the class will address at the next session. Then bring it up at the next class period when you feel better prepared.

- **Remind students of their discussion or participation agreements.** If you have not already developed guidelines, suggest a few core ideas to keep the discussion moving out of the hot moment, such as, refraining from personal attacks, being open to a variety of viewpoints, and holding each other accountable for the effects of our words on our peers.
- **Encourage students to take deep breaths, move around the classroom, or quietly sketch or write.** In some instances, simply addressing and breaking tension by taking a different action in mind or body can be productive toward moving past a difficult moment.
- **Try to connect the moment of tension to course themes or learning goals.** How does the emotion of the room relate to the importance of the material? Can any of the course content help address the discussion that follows tension? Does your course include any learning objectives related to critical thinking, considering new perspectives, or learning to precisely frame an argument that could be emphasized by how you ask students to participate?
- **Clarify comments from students that led to the hot moment.** At times, students who are struggling to understand new viewpoints or feel uncomfortable with having their previously held views challenged may unintentionally say something that is insulting or marginalizing. If you believe a student's comment comes from such a struggle, it may be appropriate to give that student the opportunity to explain their thought process e.g., "I heard you saying X; is that what you intended?" or "What did you mean by Y?") or consider asking them to rephrase their comment if it's clear they recognize they made a mistake (e.g., "Would you like to try phrasing that differently?" and then, if needed, "Why don't we discuss why that initial statement felt problematic?").
- **Establish a basis for mutual understanding.** Provide relevant facts about issues raised during the hot moment. You can provide the information yourself or encourage students to share key points. You may choose to list categories on a whiteboard (e.g., "what we know," "what's in dispute," "what we hope to learn more about") and have students suggest ideas for each category, either as the whole class or as individuals. If possible, you may also choose to explain or ask the class to determine why a particular topic or choice of language created such tension, particularly if you believe some students may not understand or even respect their peers' emotional reactions.

- **Provide students the time needed to gather their ideas in writing about the views, topics, or exchanges at issue before discussing them as a group.** You may direct them to relate their writing to course content. Asking students to write their ideas is particularly helpful when students react to hot moments with silence. You may choose to ask them, "Why is this issue so tough to talk about?" or "What is something you feel like you can't say out loud?" You may choose to collect the writing anonymously in order to best determine how to address the topic at a later time.
- **Work to depersonalize areas of dispute that arise among students.** For example, instead of discussing "what X student said and what Y student said," frame the conversation as "this disagreement about Z topic" or "using X phrase or word"). This may decrease the likelihood of students feeling defensive and encourage more participation in the discussion.
- **Ask students for additional viewpoints.** For example, "We've heard ideas X and Y — how else might you address the topic?" can redirect the discussion away from individual students toward the ideas and perspectives being raised. You could also depersonalize by addressing when a widely held belief has been offered: "There are many people who believe this. Why might that be?" Followed by: "And why may others feel disrespected by this perspective?"
- **Work with the students in conflict to find common ground.** This could involve determining a shared value ("I can tell you each are passionate about achieving X but have strong disagreement about how to achieve that goal") or involving the class ("What do these two viewpoints have in common? Where do they diverge?").
- **Give students the benefit of the doubt.** When students say things that appear to devalue or disrespect other individuals or ideas, acknowledge that it may not have been on purpose (e.g., "I don't think it was your intent but..." "You likely didn't realize how this sounded..." "I know you're trying to make a joke, however..."). While offering students the benefit of the doubt, you should also explain the possible influence of language decisions (e.g., "The term X is a phrase that's often a source of pain for those it is commonly used to describe because..." "I could see a scenario where your use of that phrase would feel insulting to people who...")

- **Following a discussion of tense topics, ask students to reflect either individually or collectively (or both) on the perspectives raised.** You may want to use a questionnaire asking students to list what they appreciated about the discussion, what they've learned, and what is still unresolved.
- **Connect outside of class with the individuals most directly influenced by the discussion.** Indicate your commitment to ensuring their success, helping them learn from the moment, and understanding more about their experience.
- **Check in with your own network of support.** This is particularly important if you felt affronted or personally targeted by the incident. It can be useful to process your personal responses with colleagues or friends that you trust in order to be able to confidently and optimistically return to your classroom.

## Conclude Class Discussions

- **Provide a summary of major ideas and themes.** To ensure students understand the key takeaways from the class discussion, write significant ideas and themes on the board or provide an online version. While it can be useful to document important contributions throughout the session, it is essential to provide a summary at the conversation's close.
- **Offer a closing question.** You can set up future discussions or assignments with a final question. For example, the question can be a thought-provoking one that encourages students to continue processing what they learned from the discussion after class has ended or it could be one that helps students relate the material to their lives outside of the classroom.
- **Be available.** Establish office hours or inform students you will be available after class or via email to answer any remaining questions that were not addressed during the discussion.
- **Always look for ways to improve.** Keep a record of class discussions and use your notes to retool and revise future discussions.

## CONCLUSION

Discussion is a time-honored teaching strategy that generates multiple educational benefits. The exchange of ideas along with a chance to ask questions can clarify content, increase comprehension, help students integrate new ideas and information into their existing knowledge, and improve class community. But it can be a challenge to generate good classroom discussion. To ensure discussions are worthwhile and an effective use of time, you need to invest time and effort into planning and preparation. This will enable you to use discussion successfully in your courses and in ways that promote student learning. Given its potential benefits, exerting the effort required to make class discussions work is an essential task for engaged teachers.

## FOCUS ON ONLINE TEACHING

The information we share in the main body of this chapter applies to both onsite and online teaching, but here we provide additional insights focused specifically on teaching online, hybrid, and blended courses.

### What: Online Discussion

Online discussions are a type of computer-mediated communication (Corich et al., 2004). They are most often text-based and employed asynchronously, although synchronous discussion is becoming more common. Online discussions are expected to reflect the features of onsite discussion by eliciting student responses to questions and demonstrating comprehension, spontaneity, and continuous feedback. Garrison et al. (2000) suggested that for higher level learning to occur in an interactive online environment, discussion should require cognitive collaboration of learners in integrating, synthesizing, and evaluating ideas.

### Why: Online Discussion

Several factors have been documented as critical to online discussion, including sustainability and depth of the interaction (Sing & Khine, 2006); cognitive collaboration of learners (Darabi et al., 2010); and the interaction between the instructor, the students, and the course content (Slagter van Tyron & Bishop, 2009). Meaningful peer interaction, facilitated discourse, and direct instruction instead of the conventional method of question and answer provide learners with a deeper understanding of the content (Bangert, 2008).

Several online discussion strategies have been documented as effective. For example, Alexander et al. (2010) found that the four-question technique (i.e., analyzing, reflecting, relating, and questioning) originally developed by Dietz-Uhler and Lanter (2009) is effective for enhancing critical thinking when compared to conventional discussion strategy of posting a question and soliciting a response. Gunter (2007) examined easy-to-implement strategies, such as frequent and specific feedback, addressing students by name, praise, and use of a supportive tone, and found that they improved students' intrinsic motivation and self-efficacy, thus leading to better learning experiences. Moreover, Richardson and Ice (2010) found that, while students preferred less complex strategies, they increased critical thinking with more complex strategies like case studies and debate. Similarly, Kanuka et al. (2007) found that when the activities are structured, defined, and require the learners to be opinionated, they evoke more responses characterized with higher levels of cognitive ability.

In a meta-analysis of online discussion, Darabi et al. (2013) examined the argument that online courses rarely use discussion strategies that are specifically designed and constructed for soliciting learners' cognitive presence and higher order thinking. The authors analyzed and synthesized studies that examined the effectiveness of discussion strategies in online learning. They found that learners performed better in a strategic discussion (e.g., application or elaborations) than when they engaged in a conventional online discussion.

They also found that:

- College students performed better in asynchronous courses that used strategic discussion.
- When compared with courses in arts and sciences, courses in the education or instruction domain provided opportunities for learners to perform better when they used strategic strategies.
- When the discussion task involved an application scenario, learners responded better to strategic and productive discussion than when they were asked to elaborate on a topic.
- When learners used strategic discussion in a convenience sampling environment, they performed better than others who were randomly selected. (p. 239)

## How: Online Discussion

Online discussions have several advantages over onsite discussions, including wider participation and potentially deeper, more thoughtful treatment of the topic. Below are tips to make your online discussions more effective.

1. **Be clear on the learning goal** for the discussion so that you can craft an engaging, focused prompt and so that you can redirect the discussion if it goes off track.
2. **Be explicit about your expectations,** including the length, quantity, and quality of contributions, deadlines, and assessment and grading criteria.
3. **Establish netiquette guidelines up front** regarding the use of appropriate language, grammar, respect for diverse opinions, and so forth.
4. **Have a plan for resolving conflicts.** While disagreements are a natural and expected aspect of meaningful discussions, it is not productive if they

escalate into arguments. Be prepared to intervene and address unacceptable behavior promptly.

5. **Be present in the discussion.** While the focus should be on student interaction, discussion is more likely to be robust, on target, and civil if students know that you are carefully monitoring it. You can establish your presence by asking probing questions that challenge students to question their assumptions or think more deeply about a topic, asking individual students to clarify or defend their positions, spotlighting particularly good contributions, refocusing or summarizing the discussion, recommending resources for additional learning, and so forth.
6. **Consider inviting someone outside of the class (such as a subject matter expert or a professional in the field) to lead the discussion.** You can ask individual students or groups of students to prepare questions in advance.
7. **Monitor participation.** If you find that certain students are not participating, consider checking in with them privately to try to determine why.
8. **Consider forming smaller groups.** Discussion boards for large groups can be overwhelming and intimidating, especially for learners who are introverted or who simply need more personal interaction.
9. **Involve students.** Identify one or two students to co-host a discussion or to write up a summary of the discussion for the whole class.
10. **Consider offering synchronous, live discussions using a shared space.** Videoconferencing tools allow for both video and audio participation as well as side chats.

*When students are interacting with other students to clarify, explain, and understand, they are actively building their own minds.*

**—K. PATRICIA CROSS**

CHAPTER 12

# Implementing Collaborative Learning

In our workshops on collaborative learning, we sometimes share a meme with the provocative question, "What's the quickest way to get your students to hate each other?" The answer: "Assign them to group work." Teachers and students alike know that collaborative learning can be challenging. Despite the difficulties, however, collaborative learning continues to attract educators' interest because it addresses several major concerns related to improving student learning. First, research has demonstrated that teachers cannot simply transfer their knowledge to students. Students must assume an active role in building their own minds through a process of integrating new knowledge into their existing understandings. Collaborative learning has a clear advantage for accomplishing this when compared with more traditional whole class discussion methods, in which only a few students (and often the same few) typically participate.

Second, willingness and readiness to engage in productive teamwork is considered by many employers to be a requirement for success. Indeed, it is a prerequisite for employment for some companies and professions. Collaborative learning offers students opportunities to learn valuable interpersonal and teamwork skills that prepare them for their future careers.

Third, it has become increasingly clear that our diverse society requires engaged citizens who respect and appreciate different perspectives. We also face daunting global, national, and local challenges that require thoughtful, long-term, collective responses. In order to solve our shared problems, the world needs people who can listen carefully, think critically, participate actively, and collaborate constructively.

Finally, colleges and universities are asking teachers to create inclusive classroom environments. In traditional lectures, students are typically treated as a single, passive, and aggregated entity. In collaborative learning, students of all backgrounds are called upon to contribute knowledge and perspectives they have developed from their unique lives. In this chapter, we offer guidance on how to design and implement collaborative learning effectively in your courses.

## KNOWING WHAT: ABOUT COLLABORATIVE LEARNING

Collaborative learning is an approach to teaching that involves two or more people working in a group in order to learn together. Participating students are able to build on each other's knowledge and skills as they aim to find meaning or understanding, develop solutions to problems, or create a project. In order for activities to be truly collaborative, several factors should be considered.

The first factor is *intentional design.* Central to effective collaborative learning is an appropriate learning task. While students are charged with taking responsibility for their learning, teachers have responsibility for designing the learning activities for student groups to complete. The assignments may involve planned discussions, or the activities could involve students solving problems with each other, teaching each other, or writing together. The key is that the assignments are intentional. This requires attending to three essential areas: (1) identifying the learning task's underlying problem and prompt, one that correlates to broader course learning goals; (2) selecting a learning activity that responds to the problem or prompt; and (3) structuring the task to address student needs and abilities.

The second factor to consider is *co-laboring,* the importance of which is exhibited in the Latin-based definition of the word *collaborative* itself. In well-designed collaborative learning assignments, each student in the group must actively participate, working with their peers toward the completion of the project. To be blunt, if one student takes on the burden of all the work while the others simply watch, then the learning is not collaborative. Students should have equitable shares of the workload, whether that involves each student receiving different tasks within a larger shared project, or each student contributing similar effort toward completing the same assignment.

The third factor in successful collaborative learning assignments is ensuring that *meaningful learning* occurs. Some would argue this is the most important factor; students working together must improve their thinking abilities or expand their knowledge. Thus, collaborative assignments should be connected to learning goals for the overall course and for the learning module.

Though collaborative learning is a more expansive term than cooperative learning, there are many features from cooperative learning proponents that could apply successfully to any group learning activity. Smith (1996) outlined five features he argued are needed for any successful learning group, listed below (see also Johnson et al., 1998).

1. **Positive interdependence:** The success of individual students should be connected to the success of the group. In order for individual students to succeed, their group must succeed so they'll be motivated to help each other accomplish shared goals.

2. **Promotive interaction:** Students should be expected to actively aid and assist each other. Group members should share their resources, while supporting each other in the pursuit of learning.

3. **Individual and group accountability:** The group should be responsible for meeting its goals; and each member of the group is responsible for their contributions to the overall project.

4. **Development of teamwork skills:** In addition to learning the course material (task work), students should develop the interpersonal skills necessary to work in a small group (teamwork). Indeed, the skills needed for teamwork should be taught "just as purposefully and precisely as academic skills."

5. **Group processing:** Each student should develop the ability to assess their own group's productivity. They should be able to describe what individual actions aid the group and which hinder the group. And then they should be able to develop plans about how to adapt moving forward. (pp. 74-76)

Therefore, collaborative learning consists of at least two students equitably working together toward preferred learning outcomes (Barkley et al., 2014). Successful collaborative learning assignments take into account a number of factors. By attending to these various elements, engaged teachers can design collaborative learning in ways that avoid common pitfalls and maximize group work's benefits.

## KNOWING WHY: RESEARCH ON COLLABORATIVE LEARNING METHODS

Why should teachers incorporate collaborative learning in their courses? Nearly all of the compilations and syntheses of the research examining group learning indicate positive results (Cuseo, 1992; Johnson et al., 1991; Johnson et al., 2014; Johnson et al., 2000; Millis &

Cottell, 1998; Natasi & Clements, 1991; Pascarella & Terenzini, 2005; Slavin, 1990; Springer et al., 1999). For instance, Pascarella and Terenzini (2005) observed, "the weight of evidence from this research is reasonably consistent in suggesting that collaborative learning approaches can significantly enhance learning" (p. 103). Additionally, Natasi and Clements (1991) demonstrated the tenor of the bulk of the research, writing:

> Cognitive-academic and social-emotional benefits have been reported for students from early elementary through college level, from diverse ethnic and cultural backgrounds, and having a wide range of ability levels... Furthermore, cooperative learning has been used effectively across a wide range of content areas, including mathematics, reading, language arts, social studies and science. (p. 111, quoted in Millis & Cottell, 1998, pp. 8-9)

David Johnson, along with his University of Minnesota colleagues, primarily focused on a comparison of learning outcomes from three different learning structures: competitive, cooperative, and individualistic. In competitive learning structures, students focus on "increasing their own achievement and on preventing any classmate from achieving higher than they do." By contrast, cooperative learning requires an environment of "promotive interaction," with students encouraging their group members in addition to pursuing their individual achievements as they relate to a shared goal. In an individualistic structure, students don't interact at all, pursuing mastery by focusing "only on improving their own achievement and ignore as irrelevant the efforts of others" (Johnson et al., 1991, p. 31). In-depth meta-analyses spanning hundreds of studies (Johnson et al., 1991; Johnson et al., 2014) indicated cooperative structures exceeded competitive and individualistic environments in numerous measures, with students generally demonstrating higher achievement, greater learning transfer to new situations, higher level thinking, and more frequent development of new solutions and ideas. Johnson and his team (1991) thus concluded:

> Cooperative learning is indicated whenever the goals of learning are highly important, mastery and retention are important, the task is complex or conceptual, problem solving is desired, divergent thinking or creativity is desired, quality of performance is expected, and higher level reasoning strategies and critical thinking are needed. (p. 40)

In light of their conclusion, it is difficult to envision any situation in a college or university setting in which the Johnson team would not recommend cooperative learning.

One of the most important conclusions to emerge in the past decades from the research examining formal learning is that cooperative learning has demonstrably clear, positive effects on several variables. Thus, one meta-analysis (Kyndt et al., 2013) of this research had two chief goals. First, the researchers aimed to replicate the research from recent studies on the primary effects of cooperative learning on three types of outcomes: achievement, attitudes, and perceptions. The second goal was to identify potential moderators of the outcomes of cooperative learning, examining the moderating effects of the method, study domain, age level, and culture. By analyzing 65 studies from 1995 and on, the meta-analysis showed positive effects of cooperative learning on student achievement and attitudes. The results also indicated that study domain, students' age level, and the culture in which the study was conducted had various moderating effects (Kyndt et al., 2013).

## KNOWING HOW: AN ACTIVE APPROACH TO MAKING GROUPS WORK

Faculty and researchers have studied and reported on collaborative methods for decades, and there is a wide range of positive anecdotal and empirical reports about their use. The information below is intended to help you feel confident about using this instructional approach. Where appropriate, we suggest a Cross Academy Technique (CAT). For more information on each CAT, visit our companion site, The K. Patricia Cross Academy, where you will find videos and downloadable templates to guide implementation in both onsite and online classrooms.

### Prepare Students for Collaborative Learning

Collaborative learning activities have become so common in education that most students come into our classrooms with some familiarity with it. If their experiences were positive, then they will likely be primed and ready to do group work in your course effectively. If their experiences were negative, however, students may be reluctant to engage in collaborative learning again. You may also have students who expect a more traditional format who are confused by and possibly fearful of engaging in group work. Ensuring students understand the benefits of collaborative learning and orienting students to their new roles can help collaborative activities be more successful.

- **Familiarize students with the prospect of group or peer collaboration early in the course.** One way to ensure successful collaborative learning is managing class expectations. Early on, introduce students to group work and explain why or have students participate in an activity that demonstrates why it is important. If you set the standard early, students are less likely to resist later. If they understand the value of group activities, they'll be more engaged and invested in their collaborative projects.

- **Ensure students develop rapport before starting an assignment.** One of the chief obstacles to effective group work is students worrying how they will be viewed by their classmates, especially ones they are only just meeting. Thus, it is useful to promote confidence and creative expression by establishing a safe and secure classroom early on through activities like icebreakers or team-building exercises.
- **Set clear rules for group participation and individual contributions.** Do not assume students know how to effectively work in groups. Many may have had poor experiences with group projects in the past. By providing structure and participation guidelines, you can set the stage so that students are able to work together constructively. One option may be to have student groups develop their own lists of expectations.
- **Work with students to develop the necessary skills for success in group work.** Not every student will enter your classroom with the skills they need to successfully contribute to group projects. Some may need better communication skills, guidance on how to resolve conflicts, or help with persuasion and influence. Others may need assistance with organization and planning, or with general decision-making. Using activities like team-building exercises or embracing self-reflection activities may help students develop the skills they need to succeed later in the semester. Another idea to consider is assigning students specific group roles that help them understand the responsibilities they should take on, such as coordinator, planner, notetaker, summarizer, and so on.

## Design Collaborative Activities Carefully

Central to implementing collaborative work successfully is creating an effective learning task. This requires careful thought and planning. Consider the following guidelines as you craft your group work assignments.

- **Make sure your collaborative assignments align to student learning goals and objectives.** For students to take collaborative learning tasks seriously, the tasks must be relevant and not seem to be superfluous busywork. One way to accomplish this is making sure the assignment is integral to achieving stated course learning goals. Thus, begin by answering the question, "What is it that you want students to learn?" See Chapter 4: Designing Significant Learning Goals, Objectives, and Outcomes for guidance on goal formulation. Once you know what learning goal the task is intended to accomplish, one option is to discuss with students how the group activity ties directly to a specific goal and then to follow up the activity with a discussion of whether it helped students accomplish that goal.

- **Choose collaborative learning techniques with proven success rates.** Many teachers put pressure on themselves to invent new teaching methods, but there are plenty of collaborative learning strategies with decades of research to prove their efficacy. You don't need to reinvent the wheel; rather, you can implement proven structures for group activities and then adapt them to your classroom's needs. Our companion site, The K. Patricia Cross Academy (*kpcrossacademy.org*), offers free videos with downloadable templates for 50 teaching techniques, of which many can be adapted easily for group work. These techniques can be further sorted by "group work" to identify activities that we believe are especially well-suited for collaborative learning.
- **Build individual accountability into group assignments.** Design your collaborative activity so that labor is distributed equitably throughout the group and that students contribute their own work first. For example, in CAT 33: Test-Taking Teams, students work in groups to prepare for a test and then take the test individually. Before learning their grade on the individual test, students rejoin their group to take the test again, reaching consensus on each answer. They then submit the test as a group. Each student receives an instructor-weighted combination of the two test scores. For example, each student's composite score could reflect 80% on their individual test and 20% on the group score. Because each student first takes the test independently, this technique emphasizes individual accountability. By retaking the test as a team, individual students benefit if their group performs well. Researchers like Michaelsen et al. (2014) have shown that groups typically test better than individuals, so in addition to ensuring student accountability, this technique is also useful for demonstrating the value of group work.

## Introduce Collaborative Learning

Setting aside sufficient time to form groups carefully and establish a clear framework for completing the task is important for effective group functioning. We offer ideas for how to approach this below.

- **Be deliberate when dividing students into groups.** Be thoughtful about the type of group you're creating. Informal groups are better for quick assignments, formal groups work better for slightly longer projects, and base groups are ideal for long-term assignments. Also, be intentional about group composition, whether homogenous or heterogeneous, and whether the groups should be assigned by random selection or purposefully.

- **Consider group size as well as group dynamics.** Research indicates that while dyads are effective for short, informal interactions, groups of five function best for more substantive assignments. Groups of six are almost as effective. Anything larger can be unwieldy and unproductive. Groups of four often split into two pairs, whereas groups of three often divide into one pair and one outsider.

- **Introduce the group task along with the project's parameters.** Students need to be provided with relevant details about their project before it begins. For example, share the course goal for the activity, tell students that they will divide into groups of five for an activity, inform them how long they'll have to work on the project, and be specific about how they should report their conclusions.

- **Take care in explaining to students how they will be graded and assessed.** There continues to be significant debate about how to assess and grade group projects. Methods like self- and peer-grading can provide teachers with useful information about the success of the group learning process. You can encourage individual accountability by giving greater weight to individual contributions (for example, establishing that 80% of the grade will be based on individual contributions). But there should be a significant enough portion of the grade based on the group results to promote successful interdependence (for example, 20% of the grade). You can also consider including peer evaluation.

- **Provide students with time to create their own group work plans.** Particularly for intensive exercises, ask students to develop a plan for their project. Formalizing this task will encourage students to establish individual deadlines and assign each other responsibilities.

- **Give students enough time to engage with their project.** There are teachers who believe it is essential to give students time to work without any interference. Though we agree, we also suggest teachers show students they are engaged in the activity as well. One way to demonstrate engagement is walking around the classroom, gauging progress, and checking to see if students have questions.

- **Check in with groups periodically but suggest students handle their own issues before seeking assistance.** Particularly for base groups working on long-term projects, it is useful to have frequent check-ins in order to avert any group issues or conflicts with individuals who may be putting their work off until the last minute.
- **Debriefing is essential to collaborative learning.** Ask a few students from the class to summarize their group's conclusions. Take time to address lingering misconceptions or clear up any confusion and give students time to ask questions.

## Grade Collaborative Learning

Because faculty, institutions, and courses have widely divergent value systems, there is no single best approach to grading collaborative activities. Here are some suggestions for how to approach this challenging task.

- **Consider separating out product and process.** Your priority is likely to evaluate how well students learned the discipline-related component of the assignment. This requires grading the product itself. But many teachers who are experienced with collaborative learning also believe it is important to grade group process as well.
- **Consider assignments in which individuals and student groups are both graded.** Separate out individual and group work and grade separately. You may want to assign greater weight to individual work than to group work in the final grade (approximately 80% to 20%, respectively).
- **Ask students to complete self- and peer-assessments, but do not let them factor too largely in the student's final grade.** Tell students directly how their evaluations will be assessed and how it will influence their overall grades.

## Understand Common Problems in Group Work

Collaborative learning has many benefits to students and student learning, but it is also important to recognize certain problems commonly occur when students work in groups (Barkley & Major, 2014), including the following.

- **Resistance to group activities:** In some classes, there will be students who are resistant to group activities. In many cases, these are good students who may just not like group work. Some students may believe they've "learned to play the game" in a standard class structure and don't want to adapt. Other students may worry that their peers will drag down their grades. Student pushback to group work could manifest itself in many ways: complaining about the project, undermining their group, or displaying aggression to their group members.

- **Lack of interpersonal skills:** Some students may not have the interpersonal skills needed to succeed in group projects. They may be overly critical of their peers, lack self-awareness, over or underparticipate, not know how to effectively navigate conflict, be ill-equipped to verbally communicate, or a variety of other issues. Students who have poor interpersonal skills could wind up disrupting their group's work and dynamics or may be ignored and criticized by the rest of their team.

- **Students not getting along with their groups:** Occasionally, some students just will not get along, whether it's because of differing interests, differing values or philosophies, conflicting personalities, or even no apparent reason. One negative result of such occasions is that the whole group may be drawn into negative behavior and fail to achieve their learning goal.

- **Differing levels of ability:** Students enter the classroom with a broad range of academic achievements and abilities. Howard Gardner's (1983) examination of multiple intelligences confirmed what many instructors had long observed: Students have different skills and strengths. Gardner argued, for example, that students may have linguistic intelligence, logistical or mathematical intelligence, spatial intelligence, musical intelligence, interpersonal intelligence, naturalistic intelligence, kinesthetic intelligence, or intrapersonal intelligence. Gardner noted that in the university setting, teachers tended to place primary importance on the first two types of intelligence. Collaborative projects offer opportunities to showcase multiple intelligences, but they also present challenges. Students are required to work with peers who may have different intellectual strengths and those differences could be problematic if, for instance, a student who is high achieving by standard academic measurements feels like they aren't challenged by the group. It can also create problems for lower achieving students who may feel overwhelmed by their peers' abilities.

- **Too many (or too few) students wanting to assume leadership:** It's not uncommon for several students to vie to be group leader. If the competing personalities engage in an uncompromising power struggle, the whole group will be negatively affected. By contrast, a group may also suffer if no student is willing to take on the responsibility of leadership. Groups need someone who can steer them toward a common goal and energize the team toward action.

- **Poor group attendance or online participation:** A common source of frustration for working groups is poor attendance or participation from some members, particularly in online projects. If students don't show up or contribute their portions of the assignment on time, then their peers will struggle to get the overall project completed. Poor attendance can also lead to frustration and animosity from the members who do attend.

- **Inequitable contributions from group members:** A common challenge for group learning is unequal participation from team members. Some students are inclined to dominate projects, by monopolizing discussions or simply taking over. In response, other students may shut down and disengage. Or students may show up unprepared and offer few contributions to the overall activity, leading their team members to complain about free riders or slackers. In each instance, overall satisfaction of team members declines and grades may suffer.

- **Students not focusing during work sessions:** Putting together groups of students, particularly if they are already friends, can lead to detrimental off-task behavior. If students spend the time they should be working goofing off, arguing, or chatting, it can negatively affect their collaborative learning.

- **Groups working at differing rates:** Different groups will operate at different speeds. It's unavoidable. But it can cause problems if some groups finish early and become bored while waiting for their peers to finish. And other groups may rush to finish, feeling pressured by their peers, and their work could suffer as a result.

## Avoid Common Issues in Group Activities

Several of the issues identified in the preceding pages can be avoided by careful planning. Doing so can ensure the problems don't arise in the first place. Here we suggest ways that you can avoid specific problematic occurrences.

**Be deliberate about choosing appropriate learning activities.** Identifying the right learning task can go a long way toward accomplishing learning goals and solving specific problems, such as:

- unfocused behavior during group work sessions,
- groups working at differing rates,
- inequitable contributions from group members,
- differing student abilities, and
- lack of interpersonal skills.

**Encourage group interdependence as well as individual accountability in tasks and make sure rewards (and penalties) are clea**r. This technique can help avert several common issues, including:

- resistance to group activities,
- inequitable contributions from group members,
- unfocused behavior during group work sessions,
- differing student abilities, and
- poor participation or attendance.

**Be careful and deliberate when selecting members and forming groups.** This can address several problems, including:

- differing student abilities,
- lack of interpersonal skills,
- too many (or too few) students wanting to assume leadership, and
- unfocused behavior during group work sessions.

**Set aside time to familiarize students with the benefits of collaborative learning.** This helps to address several potential problems, including students not getting along and resistance to group activities.

**Help students develop the necessary skills for collaboration.** This helps address several issues, including:

- resistance to group activities,
- too many (or too few) students wanting to assume leadership,
- different timing and pacing among groups,
- lack of interpersonal skills, and
- students not getting along.

**Set guidelines that establish good participation at the beginning of the course.** Designing appropriate policies and rules for students can help to avoid problems, including poor attendance or participation or unfocused behavior during group work sessions.

## Resolve Problems with Collaborative Learning

In spite of our best efforts in designing effective activities, we will run into problems. While it can be tough for teachers to watch groups struggling with their assignment, don't be too hasty to jump in and solve the students' problems for them. Learning to work through issues is part of the group development process. In fact, Tuckman's (1965) article outlined the classic stages of group work, arguing that groups go through five development stages: forming, storming, norming, performing, and adjourning. During the *forming stage*, team members meet each other and develop their shared expectations for the project. During the *storming stage*, students test their relationships with each other and may grow frustrated with some members' levels of engagement. Then, when proceeding to the *norming stage*, learners will define their group norms, including individual roles and working relationships. Entering the *performing stage*, students actually do their work. In the final phase, *adjourning*, students complete their work and part from one another. While no group will follow all five stages exactly, understanding the process will help teachers understand where students are in their group development and, ideally, will avoid interfering with the natural group process.

If student groups do struggle with problems that go beyond typical group progression, it is necessary to dedicate appropriate time and effort toward resolving group issues. A good approach may be to help them identify the issue before determining how best to address it. In many cases, once the group is able to identify their problem, they can address it on their own. This is the ideal outcome for providing both a learning experience and a shared sense of accomplishment. In other cases, it may be necessary to guide students through creating workable solutions to their problems. And in some instances, the teacher should be willing to intercede and directly address problems. When intervening, some general advice includes getting to understand students on a personal level, avoiding taking student conduct personally, looking past what you might consider mild behavior, designing groups to build on personality strengths while minimizing weakness, and adjusting group size and makeup (Johnson & Johnson, 1997; Silberman, 1996).

If you have taken care to attend to our guidance on how to avoid common problems, but continue to experience it, consider the suggestions below.

**Establish teacher presence.** While lecturing or leading a full class discussion, teachers are generally quite visible, with the majority of student attention turned toward the instructor who is providing valuable information or leading the conversation. However, during collaborative learning activities, teachers must make a conscious effort to make their presence in the classroom known. Student attention is generally directed toward their group members and, in some cases, they may even forget the teacher is present. Thus, teachers must establish a strong presence by either moving throughout the room and checking in with groups or, in online settings, by posting frequently and quickly responding to student comments and questions. Establishing teacher presence may be especially effective in averting problematic behaviors, such as:

- students not getting along,
- unfocused behavior during group work sessions, and
- poor participation or attendance.

**Provide public praise to groups that work well together, promoting effective behaviors.** When students are new to collaborative learning, they may be unaware how effective groups work. By highlighting effective behavior, you may be able to resolve issues, such as:

- resistance to group activities,
- students not getting along,
- too many (or too few) students wanting to assume leadership, and
- unfocused behavior during group work sessions.

**Address the entire group about the issue.** By speaking with the entire group, you empower students to participate in creating a solution and developing their problem-solving skills. This technique may effectively help address issues, such as:

- resistance to group activities,
- students not getting along,
- too many (or too few) students wanting to assume leadership, and
- unfocused behavior during group work sessions.

**Privately address problems one-on-one with an individual student.** If one student is creating broad group dysfunction, it may be necessary to speak with that student specifically. This approach may be useful to address the following problems:

- resistance to group activities,
- inequitable contributions from group members,
- lack of interpersonal skills, and
- poor participation or attendance.

**Re-shape groups.** Teachers often wonder whether they should adjust group membership frequently (to provide students with the opportunity to work with more of their peers) or infrequently (to allow students the opportunity to develop strong working relationships). Generally, experienced teachers who use collaborative learning activities are in favor of keeping groups together as long as they can, even if the groups seem to be fraying. In those cases, Miller and colleagues (1994) suggested "teachers must have faith that in time they will pull out of their tailspin. Intervening immediately to shuffle the groups can set them back, lose hard-won experience, and force them to start all over again" (p. 40). Teachers should give groups the time needed to mature and work through their disagreements. That said, it may be necessary to reform groups at times and it could appropriately help address problems, such as:

- lack of interpersonal skills,
- poor participation or attendance, and
- students not getting along.

Most faculty and students are aware of the myriad issues that can arise from collaborative learning. If you invest the time and effort to create effective collaborative learning environments and address and revolve potential issues as needed, you will likely be able to maximize the benefits while minimizing the challenges.

## CONCLUSION

Engaged teachers recognize that the role of college instructors has shifted dramatically over the last several decades. No longer is it sufficient to be a dispenser of information. Teachers are now increasingly being held accountable for what and how much students learn. Collaborative learning is a well-researched and important pedagogical approach, but for collaborative learning to be successful, the teacher must carefully consider a host of factors. To do collaborative learning well means learning about the approach, understanding what its benefits are and where its potential challenges lie, and developing a sound plan of action.

## FOCUS ON ONLINE TEACHING

The information we share in the main body of this chapter applies to both onsite and online teaching, but here we provide additional insights focused specifically on teaching online, hybrid, and blended courses.

### What: Collaborative Learning Online

Collaborative learning is an approach that involves two or more people working in a group to learn together in an online environment.

### Why: Collaborative Learning Online

Just as with onsite collaborative learning, online collaborative learning appears to deepen student learning outcomes. A recent meta-analysis examining the effects of computer-supported collaborative learning (CSCL) in STEM courses, drew from 143 studies, published between 2005 and 2014 and examined the effects of CSCL on 316 outcomes. The researchers demonstrated a moderate but noteworthy effect regarding online collaborative learning. The influence was most significant on process outcomes and then knowledge outcomes, followed by affective outcomes. The sizes of the effects were mediated by the types of pedagogy and technology used, the educational level of the students, and the learning domains.

Additionally, the moderators interacted in a way that the effects of pedagogy and technology could vary based on the methods of collaboration, students' education levels, and the domains of education. The meta-analysis indicates the broad advantage of CSCL in online STEM education and demonstrates the necessity of understanding how the existing variables interact and contribute to CSCL effectiveness (Jeong et al., 2019).

### How: Collaborative Learning Online

Collaborative learning can be challenging in online classes, but given the ways in which it can deepen learning and decrease student isolation, it is well worth the risk. We suggest the following five Cross Academy Techniques (CATs) for collaborative learning online. You can see a video on the main technique and a video on how to implement it in the online environment as well as download additional guidance and a template on our companion site, The K. Patricia Cross Academy (*kpcrossacademy.org*).

**CAT 28: Dyadic Interviews:** In Dyadic Interviews, student pairs take turns asking each other questions that tap into values, attitudes, beliefs, and prior experiences that are relevant to course content or learning goals.

**CAT 37: Think-Pair-Share:** In a Think-Pair-Share, the instructor poses a question, gives students a few minutes to think about a response, and then asks students to share their ideas with a partner. Hence, think-pair-share.

**CAT 44: Fishbowl:** In Fishbowl, students form concentric circles with a small group inside and a larger group outside. Students in the inner circle engage in an in-depth discussion, while students in the outer circle listen and critique content, logic, and group interaction.

**CAT 4: Jigsaw:** In Jigsaw, students work in small groups to develop knowledge about a given topic before teaching what they have learned to another group.

**CAT 26: Dyadic Essays:** In Dyadic Essays, students: (1) complete a content unit, identify a central question, and draft an answer to that question; (2) exchange questions with a peer and prepare responses; and (3) pairs read and compare the model and in-class answers.

To implement these effectively, we offer the following tips:

**Form diverse groups.** Deliberately mixing students by achievement level, academic interests, or other relevant factors can enable students to work constructively with others who bring different strengths to their learning tasks.

**Keep groups small.** Group members need to interact frequently, and this can be a challenge for students learning online. Consider limiting group size to three to five members.

**Build strong group interdependence and positive interaction.** Online students need to rely on each other, but they need to do so in a positive and promotive way. You might consider offering bonus points to a group if all members score above a certain grade on an assignment, test, or paper. Better prepared students may be motivated to help their peers. Less-prepared students may work harder to avoid disappointing peers, but the group doesn't fail if they don't make it.

**Implement peer evaluation.** Peer evaluation helps to build a team because students reflect on the process and outcomes of their learning. Consider asking:

- Did all members of the group contribute?
- What could be done next time to make the group function better?
- What were the most important things I learned?
- What contributions did I make?

PART 5

# Improvement

*In what may as well be starkly labelled smug satisfaction, an amazing 94% of college instructors rate themselves as above average teachers, and 68% rank themselves in the top quarter of teaching performances.*

**—K. PATRICIA CROSS**

CHAPTER 13

# Reflecting on Teaching

Scientists continue to make amazing discoveries about the intelligence in the world around us, but as far as we know, we remain the only species that reflects on our existence. Renowned sociologist Jack Mezirow (1997) observed, "A defining condition of being human is that we have the ability to understand the meaning of our experience" (p. 5). One of the most important ways we gain such an understanding is by reflecting on those experiences. Reflection, then, is part of meaning making, and it is deeply connected to human learning.

Some professionals, such as many who work in education, social work, and nursing, engage in *reflective practice*, which is a tool that helps them synthesize, interpret, and understand their work based on their personal experiences. For educators, such reflective practice is typically focused on teaching and learning. Engaged instructors use reflective practice to seek out the best methods for teaching so that they can become more effective in their instructional roles and responsibilities. In this chapter, we share information about what reflective practice is, review the research on why it is important, and offer techniques for engaging in reflective practice.

## KNOWING WHAT: ABOUT REFLECTIVE PRACTICE

What we now refer to as reflective practice, especially as it applies to education, was developed by John Dewey in the early 20th century. Dewey (1910) defined reflective practice as "the active, persistent and careful consideration of any belief or supposed form of knowledge in the light of the grounds that support it" (p. 6). Later, Dewey (1933) further developed his ideas about reflective practice, writing that reflection "enables us to direct our actions with foresight ... It enables us to know what we are about when we act" (p. 17). Why is reflection essential to learning? Dewey (1933) argued:

> Of course, intellectual learning includes the amassing and retention of information. But information is an undigested burden unless it is understood ... And understanding, comprehension, means that the various parts of the information acquired are grasped in their relations to one another — a result that is attained only when acquisition is accompanied by constant reflection upon the meaning of what is studied. (pp. 78–79)

Thus, effective teachers not only approach classroom instruction with well-developed plans based on their knowledge of disciplinary content, pedagogical theory, and personal experience, but then they improve their understanding by constantly reflecting on how these components relate to and interact with each other.

Educators can use reflective practice, then, to seek out the best methods for teaching students and enhancing their learning. In his book *Becoming a Critically Reflective Teacher* (1995, 2017), Stephen Brookfield proposed that active reflection helps teachers:

- **Resist self-sabotage:** By deliberately examining student learning experiences, critically reflective educators may understand that their students' behavior can be affected by several factors, including external ones. Students may be resistant to learning for a host of social and political reasons, that likely fall well beyond a given teacher's failings. Thus, teachers can be more realistic in assessing their individual influence on student behavior.
- **Maintain emotional stability:** Unless instructors engage in critical reflection, they may second guess every single action in their classrooms. The slightest error or victory may confirm teachers' assumptions that they are either terrible or terrific in their work. But if they slow down and critically reflect on their own predispositions and student learning outcomes, they can assess their influence more accurately and effectively.
- **Understand why they teach:** Teachers need to consider what they believe and why. By rooting their identity and actions in well-developed values and core beliefs, teachers build and maintain credibility in the classroom. In the best circumstances, students understand what their instructors believe and why it is important (p. 23).
- **Foster a positive learning environment:** Teachers can encourage students to think critically about their own education by openly engaging in personal reflection. By demonstrating intention, self-reflective teachers can encourage students to take up the challenge of critically examining their educational pursuits and thereby maintain interest in the classroom (p. 25).

- **Act based on information:** Self-examination offers teachers the opportunity to make better informed decisions that are geared toward achieving specific results from their students. Educators are better able to explain and rationalize their behavior in the classroom to their students and third parties (p. 22).

Reflective practice is essential to active teaching and learning because for teachers in higher education, the benefits outlined above can help us become more effective in the classroom.

## Schön's Model of Reflective Practice

Dewey planted the seeds for what we now know as reflective practice and there have subsequently been several different models introduced regarding reflection (for instance, Atkins & Murphy, 1994; Brookfield, 2017; Gibbs, 1988; Kolb, 1984). But the term itself wasn't in vogue until Donald Schön's work in the 1980s.

Schön (1983) asserted that professionals and amateurs alike engage in reflection when they consider their actions (either before or after their completion) and follow that with turning thought back on action and ... knowing (p. 50). Schön stressed that in order to be effective, professionals must maintain a process of real-time reflection on their own knowledge and the quality of their work.

The model developed by Schön indicates reflection has two core components: *reflection-in-action* and *reflection-on-action.* The former indicates the immediate thinking and reaction happening in real time. For instance, in the middle of a class session, a teacher may recognize that students are struggling to follow the presentation of new material. Reflection-in-action would prompt the teacher to pause and try to determine why students aren't understanding and then alter the approach accordingly. This aspect of reflecting may result in rephrasing a description, approaching the subject from another viewpoint, offering new resources, or implementing alternative activities in the moment.

By contrast, reflection-on-action consists of the thoughts and analyses that take place following completion of the activity. In this manner, a teacher may revisit the events of a class session after it is over to examine why students didn't seem to follow the presentation and then identify possible causes and solutions. It also includes what the teacher was thinking when they chose to address the situation using one approach rather than another. Reflection-on-action generally hinges on an educator's existing expertise and experience in addition to a deeper understanding of education theories and their own style and ideals. Schön's model is an effective way to understand how and when reflection takes place. Figure 13.1: Schön's Model of Reflection summarizes the steps involved in reflective practice.

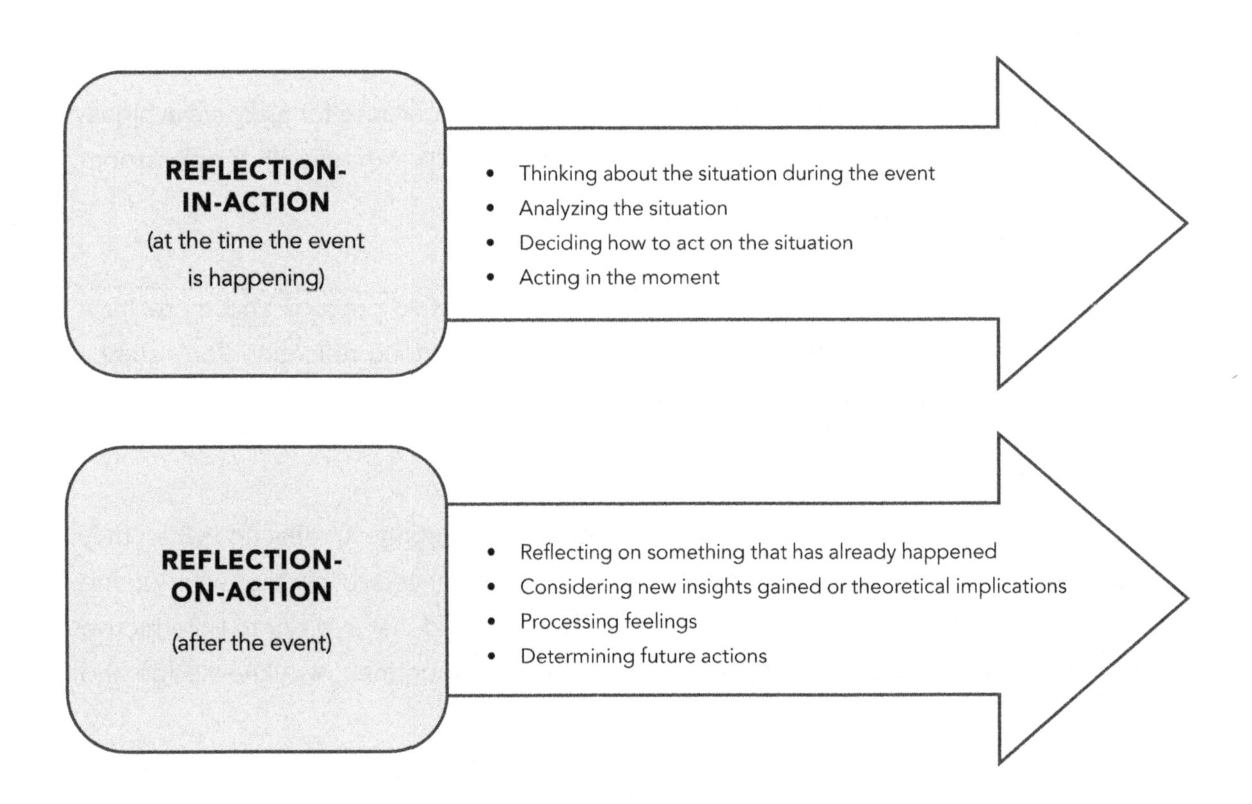


**Figure 13.1. Schön's Model of Reflection**

## Key Features of Reflective Practice

Scholars increasingly recognize the need for reflective practice among higher education teachers (e.g., Biggs, 1999; Brookfield, 2017; Clegg et al., 2002; Kreber, 1999; McAlpine et al., 1999). Day (1999) argued that reflective practice is necessary for establishing and developing teachers' ability "to think and act professionally over the span of their careers" (p. 222). But what exactly does reflective practice look like? Generally, a few key components are accepted as aspects of reflective practice in the field of education, such as:

- Reflective teaching recognizes that every action in the classroom has its own issues and obstacles to work through.

- Reflective teachers examine ideas and issues from multiple lenses, improving their ability to assess their own biases, values, and beliefs.
- Reflection is more complicated than just thinking; it involves active learning.
- Reflective practice is nonlinear; each reflection generates new ideas that inform additional lesson plans and learning stages, which then fuel additional reflection.
- Reflection advances the field of education by encouraging the adaptation of ideas and their application to new situations.

## Trends in Conceptualizations of Reflective Practice: From Descriptive to Critical

Dewey and Schön's models are not the only approaches to reflection. Over the years, the academic approach to reflection has evolved significantly. Broadly, the scholarship that has emerged since Dewey and Schön's early work has focused on the need for teachers not only to study their instructional practices but also to examine their underlying biases and assumptions about teachers, students, and the sociopolitical environment that contributes to student success in and out of the classroom (Brookfield, 2000; Fendler, 2003; Larrivee, 2000). In 1990, Mezirow argued that "reflection enables us to correct distortions in our beliefs and errors in problem-solving. Critical reflections involve a critique of the presuppositions on which our beliefs have been built" (p. 1). Osterman (1990) described reflective practice as a "mindful consideration of one's actions, specifically, one's professional actions ... a challenging, focused and critical assessment of one's own behavior as a means towards developing one's own craftsmanship" (p. 134). Korthagen (2001) offered that "reflection is the mental process of trying to structure or restructure an experience, a problem, or existing knowledge or insights" (p. 58).

Recently, scholars have begun to distinguish several different types of reflection, including technical, descriptive, instrumental, and critical reflection. They argue that *critical reflection* is distinctly different from the others (Brookfield, 2000; Larrivee, 2000; Zeichner & Liston, 2014). Brookfield stressed that reflection may just involve technical decision-making; critical reflection, however, is centered in internalizing critical theory and examining our own contributions to the power dynamics in educational spaces and existing biases.

Fendler (2003) refuted Brookfield, arguing that the distinction between critical reflection and reflection is incorrect because critical practitioners may also use technical reflection if "they believe that the efficient mastery of subject matter by their students is the most effective means of redressing social inequities" (p. 21). More recently, Zeichner and Liston (2014) argued that reflection helps teachers improve by encouraging them to examine their ideas, beliefs, and actions and to strive toward social justice. They also suggested that reflection should not just be a solo endeavor but should be a collective process.

Other researchers have suggested that reflection doesn't simply occur as a cognitive process but incorporates sensorimotor functions and emotions (Jordi, 2011; Sodhi & Cohen, 2012). Still others have noted that reflective practice also relies on the structural, sociocultural, and political environments in which educators must work (Coburn & Turner, 2012; Spillane, 2012).

Most scholars agree that critical reflection is a process of examining one's own performance as well as one's inherent biases and assumptions; however, they diverge on the purpose and targets of critical reflection. Some scholars, like Mezirow (1990) and Imel (1992), argue that the goal of critical reflection should be to eliminate individual bias and become more self-aware and objective. Imel (1992, p. 8) argued that reflective practice "involves thinking about and critically analyzing one's actions with the goal of improving one's professional practice" (see also Larrivee, 2000). Others, like Brookfield (2000) insist that critical reflection should also lead to greater societal awareness, not just self-awareness. He argued that reflective teachers should promote social justice and empowerment in the academy and that "examining power relationships and hegemonic assumptions must be integral to the definition of critical reflection" (p. 125).

## KNOWING WHY: RESEARCH ON REFLECTIVE PRACTICE

Relatively little empirical research examines reflective practice among college and university educators, particularly compared to the research on how K-12 educators reflect upon and use data. Coburn and Turner (2012) were blunt, stating that there is "shockingly little research on what happens when individuals interact with data in their workplace settings" (p. 99). That said, encouraging lines of inquiry have emerged. For example, the research suggests that effective teachers generally engage in reflective practice regarding their own performance in the classroom.

Multiple studies have demonstrated the prevalence and traits of reflective practice in addition to its role among effective teachers. For example, Kane and colleagues (2004) built on the work of Hatton and Smith (1995) and examined the methods of 17 award-winning teachers. They determined that a "common characteristic ... was that these excellent university teachers engaged in regular, purposeful reflection on their teaching practice" (Kane et al., 2004, p. 300). The types of reflection engaged by the study's participants included the following:

- **Technical reflection:** decisions made about immediate experiences
- **Descriptive reflection:** analysis and explanations of past teaching performance
- **Dialogic reflection:** the consideration of alternative methods for future teaching
- **Critical reflection:** consideration of the effects of their actions on others and the sociopolitical ideas at work in the classroom (Kane et al., 2004)

Their study indicated that of the different types of reflection, faculty engaged in technical and descriptive reflection most often. Of note, while Kane et al. examined respondents' critical reflection of their teaching methods as related to historical, political, and social context, the researchers did not do a deep analysis of specific aspects of the participants' critical reflection.

McLean and Blackwell (1997) contended that the best higher education teachers approach their craft with critical reflection that is theoretically informed. They studied how new teachers were trained to see how their preferred approach could be put into effect. The researchers determined that faculty pursuing a reflective practice approach develop ideas of instruction that improve their practice and also potentially alter how departments think about teaching and learning. They suggested that promoting reflective pedagogy could effectively engage faculty to make the necessary cultural changes to improve the overall status of the teaching profession.

McAlpine and Weston (2000) studied six successful university professors and found that their teaching was improved by reflective practice. These professors also expressed strong desire to teach, build on their own pedagogical knowledge, create a positive work environment, include moments for reflective practice, and take advantage of pedagogical training. The researchers learned that all professors involved in the study had and used extensive knowledge about learners, as individuals and as groups, and applied that knowledge when reflecting on the influence of their instruction of students. They determined that reflection had a significant relationship with the development of teaching knowledge.

Other research has pointed to multiple challenges to faculty engaging in reflective practice. For example, some teachers are not given sufficient time to reflect (Kuit et al., 2001). Other teachers, who are overworked or undermotivated, simply lack interest in reflective practice (Davis, 2003).

Hora and Smolarek (2018) identified three distinct modes of faculty reflection: instrumental, social-critical, and structural-critical. They argued that, even among faculty who consistently made time for reflective practice, their reflection could be affected by individual biases or institutional limitations. Hora and Smolarek suggested that instructors should be given more institutional support (e.g., space, time, and institutional guidance for reflective practice) in order to better serve their students, especially those from groups that are historically underrepresented. Faculty also need the opportunity to voice their concerns, and their institutions must be willing to make the necessary adjustments.

## KNOWING HOW: AN ENGAGED APPROACH TO REFLECTIVE TEACHING

College teachers face several obstacles to engaging in reflective practice. These include finding the time or the motivation to engage in critical reflection. But critical reflection is an essential component for being a truly engaged teacher. So how can we adopt and internalize reflection and be effective and intentional in our approach?

### Steps for Reflective Practice

If you are new to the practice, there are six key steps, sometimes identified as the Six Rs, that will help you maximize the effect of your reflections: reacting, recording, reviewing, revising, reworking, and reassessing. Consider asking yourself the questions corresponding to these steps as outlined in Table 13.1: Six Key Steps to Enhance Reflections.

### Tools for Reflective Practice

The strategies and questions outlined in Table 13.1 offer a useful framework, especially when used in combination with specific steps to help instructors record and document their reflections. Documentation can lead to action and implementation. Consider the following approaches to record reflections.

#### INDEX CARDS AND STICKY NOTES

Index cards or sticky notes can be useful for jotting ideas down as soon as they occur. You can simply take a note of something you would like to be sure to include in a future class or something that you think you could do better. This tool is also flexible, allowing you to shuffle and sort your notes into groups. In this way, you can develop key themes from your reflections or identify areas that you want to enhance or improve.

**FREEWRITING**

When freewriting, rather than reflecting on a specific class session or module, determine a teaching experience or moment and write about it continuously in full sentences and paragraphs. Set a timer for 5 to 10 minutes and write for the entire time, without self-censoring or editing. In the process of writing whatever is on your mind, you may identify some ideas and/or beliefs for further exploration and consideration.

| STEP | ACTIVITY | DESCRIPTION | KEY QUESTIONS |
|---|---|---|---|
| 1 | Reacting | Making an informed decision | What should I do? What areas of my practice need attention? |
| 2 | Recording | Logging your reflections | How will I document my reflections? When will I log my reflections? |
| 3 | Reviewing | Understanding your current teaching practices and methods | What worked well, and how do I know this? What did not work as planned? |
| 4 | Revising | Adapting your teaching by trying new strategies | What will I change or adapt? Will I change the entire task or something specific about the task? |
| 5 | Reworking | Understanding how these new strategies affected learning | How will I put the change in place? What materials do I need to make the change? |
| 6 | Reassessing | Understanding how these new strategies affected learning | How successful were the new strategies? What will I change for the next time? |

**SOURCE:** Cambridge International Teaching and Learning Team. (n.d.) Getting started with reflective practice. *(https://www.cambridge-community.org.uk/professional-development/gswrp/index.html)*

**Table 13.1. Six Key Steps to Enhance Reflections**

## READING JOURNAL

One efficient method for documenting reflections is to create and maintain a reading journal. Establishing a dated journal to collect your thoughts while reading is a good way to capture summaries and reflections about books and articles designed to improve your teaching. For example, you might log a reading by title, date, a brief summary and then include your personal reaction to it. You may also prefer a less formal style, choosing to just write down key ideas and thoughts in the moment. No matter your approach to journaling, taking this first step sets a habit for engaged reflection.

## TEACHING JOURNAL

Instead of a journal built around reflecting on individual readings, this type of journal is a space to record your notes, ideas, observations, and other materials related to your time in the classroom. After each course period, spend some time recording your observations about what worked and what didn't, which techniques to maintain and what new approaches to try. Teaching journals offer a space for self-evaluation but can also serve as a repository for student questions and ideas that need to be addressed in upcoming class sessions.

## STRUCTURED SELF-EVALUATIONS

Some teachers may want or need reflections that are more structured than freeform journals. Structured self-evaluations serve a similar purpose to freeform journals but the format is more clearly established and entries are made in a routine sequence that is followed regularly. To implement a structured self-evaluation, establish a series of questions to answer after each class session that will help you gauge your strengths and areas for improvement. The format and routine are useful for establishing the habit of reflective practice while also recording your observations of student productivity. Some sample questions could include:

- How engaged were my students during this session? What captivated them? Where did I lose them?
- What obstacles did I encounter during the period? How did I deal with them?
- What topics did students struggle with? How can I approach the subject matter differently next time?
- What did I do well this period? How can I replicate it?
- What do I want to retain from this session? What do I want to do differently next time?

### AUDIO RECORDING

You need not always reflect in writing. Indeed, capturing your thoughts in an audio recording can be a useful way to document your reflections, which may be as simple as sharing what you thought went well or what you would like to improve moving forward.

### MICROTEACHING VIDEOTAPE

A more intensive approach to reflective practice involves making a video recording of your course and reviewing it with or without a third party. Schedule a time with a videographer to record a class session, asking them to make sure to film you as well as students' reactions. Then, review the tape either by yourself or, ideally, with a colleague or an expert from your university's teaching center. Sometimes the reality of a class session is quite different from what we imagined it to be. Watching a video recording affords you the opportunity to know what your teaching process really looks like in the classroom. Put together a checklist to determine what you should and should not do in future sessions. Some sample questions include:

- How does this compare to my perception of how the class went?
- What are my strengths? Weaknesses?
- When are the students most engaged? When do they seem disengaged?
- What are two specific areas for improvement?

### OBSERVATIONS

In some cases, reflective practice may improve with third party observation. Work with a colleague or an expert from your university's teaching center to determine a specific area of emphasis for an observation period. Thus, instead of soliciting a blanket observation, you ask the observer to focus on something particular such as student engagement during a lecture, participation during group activities, and so forth. By agreeing upon an area of focus, the observer's feedback will offer the kind of precise data that will be more useful for your personal reflection and revision. You may wish to have your colleague observe multiple sessions so they can monitor your progress and offer ongoing ideas for further development.

### SHARED PLANNING

There is power in collective reflection in addition to personal reflective practice. Consider working with colleagues in your department to develop and plan class sessions or course modules, building on each other's strengths and ideas to develop better lessons. You might even work with colleagues to develop courses from beginning to end. In other cases, you might adapt lesson plans that your colleague has already produced, and vice versa. Working with your colleagues leads to self-reflection as it requires you to determine what exactly works about teaching strategies and lessons and how they can be replicated and adapted.

#### FACULTY DISCUSSION GROUPS

Another opportunity for collective reflection is the establishment of a faculty discussion group. Each group typically involves two to six members hosting peer-led conversations that foster an environment of active collaboration, support, and reflection. Teachers discuss best practices from their class sessions as well as moments of difficulty, with other participants offering alternatives for improvement.

#### STUDENT DIALOGUE

It's not just colleagues who can play a role in your reflective practice. Encouraging students to reflect on how lessons and courses went and to offer feedback for ways to improve serves two goals: (1) it helps student develop their own habits of reflection and (2) it offers teachers better information for their own practice. Encourage students to keep their own journals where they record key moments from lessons, areas for improvement, likes and dislikes, and more. Consider holding a discussion with students, reflecting together on what went well and what could be improved.

#### QUESTIONNAIRES AND CHECKLISTS

Develop questionnaires or checklists to be completed by students or colleagues, but also make sure to complete them yourself. How do students' or colleagues' answers differ from your own? Examine the answers collected with a third party to help you talk through the data and determine what the answers mean for your teaching performance. If there are many commonalities among the answers, that may improve your confidence that your approach to teaching is working. Areas where the answers diverge may suggest aspects of your teaching methods that need to be refined and improved.

### Tips for Reflective Practice

The most important thing to remember about reflective practice is that it requires personal honesty. When you reflect, avoid self-censoring. Be willing to go to uncomfortable places and examine hard truths in order to improve your teaching. Remember that everyone has weaknesses and challenges, so don't be hard on yourself, but still look for areas to improve.

Don't be afraid to turn to others for feedback and support. It may feel tough or awkward to maintain objectivity when assessing your own performance. It is easy to rationalize or explain missteps or obstacles as anomalies. But if you really want to improve as a teacher, you have to be able to examine your performance critically. If you are struggling with talking to others about your performance, try examining yourself as if you were a third party. Pretend you are offering feedback to a peer instead of yourself. Be specific with your feedback. General reflection can be helpful but also daunting. It helps to focus on specific moments or aspects of your teaching and then identify ways to develop and improve those targeted aspects. Adapting some of the techniques that you ask your students to use to reflect can be beneficial to you as well. For example, CAT 3: Contemporary Issues Journal and CAT 47: What? So What? Now What? Journals can be great activities for reflecting on teaching. Remember that teaching is an interactive process, and you should and will improve in different areas over the course of your career.

## CONCLUSION

Because teaching is so critical to our roles as faculty members, we should always be looking for ways to improve our performance in the classroom as well as to help our colleagues excel. Reflective practice is an essential tool for developing and enhancing teacher knowledge and innovation. Engaged teachers use reflective practice to improve their teaching and students' learning and, hence, look for ways to incorporate it into their regular routines.

## FOCUS ON ONLINE TEACHING

The information we share in the main body of this chapter applies to both onsite and online teaching, but here we provide additional insights focused specifically on teaching online, hybrid, and blended courses.

### What: Reflection on Online Teaching

Reflective practice is critically examining your own actions to engage in a process of continuous learning. As we have noted in the main body of this chapter, reflective practice can improve teaching and make it more satisfying. Teachers who engage in some form of reflective practice will likely learn more from their experience teaching than they would otherwise. Reflecting on an online course is much like reflecting on an onsite one, and it yields similar benefits.

### Why: Reflection Online Teaching

It stands to reason that reflecting on teaching online would lead instructors to engage in their teaching more deeply, which would in turn shape their teaching practices. The research seems to support this basic idea. Laprade et al. (2014), for example, created a formative evaluation instrument for online faculty reflection. The instrument asked faculty questions regarding key areas: communication, engagement, expertise, and use of quality instruction techniques. They then conducted a quasi-experimental study with 50 online instructors, with equal numbers in the control and experimental group. Participants in the experimental group self-evaluated and reflected on their online instruction capabilities and practices, while participants in the control group did not. The researchers analyzed course data and examined performance in the key areas. They found positive effects that were statistically significant related to the use of evaluation and reflection for online faculty both in their participation in online discussion forums and their use of high-quality instructional techniques.

### How: Reflection Online Teaching

The processes for reflecting on online teaching are similar to those for reflecting on online. Following are tips for engaging in reflection for online teaching:

#### SEEK FEEDBACK

It is possible to gain quick and meaningful feedback in an online environment, and there are many ways to gather it. Consider student polls focused on how the module went. Ask students open-ended questions in the chat or discussion forum about how to improve the module. Have students answer multiple-choice questions in quiz format after each module to determine how much they learned and how and where they struggled. You can also ask peers for feedback. They can review online course materials, the course site, or even attend a synchronous session for an observation.

### ASK YOURSELF WHAT YOU LEARNED FROM A PARTICULAR MODULE

Just as at the end of each onsite class or unit, it can be beneficial to consider what you have learned at the end of an online learning module. Begin by analyzing the feedback you received from students. Consider the questions the students are asking you on email, in the discussion forum, or through the LMS messaging center. Reflect on the times when your students were more active and engaged online and when they were less so.

### IDENTIFY YOUR STRENGTHS

It is easy to fall into the trap of looking only for weaknesses in teaching, and since many of us are new to teaching online, it can be even easier to look for weaknesses there. Make it a point to consider what you are doing well in your online course. Are you good at giving timely feedback? Are you great at encouraging communication on the discussion boards? Is your course plan and structure particularly effective? Have you used great images to engage students? Rather than making reflection about addressing deficits, you can and should also consider your strengths. You may well find strengths that you wish to capitalize on the next time you teach onsite.

### USE A STRUCTURE

Use a structure, like the 6-step reflective model we described above in the "Knowing What" section of this chapter, to reflect on your online course. A structure provides a guideline for your thinking that may yield different information than you would have generated otherwise. It can be particularly important when teaching online, as this is a new environment for many, and a structure can help us maintain focus.

*The problem with student evaluations is not so much that they lack validity, as that they are not very helpful to teachers.*

**—K. PATRICIA CROSS**

CHAPTER 14

# Assessing and Evaluating Teaching

As teachers today, we deal with an almost dizzying array of challenges. These include how to best teach an increasingly diverse set of learners and how to prove to a wide range of stakeholders that students in our courses are learning. Instead of relying on time-honored routines, we need to become ever more skillful in our ability to assess our teaching situations and adapt our approaches as needed. The best method of assessing and evaluating teaching involves using multiple sources of data. No one data source — whether student evaluation forms, peer review, or publications in the scholarship of teaching and learning (SoTL) — allows for a full, nuanced evaluation of the complex teaching process. Whatever combination of sources you choose to use, make the effort to design, execute, and report the results appropriately. You want to present your teaching in the best possible light, which is dependent upon the quality of evidence you collect and the clarity with which you document and present it. Assessing and evaluating your teaching is a critical component of being an effective and engaged teacher. This chapter is designed to help you do so.

## KNOWING WHAT: ABOUT ASSESSING AND EVALUATING ACTIVE TEACHING

In general, what we mean by the assessment and evaluation of teaching is a systematic process for gauging the effectiveness of our teaching. This process can provide teachers with feedback about their teaching that promotes professional growth so that they can make improvements that will in turn enhance student learning.

As we mentioned in the first chapter of this book, teaching effectiveness historically has been evaluated solely by way of student ratings. This approach has some challenges, including the fact that it relies on a single, questionable measure (student evaluations of teaching) as well as the fact that it is largely used for one purpose: summative evaluation of teaching for formal review. In the 1990s, we began to see some signs of change to the traditional norm in the growth of the peer review of teaching movement. With the publication of Boyer's (1990) *Scholarship Reconsidered* and Glassick and colleagues' (1997) *Scholarship Assessed*, we also saw greater push to treat teaching and its attending assessment and evaluation more seriously.

Gaining a true sense of how effective our teaching has been, including a close look at what is working and what is not, however, takes a thoughtful and holistic approach. This approach can be informal, done for our own knowledge and continuous improvement of teaching, or it can be a more formal process that our institution employs for the purpose of reviewing and rating a teacher's performance and effectiveness in the classroom. Engaged teachers use multiple measures to assess their teaching, which can in turn allow the data collected to be used for multiple purposes. These purposes include formative and summative ones and those that range from gathering information only for our own use to those required as part of the hiring, tenure, and promotion review process.

## KNOWING WHY: RESEARCH ON ASSESSING AND EVALUATING TEACHING

Why should we care about assessing and evaluating teaching? One of the key reasons is that when we have good evidence, we can typically make better teaching decisions. Yet most research on assessment and evaluation of teaching to date has focused on student evaluations of teaching. Student evaluations of teaching are the surveys administered by colleges and universities directly to students enrolled in the course, most often at the end of the academic term. These surveys also are called student ratings of instruction, teaching evaluations, and course evaluations. Although student evaluations were used as early as the 1920s, their use expanded in the United States in the late 1960s and early 1970s (Uttl et al., 2017). Now, nearly all higher education institutions employ student evaluations of teaching and use them as the measure of teaching effectiveness. Their extensive use has led researchers to seek to answer several key questions.

### Are Student Evaluations and Student Learning Related?

The answer to the question of whether student evaluations and student learning are related has changed over time. Cohen (1981) was the first to conduct a meta-analysis of multi-section studies of student evaluations of teaching. He found a correlation between student ratings and student learning and wrote: "The results of the meta-analysis provide strong support for the validity of student ratings as a measure of teaching effectiveness" (p. 281) and "... we can safely say that student ratings of instruction are a valid index of instructional effectiveness. Students do a pretty good job of distinguishing among teachers on the basis of how much they have learned" (p. 305). Since its publication, this article has been frequently cited to support the use of student ratings to evaluate faculty's teaching effectiveness. The assertion was that students learn more from professors with high ratings, which became a widely unchallenged claim.

More recently, however, studies have leaned in the other direction, suggesting that there is not a significant relationship between student ratings and student learning. Clayson (2009), for example, conducted a meta-analysis of multi-section studies and concluded that student evaluations were not directly correlated with student learning. Clayson also found that weighting the correlations by sample size reduced the student evaluation–learning correlation. In addition, studies with few sections had the highest correlations, while studies examining more sections reported smaller correlations. In another study, Uttl et al. (2017) reanalyzed previous meta-analyses of multi-section studies and also found that students did not learn more from professors with higher student evaluations of teaching than they did from those with lower ratings.

On the whole, then, more recent studies suggest that student ratings and student learning are unrelated. It is important to remember that student ratings instruments gather student views of their experiences (Abrami, 2001; Arreola, 2007; Hativa, 2013). They are student perception data, or evidence of student satisfaction, instead of direct evidence of teaching effectiveness (Nilson, 2012).

## Does Course Difficulty or Workload Correlate With Student Ratings?

Research has been more decisive on the question as to whether or not student ratings correlate with course difficulty or workload. While it is commonly believed that more difficult instructors or courses get lower ratings, and easier instructors or courses get higher ones, research studies do not support this belief. Studies generally show no correlation between course difficulty and student ratings (Beran & Violato, 2010; Willits & Brennan, 2017). What these studies suggest is that it is not likely faculty can influence student evaluations through leniency, particularly if student expectations for course difficulty are met (Addison et al., 2006; Joyce, 2017).

## Do Expected Grades Show Any Correlations with Student Ratings?

Researchers have also examined the effects of grades on student evaluations. The results have been mixed. Some studies on expected grades have shown no correlation between the grades students expected to earn and their ratings of instructors (e.g., Centra, 2003, 2009; Feldman, 1997; Gigliotti & Buchtel, 1990; Marsh & Roche, 1997; Winer et al., 2016). If correlations were found, they were found to be insignificant. On the other hand, some research studies have found students' grades to be positively correlated (low to moderate correlation) with student evaluations (Abrami, 2001; Arreola, 2007; Benton & Li, 2015; Eiszler, 2002).

The reasons for the differences in findings are not clear, but it may have something to do with the research methods employed. By design, many of the studies have had a limited sample size. In addition, researchers have found it difficult to include some key variables in their analyses, such as the discipline or field in which the course was offered. Alternately, the correlation, or lack thereof, may indicate an underlying yet untested relationship. Marsh (2007), for example, argued that most research studies in this area support the hypothesis that students who learn more tend to earn higher grades and thus also tend to give higher ratings. Clayson et al. (2006) suggested a reciprocity effect may be at play. Thus, while it is not clear what the issue is, what is clear is that we cannot depend on student ratings of instructors or instruction to be indicative of student learning. Benton and Li (2015) found that when students took on some share of responsibility for learning, they gave the instructor higher ratings. Thus, whether or not a relationship exists, there may be alternative explanations for the result.

## Are Student Evaluations Valid and Reliable?

Some studies of student evaluations of teaching indicate that they are, at least from a statistical perspective, reliable and valid measures of teaching effectiveness. Studies also show a high correlation with student evaluations and other measures of teaching effectiveness, such as peer observation and external peer review of materials (Abrami et al., 1990; Berk, 2013). On the other hand, in a review of the research, Spooren et al. (2013) found the utility and validity ascribed to student evaluation of teaching to be questionable:

> Our systematic use of the meta-validity framework of Onwuegbuzie et al. (2009), however, shows that many types of validity of SET remain at stake. Because conclusive evidence has not been found yet, such evaluations should be considered fragile, as important stakeholders (i.e., the subjects of

> evaluations and their educational performance) are often judged according to indicators of effective teaching (in some cases, a single indicator), the value of which continues to be contested in the research literature. (p. 32)

Thus, the research is not entirely conclusive on this issue.

## Are Student Evaluations Biased?

For many years, studies showed no gender bias in ratings, particularly in studies where the researchers analyzed large numbers of courses from multiple disciplines (Li & Benton, 2017). Several meta-analyses and research summaries also failed to find meaningful gender differences and, thus, concluded there was no gender bias in student ratings (for example, see Algozzine et al., 2004; Arreola, 2000; Centra, 2009; Gravestock & Gregor-Greenleaf, 2008; Huston, 2005; Theall & Franklin, 2001; Wright & Jenkins-Guarnieri, 2012). Li and Benton (2017) had a sample of 25,243 instructors from 256 U.S. institutions and found that that "Instructor gender has no meaningful effects on student ratings of either overall summary measures or instructor use of teaching methods, in both STEM or non-STEM fields" (p. 10). They also criticized and rejected findings of studies that found gender bias, arguing that these results are:

> More an artifact of research design than students' favoritism of one gender over the other. When gender differences have been found in SRI, they have usually occurred in laboratory studies, where students rated descriptions of fictitious teachers who varied in gender ... In contrast, in studies conducted on ratings of actual teachers in the classroom, researchers have found, as we did, no meaningful differences due to gender or only a very weak relationship that favors female instructors. (p. 10)

A growing number of studies, however, suggest that student biases may affect their ratings of instructors, particularly bias against women (e.g., Anderson & Smith, 2005; Davis, 2010; Gilroy, 2007; Lazos, 2011; Martin, 2016; Mengel, et al., 2019; Mitchell & Martin, 2018; Reid, 2010; Smith, 2007, 2009; Smith & Hawkins, 2011; Smith & Johnson-Bailey, 2012). For example, researchers have found that gender bias can cause female instructors to be rated worse than objectively less effective male instructors (Boring et al., 2016). Bias can affect ratings of "objective" items like promptness (Boring et al., 2016; MacNell et al., 2015), it can vary by discipline (Boring et al., 2016; Mengel et al., 2019), and it can be associated with ethnicity and gender (Chisadza et al., 2019). Thus, bias does appear to be a concern with student ratings.

Esarey and Valdes (2020) conducted a simulation in which they assumed the most positive findings possible from previously published research reports. That is, assumed that student evaluations were correlated with teaching effectiveness, that they were reliable measures, and that they did not discriminate due to biases not related to instruction. They found that, even under these ideal circumstances, student evaluations of instructors and instruction can produce an unacceptably high error rate. That is, scores failed to reliably identify the best teachers. The researchers attributed the problem to imprecision in the relationship between the evaluations and the instructor quality. They recommended evaluating instruction using multiple measures, all of which are imperfect, in order to achieve a fairer and more useful result.

Our takeaway from research on student ratings is that student evaluations can add value to the process of assessing and evaluating teaching because they are an indicator of student satisfaction. However, they are also sufficiently questionable as a measure because of the issues and challenges outlined here, and, therefore, should not be accepted as the sole measure of effective teaching. Instead, a better approach is to have multiple measures to document, assess, and evaluate teaching effectiveness.

## KNOWING HOW: AN ACTIVE APPROACH FOR ASSESSING AND EVALUATING TEACHING

There are many ways to collect information about teaching activities, accomplishments, and effectiveness. We suggest that an engaged teacher take an active stance by thinking through the various measures and selecting the best ones to capture their intellectual effort.

### Gather Evidence from Students

When we think about and reflect on our teaching, we tend to do so in isolation. Students, however, can be a great source of feedback on teaching and learning. There are several strategies that will allow you to gather data from students related to your effectiveness, the course, or student learning. Following are a few suggestions.

#### DIRECT EVIDENCE

According to Bain (2004), effective college teachers are constantly looking for results of learning, and in particular, they focus on the progress students are making. That means an initial assessment of the students' level followed by consistent assessment of the progress students have made during the course with the teacher's guidance. In addition to their focus on gauging student learning, effective faculty are also concerned about their own learning and growth as teachers. The best teachers excel at improving student learning, especially students from weaker academic backgrounds, and incorporate systemic strategies for monitoring student progress as well as soliciting student feedback to evaluate the teacher's own progress (Bain, 2004).

To gather such evidence, collect examples of student work that documents what each student has accomplished during the term (Barkley & Major, 2016). For example, you might review examples of work for students who earned an A, B, C, and so forth along with a grade distribution to determine and document growth and development. Or you might consider a technique such as First Day Final. In this strategy, students take a non-graded test the first day of the term that consists of questions that are similar to the final exam, and then identify the questions they found easiest and those they found most difficult. At the end of the term, students take the real, graded final exam, and the results are used as a reference point to demonstrate learning gains and achievement over time. See our publication *Learning Assessment Techniques: A Handbook for College Faculty* (pp. 78-84) for specific guidance.

### INDIRECT EVIDENCE: STUDENT OPINIONS

Student perceptions of you as the instructor, the course, and of their own success at learning can also provide good information for assessment and evaluation of teaching. Consider the following options:

- **Early feedback form:** Use an early feedback form, similar to the one that will be on the course evaluation at the end of the term, to gather anonymous responses and suggestions for improvement while there is still time to make change.
- **Midterm feedback form:** Use a form to gather information you will use for improvement. It could be as simple as asking students to say what is going well and what could be improved.
- **Cross Academy Techniques (CATs):** Several of the techniques on our companion site, The K. Patricia Cross Academy (*kpcrossacademy.org*), enable you to get feedback from students on teaching. Indeed, under "Activity Type," you can sort the techniques by "Learning Assessment." For example, CAT 21: Post-Test Analysis is a two-stage process that is divided into several steps designed to help students develop greater awareness of their test-preparing and test-taking skills. The information students provide can offer you rich insight in to how well they believe they are learning the material you are teaching.

## Gather Evidence from Colleagues

While peer review of research is standard practice in most professional fields, peer review of teaching did not become well-established until the late 20th century. Although designed as a way to improve the quality of evidence for tenure and promotion decisions, peer review has promoted a greater emphasis on faculty collaboration for the purpose of ongoing improvement. Reciprocal classroom visits, new faculty mentoring, and team teaching are just a few ways that peer review of teaching has encouraged faculty members to work with each other. Possible options include the following:

- observations of classroom teaching,
- review of course materials (e.g., syllabi, assignments, rubrics),
- review of student work,
- interviews with students, and
- review of teaching and course portfolios.

## Gather Evidence From Yourself

Many faculty gather evidence from students, and a few work collaboratively with their colleagues. Fewer, however, consider themselves to be useful sources of information. Yet self-generated data can be a particularly useful source of information for documenting teaching. Consider the following strategies:

- Videotape yourself teaching.
- Create a teaching log or journal.
- Write out your philosophies.
- Capture your written work products, including syllabi, assignments, and assessments.
- Keep your course planning notes.
- Write a self-reflection.

The main questions to consider are the following:

- What did I do well?
- What could I have done better?
- What kept the students engaged?

- Where did students have difficulties?
- When did students get lost or lose interest?
- If I could do this session over again, what would I change?
- How could I go about making those changes?

In Figure 14.1: Three Sources of Teaching Assessment Data, we provide an illustration (adapted from Brent & Felder, 2004) and offer some commentary about the kinds of data individuals can provide.

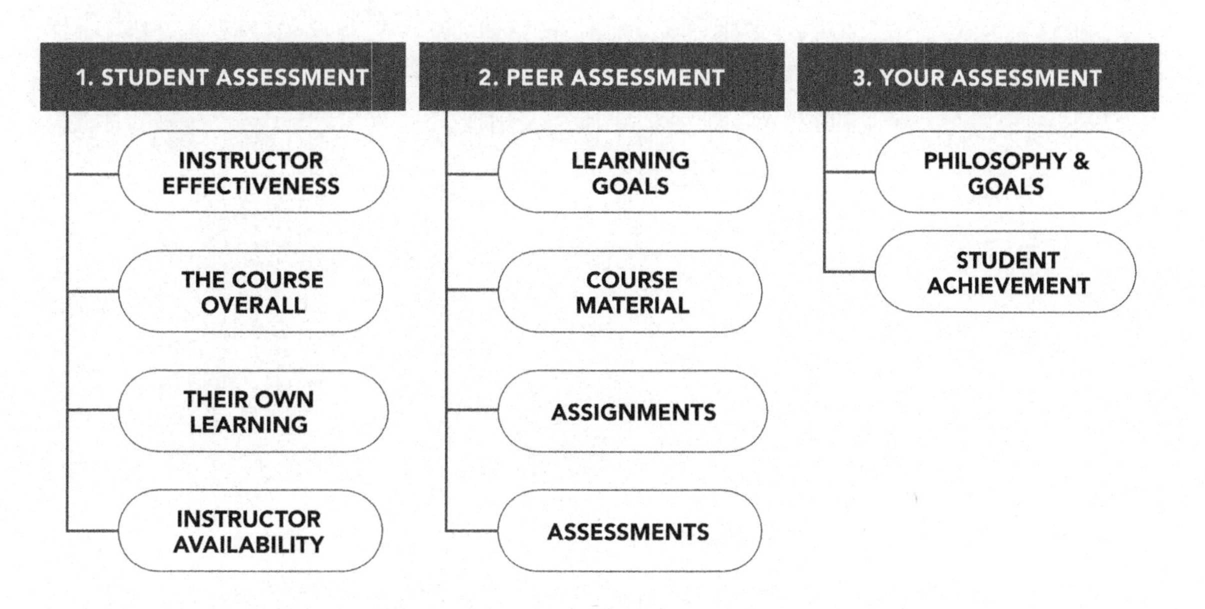


**Figure 14.1. Three Sources of Teaching Assessment Data**

## Document Your Work in Each Functional Area of Engaged Teaching

While thinking of the different sources of information is important, so is thinking through how to document your knowledge. Consider the suggestions in Table 14.1: Documenting Your Knowledge of Specific Domains in Engaged Teaching. The bottom line is to consider the process of teaching from multiple sources of data in order to provide a more holistic view of your teaching.

## CONCLUSION

If you teach long enough, you are bound to get an evaluation that includes a comment from a student or supervisor that stings. The feedback can feel unfair, mean-spirited, or simply wrong. We have both received such constructive criticisms in our decades-long careers, and even though the fault-finding statements are surrounded by largely positive ones, it is these negative ones that stand out and continue to irk us years later. Evaluations of our teaching can be uncomfortable, but they are the only way we can be keenly aware of what is and what is not working in our courses. Thus, we need to have our teaching assessed and evaluated with sophistication and regularity. As an engaged teacher, you can assume an active stance toward assessing and evaluating your own teaching, thus ensuring that it is not only fair and accurate, but that it also represents the effort you invest in it.

| DOMAIN | DESCRIPTION | SAMPLE EVIDENCE THAT CAN BE ASSESSED OR EVALUATED |
|---|---|---|
| **DEVELOP A FOUNDATIONAL KNOWLEDGE BASE** | Your knowledge of your field as well as your knowledge of pedagogical practices and student learning | • Attendance at discipline- or teaching-focused conferences and conference sessions<br>• Evidence of professional development courses and workshops completed<br>• List of books related to teaching that you have recently read<br>• A teaching philosophy statement |
| **PLAN THE COURSE** | A focus on the clarity of the learning outcomes and alignment of the instructional activities and course materials with those outcomes | • List of goals and objectives linked to instructional activities and assessments<br>• Sample course syllabi, homework assignments, lesson plans, assignment prompts<br>• A completed course design template following Backward Design or Teaching for Significant Learning principles<br>• Exams, quizzes, samples of written feedback on graded work, graded student exams or papers |
| **ESTABLISH THE CLIMATE** | Course accessibility as well as your own responsiveness and sensitivity to the diversity of the student population, including rapport with students and your knowledge of student resources and services | • List of activities to make students feel welcome and valued<br>• List of course materials and activities that document efforts to promote equity and inclusion<br>• List of efforts to build class community |
| **CHOOSE THE BEST INSTRUCTIONAL METHODS** | Your choice of instructional activities guided by research on learning and the means by which you facilitate these activities | • Lecture outlines or lesson plans<br>• List of instructional methods used, with research articles that document their efficacy<br>• Video recordings of teaching<br>• Classroom observation records<br>• Instructional materials such as handouts or problem sets |
| **CONTINUOUSLY IMPROVE TEACHING** | Evidence of student learning and engagement using direct and indirect measures, participation in professional development events and programs, and reflective practice | • Student or peer evaluations (formal or informal)<br>• List of assessment of teaching measures undertaken<br>• Samples of completed student work (with their permission) such as pre-tests and post-tests that show student progress towards meeting the learning outcomes, comparisons of student work at the beginning and end of term to document growth, sample student projects, students' lab books, and so forth<br>• Documents capturing reflective practice<br>• Attendance at teaching-focused conferences along with sessions attended<br>• List of SoTL publications read or written |

**Table 14.1. Documenting Your Knowledge of Specific Domains in Engaged Teaching**

## FOCUS ON ONLINE TEACHING

The information we share in the main body of this chapter applies to both onsite and online teaching, but here we provide additional insights focused specifically on teaching online, hybrid, and blended courses.

### What: Evaluating Online Teaching

Assessment and evaluation of online teaching means engaging in the systematic process of determining whether we have accomplished our goals and enhanced student learning. The teaching goals and anticipated learning outcomes are likely similar to those that we have for our onsite teaching, but we may gather information in different ways.

### Why: Evaluating Online Teaching

As we noted in the main body of this chapter, student evaluations of teaching have some value, but they also have some distinct challenges. We have argued that to have truly useful information, you need to go beyond student evaluations and gather other evidence to be able to understand and document your teaching effectiveness. This holds true for online teaching as well, and gathering data from online courses for the purpose of assessing and evaluating teaching online is essential for an engaged teacher. It is critical to the improvement of teaching and learning online, and it is also likely important to gather information to provide to external stakeholders.

### How: Evaluating Online Teaching

When assessing and valuating online teaching, consider the following questions:

#### WHAT COMPONENTS OF ONLINE TEACHING SHOULD BE EVALUATED?

How can we effectively measure aspects of online teaching such as instructional design, course content, or instructor presence? Consider what exactly it is you are evaluating. The topics of the chapters in this book provide a good starting point, for example you could evaluate any of the following:

- course goals, objectives, and outcomes;
- grading and assessment methods;
- visual design;
- student engagement;
- community;
- inclusivity and accessibility;
- lecturing effectiveness;
- discussion effectiveness; and
- collaborative learning effectiveness.

#### WHAT IS YOUR PRIMARY PURPOSE FOR EVALUATING ONLINE TEACHING?

Consider whether you are evaluating your course for formative reasons, for example to improve your online teaching, or whether it is for summative reasons, for example to share with a promotion and tenure or merit committee or for part of an online program evaluation. The purpose will likely guide your decisions.

#### WHAT DATA SHOULD YOU GATHER?

Remember from earlier in this chapter that you may want to collect data from students, such as direct evidence of their work or indirect evidence such as their opinions about their learning. Data collection can be efficient in an online environment, where you have many data collection tools at your disposal (for example, polls, quizzes, and discussions). You may want to consider having a colleague review your online course materials or observe a synchronous session. And you may want to use information you gathered through reflection on online teaching as a part of your evaluation; it is a form of data.

#### HOW WILL YOU ANALYZE THE DATA?

Consider the forms of data you have as well as typical approaches to evaluation of these data.

- **Quantitative data analysis.** Data may be quantitative, which means that they come in the form of numbers. Test and quiz scores are a form of quantitative data, as are rubric evaluations. The following are forms of quantitative data analysis:
  - » **Simple counts and tallies** are the sums or totals of several numbers together.
  - » **Descriptive statistics** refer to what researchers use to describe sets of numbers, such as student test scores.
- **Qualitative data analysis.** Data may be qualitative. These data tend to be associated with words or narrative, such as those in student discussion postings, essays, and papers. Qualitative data are also available in artistic representations. Two common qualitative analytic approaches are as follows:
  - » **Key Word Analysis** involves examining words that have some sort of meaning in the larger context of the data. Key word analysis then is a way of summarizing a narrative data set, such as a set of essays.

» **Thematic analysis** is a method of identifying, analyzing, and reporting patterns in the data (Braun & Clarke, 2006). Thematic analysis at a fundamental level is "the process of recovering the theme or themes that are embodied and dramatized in the evolving meanings and imagery of the work" (van Manen, 1990, p. 78). This approach to analyzing a qualitative data set provides a general sense of the information through repeated reading and manipulation of the data.

### WHAT WILL YOU DO WITH THE INFORMATION?

One of the primary purposes for evaluating online teaching is to improve it going forward. You should consider the kinds of improvements you can make to your class based on what you have learned. Another important step is to consider how you will share the information with stakeholders or peers. Might you consider presenting or publishing based on what you have learned? If you answered yes, consider our final chapter on the scholarship of teaching and learning (SoTL).

*I can think of no action that would do quite as much for the improvement of teaching and learning as to let a thousand classroom laboratories bloom across the nation.*

**—K. PATRICIA CROSS**

CHAPTER 15

# Engaging in the Scholarship of Teaching and Learning (SoTL)

When Lee Shulman became president of the Carnegie Foundation for the Advancement of Teaching in 1997, he had several items on his agenda, but among the top were to move the foundation's headquarters from Princeton to Stanford, to recruit K. Patricia Cross to the foundation's board, and to change the culture of academia. He achieved all three. While the first two are likely under the radar of most college educators, the third has impacted everybody teaching in higher education today. Shulman and his colleagues, particularly Pat Hutchings and Mary Huber, worked tirelessly to elevate the status of teaching by supporting the development of a new discipline: *the scholarship of teaching and learning* (SoTL). SoTL is the systematic investigation of teaching and learning to advance the practice of teaching by making inquiry findings public so that they can be extended to other settings. In this way, SoTL provides the evidentiary basis for improving classroom teaching practice in higher education. How does this relate to engaged teaching?

Engaged teachers invest the intellectual effort required to improve their teaching so that they can improve student learning. One of the first steps toward achieving this is acquiring expertise not only in one's content area, but also in pedagogy. It also requires gathering evidence of student learning outcomes and the effectiveness of one's teaching methods in order to assess and improve both. Additionally, it means moving out of one's comfort zone to experiment with and then reflect upon new pedagogical processes and strategies. But at its best, engaged teaching also means sharing what we have learned in order to contribute to a base of pedagogical knowledge that can be accessed by our peers. Thus, truly engaged teachers not only focus on making their own teaching effective, but they also make their work visible and share it with other teachers who can benefit from the effort. In this chapter, we offer guidance on how you can build upon your work as an engaged teacher to contribute to the scholarship of teaching and learning.

## KNOWING WHAT: ABOUT SCHOLARSHIP OF TEACHING AND LEARNING

True scholarly work builds upon the work of others. When Shulman chose to focus the Carnegie Foundation's work on elevating teaching, he was following in the footsteps of those who preceded him, including Andrew Carnegie himself. The charter mission statement of the foundation asserts that it was established "To do all things necessary to encourage, uphold, and dignify the profession of teaching" (Carnegie Foundation, 2021). Shulman was also drawing on the work of K. Patricia Cross, who in the decade before Shulman's presidency, argued that college teachers offered the most powerful means for improving learning in higher education and proposed that they use their classrooms as laboratories for the study of learning and make the results of their research public.

In *Scholarship Reconsidered: Priorities of the Professoriate*, Ernest Boyer (1990), Shulman's immediate predecessor as president of the Carnegie Foundation, responded to the criticism that the academy was privileging research over teaching at the college and university level. He urged faculty to reevaluate the purpose of scholarship, arguing "the time has come to move beyond the tired old 'teaching versus research' debate" and to "honor the full scope of academic work" (p. xii). Boyer proposed that educators focus their work on four distinct but overlapping domains of scholarship: discovery, integration, application, and teaching. He argued that these four scholarship functions are inseparable and depend on "recognition that knowledge is acquired through research, synthesis, practice, and teaching" (p. 24). Of those four functions, the scholarship of teaching was the one that resonated most with educators. Teachers also appreciated its acknowledgement of the intensive scholarly and intellectual effort required to design and deliver information; of the four functions, this area has enjoyed the most scrutiny in research.

### The Goals of SoTL

Ever since the publication of Boyer's book and Shulman's essays in 1987 and 1991, respectively, educators have been occupied with the question of why they should engage in the scholarship of teaching (Major & Braxton, 2020). Researchers like Rice (1991), Hutchings and Shulman (1999), Kreber (2002), and Chick and Poole (2013) offer insight on the goals as well as the objectives of the scholarship of teaching. For example, Hutchings and Shulman (1999) argued that the scholarship of teaching is a method for advancing the teaching profession, with its dual focus on the improvement of one's own instruction as well as the improvement of the practice of teaching as a whole. They argued further that the purpose of the scholarship of teaching is to advance student learning, specifically by pursuing knowledge about how learning occurs and the conditions under which students best learn. Their pursuits directly connected teaching and learning, and like much of the scholarly research, contributed to the prevalence of the term, scholarship of teaching and learning. Chick and Poole (2013) wrote that SoTL provides a framework for faculty development and also a path for ongoing improvement in their teaching by giving teachers a more cohesive and informed manner to consider their work as teachers and their students' efforts as learners.

## The Practice of SoTL

Multiple methods, frameworks, models, and other schema have been offered to establish what SoTL is (for example, see Felton, 2013; Gayle et al., 2013; Glassick et al., 1997; Gurung & Wilson, 2013; Huber & Hutchings, 2005; Huber & Morreale, 2002; Hutchings et al., 2011; Kern et al., 2015; Kreber, 2001; McKinney, 2013; Miller-Young & Yeo, 2015; Murray, 2008; Trigwell et al., 2000; Wilson-Doenges & Gurung, 2013). For instance, Huber and Hutchings (2005) wrote that SoTL entails "... viewing the work of the classroom as a site for inquiry, asking and answering questions about students' learning in ways that can improve one's own classroom and also advance the larger profession of teaching" (p. 1). And Hutchings et al. (2011) further argued:

> The scholarship of teaching and learning encompasses a broad set of practices that engage teachers in looking closely and critically at student learning for the purpose of improving their own courses and programs. It is perhaps best understood as an approach that marries scholarly inquiry to any of the intellectual tasks that comprise the work of teaching — designing a course, facilitating classroom activities, trying out new pedagogical ideas, advising, writing student learning outcomes, evaluating programs. When activities like these are undertaken with serious questions about student learning in mind, one enters the territory of the scholarship of teaching and learning. (p. 7)

Thus, SoTL includes an intellectual investigation into the processes of both teaching and learning. In addition to the intent and pursuits of SoTL, there is also the expectation of sharing the results and using those findings to make improvements. As Chick (n.d.) outlined, SoTL does not just involve raising important questions and providing answers rooted in visible student learning and systemic analysis. It also involves sharing the results of that analysis publicly to invite review and to contribute to the body of knowledge on student learning in a variety of contexts and aims to improve student learning by strengthening the practice of teaching (one's own and others'; para. 2).

Likewise, Trigwell and Shale (2004) stressed the necessity of widely sharing findings and the peer review process in establishing teaching and learning as a scholarly pursuit:

> We see scholarship as being about making scholarly processes transparent and publicly available for peer scrutiny ... We see teaching as a scholarly process aimed at making learning possible. It, therefore, follows that we see the scholarship of teaching as about making transparent, for public scrutiny, how learning has been made possible. (p. 525)

Similarly, Healey (2000) emphasized the need to share SoTL thus:

> Developing the scholarship of teaching is more than striving to be an excellent teacher or being scholarly. Whereas striving for excellence involves a high level of proficiency in stimulating students and fostering their learning in a variety of appropriate ways, a scholarly approach to teaching entails being familiar with the latest ideas in one's subject and also being informed by current ideas for teaching that subject. A scholarly approach also involves evaluating and reflecting on one's teaching practice and the student learning which follows. The scholarship of teaching shares these characteristics of excellent and scholarly teaching, but, in addition, involves communicating and disseminating about the teaching and learning practices of one's subject. It also entails investigating questions related to how students learn within a discipline. (p. 172)

Therefore, though SoTL differs from the scholarship of discovery in its single-minded examination of course-level instruction and learning, it is related to discovery as it requires establishing concrete research questions, undergoing reviews of the most effective scholarship on the topic, completing methodical examinations, compiling thorough data analyses, and publicly sharing findings in methods like scholarly publications or conference presentations (Major & Braxton, 2020). Additionally, publication involves critical peer evaluation. Also, similarly to the scholarship of discovery, SoTL demands researchers use past findings as a basis for further investigation.

## Article and Analytic Type

Drawing from Weimer (2006), article types for SoTL include personal accounts of change, recommended practice reports, recommended content reports, and personal narratives. These different article types can be described as follows.

- In **personal accounts of change**, faculty share their own experiences of introducing new instructional strategies, methods, or techniques into their courses.
- In **recommended practice reports**, instructors generally share recommendations about pedagogical methods, techniques, or strategies. The advice may be broad or it may be specific to a given course or subject. And the recommendations may be based on personal experience, research, or a blend of the two.
- In **recommended content reports**, teachers offer advice about specific content to teach or specific ways to teach a subject, focusing less on pedagogy and more on the skills, perspectives, or ideas necessary to transmit material or how it should be delivered.
- In **personal narratives**, teachers generally do not offer advice but instead intend their work to be a self-reflective analysis in which the author critically examines their professional development. Some examples of personal narratives are personal teaching philosophies, position papers, or any pedagogical content that includes a personal opinion.

Weimer (2006) also described multiple analytic types: descriptive research, quantitative investigations, qualitative studies, mixed methods, literature reviews, and personal reflections. Descriptions of each type follow.

- Scholars use **descriptive research** to collect and assess data, either quantitative or qualitative, describing innovations or approaches to teaching. This research is neither experimental nor quasi-experimental; instead, the goal is to summarize the current state of something, not to determine causation.
- **Quantitative investigations** are experiments that include treatment and control groups, and manipulate variables between or across the groups.
- **Qualitative Studies** are an expansive analytic type that can differ from one discipline to another. Inductive studies generally depend on interviews

or analyses of written materials with the intent to study phenomena in their natural settings. Analyses are then built from these interpretations. Analyses are then built from these interpretations.

- Scholars engaged in **personal reflections** typically write reflections, with the intent to explore their personal experiences, reflections on events, or perhaps thoughts and feelings that relate to instruction and learning in higher education.

Engaged teachers who who choose to engage in SoTL benefit from understanding the various approaches to the genre.

## KNOWING WHY: RESEARCH ON SCHOLARSHIP OF TEACHING AND LEARNING

Engaged teachers are exceedingly busy individuals. They constantly invest energy and effort into the process of teaching as they aim to improve student learning. Why should they care about the SoTL?

### Continuous Increase in SoTL Publications

We continue to see a rising interest in the development and publication of articles that focus on SoTL. Indeed, a search of Google Scholar to find articles that include the term *Scholarship of Teaching*, shows that the number of published pieces has increased each year over the past decade. Additionally, between 2010 and 2020, researchers published almost 50,000 articles concerning SoTL. We show the yearly breakdown in Table 15.1: Number of Articles Including the Term *Scholarship of Teaching and Learning*, 2010–2020.

| YEAR | NUMBER OF ARTICLES |
|---|---|
| **2020** | 7,280 |
| **2019** | 6,030 |
| **2018** | 5,690 |
| **2017** | 5,330 |
| **2016** | 4,630 |
| **2015** | 4,180 |
| **2014** | 3,630 |
| **2013** | 3,390 |
| **2012** | 3,010 |
| **2011** | 2,660 |
| **2010** | 2,220 |
| **TOTAL** | **48,050** |

**Table 15.1. Number of Articles Including the Term *Scholarship of Teaching and Learning*, 2010–2020**

Additionally, as Tight (2018) observed, pieces concerning SoTL continue to be published around the English-speaking world. This is just a handful examples of publications from the last decade, listed by nation:

- **Australia:** Greaves, 2015; Bennett et al., 2016
- **Canada:** Simmons and Poole, 2016
- **Ireland:** O'Sullivan, 2011
- **Malaysia:** Harland et al., 2014
- **New Zealand:** Haigh et al., 2011
- **Singapore:** Geertsema, 2016
- **South Africa:** Leibowitz and Bozalek, 2016; Mtawa et al., 2016
- **Sweden:** Lindberg-Sand and Sonesson 2008; Martensson et al., 2011
- **Trinidad and Tobago:** Blair, 2014
- **United Kingdom:** Craig, 2014
- **United States:** Willingham-McLain, 2015; Burns, 2017

Although there are now thousands of articles on SoTL, there is a relative dearth of reviews or syntheses of the extant literature. There are, however, some notable exceptions. For instance, Gurung et al. (2008) examined the state of SoTL, with a specific focus on psychology as a discipline. Additionally, Fanghanel et al. (2015) reported on SoTL's characteristics, definitions, and purposes in the United Kingdom. And Tight (2018) provided a review of SoTL articles contained in Scopus and Google Scholar, but focused primarily on the descriptions of SoTL and not the articles presenting SoTL findings. Meanwhile, Divan et al. (2017) studied research from a two-year window that could be found in three journals that focus on SoTL. Similarly, Booth and Woollacott (2018) reviewed SoTL studies with a focus on work found in Google Scholar from 2010 to 2016. These works suggest a steadily growing scholarly interest in SoTL.

## SoTL's Influence on Students

Engaging in SoTL can influence student learning (Condon et al., 2016; Trigwell, 2013). Trigwell (2013), for example, found support for connections between teachers using certain aspects of SoTL and the likelihood of improving their students´ learning. In a survey of 56 faculty members, he found that when the faculty viewed teaching as scholarly inquiry, went through the process of peer review, and made their findings public, there was a stronger likelihood of improving student learning outcomes. Moreover, academic reports of university-level SoTL programs generally describe favorable outcomes. For example, 66% of the SoTL projects at Southeast Missouri State (i.e., 100 courses involving 4,500 students) showed enhanced student learning (Waterman et al., 2010).

### SoTL and Improvements to Faculty Work

SoTL also can positively influence faculty (Cox, 2004; Voelker & Martin, 2013). For example, faculty employed in the University of Wisconsin System who engaged with SoTL reported positive benefits from their participation. Sixty-two percent of participants published SoTL-related works (Voelker & Martin, 2013). In addition, Marcketti et al. (2015) found that faculty chose to engage in SoTL work for many different benefits, even beyond the benefits provided in promotion and tenure. The researchers also looked at the influence SoTL had on the "SoTL champions" on one university campus. Professors who engaged in SoTL reported continuing their SoTL research even after promotion and tenure due to the synergy it generated between research and teaching and the way that SoTL allowed for building additional community beyond traditional disciplinary silos.

## KNOWING HOW: AN ENGAGED APPROACH TO SCHOLARSHIP OF TEACHING AND LEARNING

SoTL involves the systematic inquiry into student learning which advances the practice of teaching in higher education by making inquiry findings public. Building on this definition, Felton (2013) suggested five principles for good practice in SoTL: (1) inquiry focused on student learning, (2) grounded in context, (3) methodologically sound, (4) conducted in partnership with students, and (5) appropriately public. We use these five principles for good practice in SoTL to offer some specific suggestions for engaging in SoTL.

### Identify the Problem You Hope to Solve

SoTL generally starts with determining the problem you aim to solve. Typically, the problems are rooted in our own classrooms and, often, focus on how best to help students learn.

### Determine the Research Question

This is how Bernstein and Bass (2005) framed the questions that often motivate academics engaging in SoTL: "How did they know that their students were learning?" as well as "Did the students' learning promise to last?" They suggested, "By asking these questions, many faculty discovered early on whatever most interested — or eluded — them about their students' learning that could not be answered simply by looking at regularly assigned course work" (p. 39). Likewise, Hutchings (2000) argued there are four primary types of questions in SoTL:

- **"What works" questions** pursue evidence about the efficacy of teaching approaches or compare teaching styles in individual contexts.
- **"What is" questions** aim to describe but not assess the efficacy of different teaching styles, or to describe the ways students learn.
- **Visions of the possible questions** relate to teaching and learning goals that have not yet been met or are new to the instructor.
- **Theory building questions** are intended to develop theoretical frameworks for SoTL similar to those used in other fields.

Examining the existing body of published scholarship, "What Works" and "What Is" questions are the most common.

## Choose a Design

Considering Pat Hutchings's (2000) "What Is" and "What Works" question types, we should evaluate the following question designs:

### "WHAT IS" DESIGNS

"What Is" projects can vary in size and scope, from small (e.g., case studies involving one student, one class period, or a small individual course) to large (e.g., many students [a "large N"] participating in several activities over time). Often, "What is" designs necessitate long descriptions, overviews of learning dynamics, or other specific details examining student learning, or what occurs during moments of learning.

### "WHAT WORKS" DESIGNS

"What Works" designs examine the efficacy of or change created by an assignment, tool, or other action. These projects typically necessitate traditional experiments involving randomly assigned control and intervention groups. However, in SoTL, this model isn't always feasible, and quasi-experimental methods may be implemented as a result.

## Identify Evidence

SoTL generally includes collection of the evidence of learning, which can come in forms that may not be traditionally used to gauge student achievement. Though the reflections of a faculty member, their peers, the self-reflection of students, and theories can help answer some questions about student learning, SoTL also necessitates the prioritization of direct evidence that student learning has occurred. This evidence can take the form of quantitative or qualitative data, and can include:

- test scores;
- written, oral, and visual projects;
- grades; and
- formative and summative evaluations (Barkley & Major, 2016).

## Determine Data Collection Methods

When outlining your data collection, make sure you provide detailed descriptions of the participants, including sample size, how they ere selected and recruited, and the relationship between the participants and the researcher. Also, provide detailed descriptions of how the data were collected, including instruments or protocols used; when data were collected; and how the data were stored, managed, and analyzed. Additionally, describe your efforts to maintain the quality of your research design and findings (i.e., trustworthiness, validity, realiability, and so forth).

## Remember the Institutional Review Board

Because SoTL research includes an examination of student learning, it is considered research that involves human subjects. Each college and university has its own ethics review committee, generally called an Institutional Review Board (IRB), but also referred to as an Ethics Review Board (ERB) or a Research Ethics Board (REB). This process may be unfamiliar to academics who have not completed research involving living human beings:

> [Because] SoTL researchers in some disciplines are unaccustomed to needing IRB approval for their disciplinary research (i.e., it does not involve human participants), there has been ambiguity among these SoTL researchers regarding the IRB process, and similar ambiguity among IRB evaluators as to what review category best fits SoTL research. (Meyers, 2007, para. 1)

Academics pursuing SoTL should be aware of any ethical concerns regarding their work involving students. One reason for concern is the inherent difference in power between faculty and students (i.e., the power to assign grades, affect status in a degree program, write letters of recommendation, and so forth). Incorporating some basic ethical practices, as outlined by an IRB, can offset this power dynamic.

## Analyze Evidence

Historically, social science research has depended on quantitative analyses, which are strong at assessing how many or how much; implementing structures to predict, confirm, deduce, or test hypotheses; and aspiring to specific, representative conclusions. Some examples include Likert-scale surveys, content analyses of texts, and counts. SoTL scholar and biologist Craig Nelson (2003) recommended the use of qualitative instruments and models "to help counter the tendency in some circles to attempt to apply to SoTL the models of research that recognize only quantitative studies" (p. 90). Meanwhile, William M. K. Trochim author of *Research Methods Knowledge Base* (2006) wrote that "All quantitative data is based upon qualitative judgments; and all qualitative data can be described and manipulated numerically" (para. 3). Remember that quantitative and qualitative data have varying goals and strengths and should be used with deliberation.

## Consider Publishing

One of the features of SoTL is dissemination of findings to a broader audience who can benefit from the findings. Following are suggestions when you consider publication:

1. When developing a manuscript, remember to consider the mission, format, and requirements of your target publication, in addition to your own purpose.
2. Define your purpose and your target audience prior to starting your work.
3. Determine possible target publications (e.g., journals, newsletters, scholarly magazines, and edited books) before completing your manuscript. Make sure your purpose aligns with the mission of the publication and your content aligns with submission guidelines. In short, find the right fit for your contribution.
4. Determine whether your manuscript is a better fit for discipline-specific journals or broader pedagogical publications.
5. Research your target outlet long before finishing your work. Then, when writing your manuscript, focus on the mission, format, and requirements of the outlet, in addition to your purpose and material.

6. Ensure your literature review is updated and comprehensive. Make sure you cite any relevant material published in the same outlet to which you are submitting. Make sure you cite key scholars in the field.

7. Use accepted formats for education research. Unless you are writing personal reflections, literature reviews, or scholarly essays, most SoTL publications will include the same sections: introduction, literature/research review, a method section including specific forms of evidence, conclusions, and recommendations. The exact format, however, will differ by publication, audience, and discipline.

## CONCLUSION

The Scholarship of Teaching and Learning has roots that extend back through the history of education. Whenever teachers have pondered why and how students learn, there has been some version of SoTL. As a more systematic approach that is recognized as its own scholarly discipline, however, it is relatively new. Scholars who have been taught to publish according to individual fields or disciplinary standards may initially be uncomfortable with writing and publishing SoTL research. This may be due partly to the relative absence of training in this field of scholarship in masters or doctoral programs for academic disciplines (Austin, 2002; Bess, 1977; Jencks & Riesman, 1977). Fortunately, there are now multiple resources available to guide you in your efforts should you decide to pursue scholarship in this area. Investigating the connections between your teaching and students' learning is essential to engaged teaching. Using the knowledge you gain through that process to help your peers takes your work to a whole new level.

## FOCUS ON ONLINE TEACHING

The information we share in the main body of this chapter applies to both onsite and online teaching, but here we provide additional insights focused specifically on teaching online, hybrid, and blended courses.

### What: SoTL for Online Teaching and Learning

SoTL in online courses means a systematic investigation conducted to advance online teaching practice through a public presentation of findings.

### Why: SoTL for Online Teaching and Learning

As we noted in the main part of this chapter, publishing in the SoTL field is gaining in popularity across the globe. Perhaps not surprisingly given the shift to remote teaching and learning during the COVID-19 pandemic, citations for SoTL carried out in online courses are also on the rise. As of August 31, 2021, a search of Google Scholar using the terms *scholarship of teaching* and *online learning* returned 2,690 publications.

Engaging in SoTL is an important way to improve online teaching practices, both your own as well as the practices of those who might learn from your work. For this reason, engaging with SoTL in online courses is imperative. We need to discover what works best in online courses and to share that information with others who can use it to improve their own courses.

### How: SoTL for Online Teaching and Learning

Consider the following tips for engaging with SoTL when teaching online:

**Identify the topic.** Consider the rationale for engaging in SoTL for your particular online course. What is the problem of online teaching and learning practice you will solve? Who will find this information most useful and why?

**Identify relevant scholarship.** What other scholarship has been done on this topic in online environments? Consider how your work will add to the existing body of scholarship.

**Identify the research question.** What exactly do you want to know about online learning in your particular course?

**Design the study.** Will you implement a quantitative or qualitative study? Why did you make this choice, and why is it the best choice for investigating teaching and learning in your online course?

**Collect the data.** How will you gather data online? Surveys? Videoconference interviews? Collection of learning artifacts? Online surveys? Or other?

**Analyze the data and draw conclusions.** You will likely choose an analytic approach based on your research design. See our Focus on Online Learning section in Chapter 14: Assessing and Evaluating Teaching for additional information.

**Present and publish your SoTL project.** There are several journals that focus on teaching and learning in online environments. These include the *Journal of Educators Online, The Internet and Higher Education, The MERLOT Journal of Online Learning and Teaching (JOLT),* and others.

Don't forget that in order to engage in SoTL in your online course, even though much of the data may be readily available already, particularly if you are using student learning artifacts, you will need to go through the IRB process at your institution in order to present or publish your findings.

# Appendix 1:

## CROSS ACADEMY TECHNIQUES (CATS) AND BOOK CHAPTERS

| CAT # | NAME | CHAPTER |
|---|---|---|
| 1 | Digital Story | 4 (p 73), 5 (p 94), 6 (p 105) |
| 2 | 3-2-1 | 3 (p 45) |
| 3 | Contemporary Issues Journal | 5 (p 90, 94), 8 (p 149), 13 (p 252) |
| 4 | Jigsaw | 11 (p 208), 12 (p 235) |
| 5 | Group Grid | 3 (p 47) |
| 6 | Analytic Teams | 4 (p 73) |
| 7 | Team Jeopardy | 7 (p 139) |
| 8 | Paper Seminar | 9 (p 165) |
| 9 | Three-Minute Message | 5 (p 94) |
| 10 | Quick Write | 3 (p 44), 5 (p 90), 7 (p 135), 10 (p 185, 192), 11 (p 208) |
| 11 | Active Reading Documents | 3 (p 51), 4 (p 73) |
| 12 | Fact or Opinion | 3 (p 44) |
| 13 | Sketch Notes | 4 (p 73), 6 (p 105) |
| 14 | Update Your Classmate | 3 (p 44), 10 (p 185) |
| 15 | Translate That! | 3 (p 48), 10 (p 193) |
| 16 | Guided Notes | 3 (p 52), 5 (p 94), 10 (p 185, 191) |
| 17 | Lecture Engagement Log | 3 (p 52) |

| CAT # | NAME | CHAPTER |
|---|---|---|
| 18 | Support a Statement | 5 (p 90), 7 (p 136), 10 (p 185) |
| 19 | Personal Learning Environment | 2 (p 27), 3 (p 45) |
| 20 | Lecture Wrapper | 3 (p 49) |
| 21 | Post-Test Analysis | 3 (p 46, 51), 4 (p 73), 5 (p 90), 14 (p 262) |
| 22 | Test-Taking Teams | 8 (p 149), 12 (p 224) |
| 23 | Role Play | 3 (p 39), 5 (p 88), 8 (p 146, 148—149) |
| 24 | Case Studies | 5 (p 89), 9 (p 161), 11 (p 214), 15 (p 280) |
| 25 | Triple Jump | 4 (p 73), 5 (p 89) |
| 26 | Dyadic Essays | 12 (p 235) |
| 27 | Variations | 4 (p 72) |
| 28 | Dyadic Interviews | 4 (p 73), 12 (p 234) |
| 29 | Advance Organizers | 6 (p 103) |
| 30 | IRAs | 7 (p 134) |
| 31 | Background Knowledge Probe | 3 (p 44, 51), 6 (p 105) |
| 32 | Online Resource Scavenger Hunt | 7 (p 134) |
| 33 | Frames | 11 (p 208) |
| 34 | Invent the Quiz | 7 (p 131) |
| 35 | Letters | 11 (p 208) |
| 36 | Class Book | 9 (p 165) |
| 37 | Think-Pair-Share | 5 (p 88), 8 (p 147), 10 (p 185), 11 (p 208), 12 (p 235) |

| CAT # | NAME | CHAPTER |
|---|---|---|
| 38 | Affinity Grouping | 9 (p 165) |
| 39 | Comprehensive Factors List | 5 (p 90) |
| 40 | Crib Cards | 5 (p 88) |
| 41 | Cued Notes | 7 (p 136) |
| 42 | Note-Taking Pairs | 7 (p 136) |
| 43 | Punctuated Lecture | 10 (p 193) |
| 44 | Fishbowl | 11 (p 208), 12 (p 235) |
| 45 | Individual Readiness Assurance Tests | 5 (p 89) |
| 46 | Quotation Summaries | 11 (p 208) |
| 47 | What? So What? Now What? Journals | 3 (p 46), 13 (p 252) |
| 48 | Think-Aloud-Pair Problem Solving (TAPPs) | 5 (p 88) |
| 49 | Briefing Paper | 5 (p 94) |
| 50 | Sentence Stem Predictions | 3 (p 44) |

# Appendix 2:

## BOOK CHAPTERS AND CROSS ACADEMY TECHNIQUES (CATs)

| PART 1: FOUNDATIONS | | |
|---|---|---|
| CHAPTER | TITLE | CROSS ACADEMY TECHNIQUES (CATs) |
| 1 | Engaged Teaching—<br>What It Is and Why It Matters | |
| 2 | Developing Pedagogical Content Knowledge | 19 Personal Learning Environment |
| 3 | Understanding Student Learning | 2 3-2-1<br>5 Group Grid<br>10 Quick Write<br>11 Active Reading Documents<br>12 Fact or Opinion<br>14 Update Your Classmate<br>15 Translate That!<br>16 Guided Notes<br>17 Lecture Engagement Log<br>19 Personal Learning Environment<br>20 Lecture Wrapper<br>21 Post-Test Analysis<br>31 Background Knowledge Probe<br>47 What? So What? Now What? Journals<br>50 Sentence Stem Predictions |

| PART 2: PLANNING | | |
|---|---|---|
| **CHAPTER** | **TITLE** | **CROSS ACADEMY TECHNIQUES (CATs)** |
| **4** | Identifying Significant Learning Goals, Objectives, and Outcomes | 1 Digital Story<br>6 Analytic Teams<br>11 Active Reading Documents<br>13 Sketch Notes<br>21 Post-Test Analysis<br>25 Triple Jump<br>27 Variations<br>28 Dyadic Interviews |
| **5** | Assessing and Grading Learning | 1 Digital Story<br>3 Contemporary Issues Journal<br>9 Three-Minute Message<br>10 Quick Write<br>16 Guided Notes<br>21 Post-Test Analysis<br>23 Role Play<br>24 Case Studies<br>25 Triple Jump<br>37 Think-Pair-Share<br>39 Comprehensive Factors List<br>40 Crib Cards (p 10)<br>45 Individual Readiness Assurance Tests<br>48 Think-Aloud-Pair Problem Solving<br>49 Briefing Paper |
| **6** | Attending to Visual Elements in Teaching | 1 Digital Story<br>13 Sketch Notes<br>31 Background Knowledge Probe |
| **PART 3: CLIMATE** | | |
| **7** | Engaging Students | 7 Team Jeopardy<br>10 Quick Write<br>30 IRAs<br>32 Online Resource Scavenger Hunt<br>34 Invent the Quiz<br>41 Cued Notes<br>42 Note-taking Pairs |
| **8** | Supporting Community | 3 Contemporary Issues Journal<br>22 Test-Taking Teams<br>37 Think-Pair-Share |
| **9** | Promoting Equity and Inclusion | 8 Paper Seminar<br>36 Class Book<br>38 Affinity Grouping |

| PART 4: METHODS | | |
|---|---|---|
| CHAPTER | TITLE | CROSS ACADEMY TECHNIQUES (CATs) |
| 10 | Lecturing Effectively | 10 Quick Write<br>14 Update Your Classmate<br>15 Translate That!<br>16 Guided Notes<br>18 Support a Statement<br>20 Lecture Wrapper<br>37 Think-Pair-Share<br>43 Punctuated Lecture |
| 11 | Facilitating Discussion | 4 Jigsaw<br>10 Quick Write<br>33 Frames<br>35 Letters<br>37 Think-Pair-Share<br>46 Quotation Summaries<br>44 Fishbowl |
| 12 | Implementing Collaborative Learning | 4 Jigsaw<br>22 Test-Taking Teams<br>26 Dyadic Essays<br>28 Dyadic Interviews<br>37 Think-Pair-Share<br>44 Fishbowl |
| PART 5: IMPROVEMENT | | |
| 13 | Reflecting on Teaching | 3 Contemporary Issues Journal<br>47 What? So What? Now What? Journals |
| 14 | Assessing and Evaluating Teaching | 21 Post-Test Analysis |
| 15 | Engaging in the Scholarship of Teaching and Learning | |

# Subject Index

# Author Index

# Master References

Abrami, P. C. (2001). Improving judgments about teaching effectiveness using teacher rating forms. *New Directions for Institutional Research*, 109, 59-87. https://doi.org/10.1002/ir.4

Abrami, P. C., d'Apollonia, S., & Cohen, P. A. (1990). Validity of student ratings of instruction: What we know and what we don't. *Journal of Educational Psychology*, 82(2), 219-231. https://doi.org/10.1037/0022-0663.82.2.219

Addison, W. E., Best, J., & Warrington, J. D. (2006). Student perceptions of course difficulty and their ratings of the instructor. *College Student Journal*, 40(2), 409-416.

Adesope, O. O., Zhou, M., & Nesbit, J. C. (2015). Achievement goal orientations and self-reported study strategies as predictors of online studying activities. *Journal of Educational Computing Research*, 53(3), 436-458.

Addy, T.M. Dube, D., Mitchell, K.A., & SoRelle, M. (2021). *What inclusive instructors do: Principles and practices for excellence in college teaching.* Stylus.

Ahn, B., & Bir, D. D. (2018). Student interactions with online videos in a large hybrid mechanics of materials course. *Advances in Engineering Education*, 6(3), 1-24.

Akerheilm, K., Berger, J., Hooker, M., & Wise, D. (1998). *Factors related to college enrollment. Final report* (ED421053). Department of Education, Office of the Under Secretary. https://files.eric.ed.gov/fulltext/ED421053.pdf

Alexander, M. E., Commander, N., Greenberg, D., & Ward, T. (2010). Using the four-question techniques to enhance critical thinking in online discussions. *MERLOT Journal of Online Learning and Teaching*, 6(2), 409-415.

Algozzine, B. Gretes, H., Flowers, C., Howley, L., Beattie, H., Spooner, F., Mohanty, G., & Bray, M. (2004). Student evaluation of college teaching: A practice in search of principles. *College Teaching*, 52(4), 134-141. https://doi.org/10.3200/CTCH.52.4.134-141

Alpert, D. (1985). Performance and paralysis: The organizational context of the American research university. *Journal of Higher Education*, 56(3), 241-281. https://doi.org/10.2307/1981734

Ambrose, S. A., Bridges, M. W., DiPietro, M., Lovett, M., Norman, M., & Mayer, R. (2010). *How learning works: Seven research-based principles for smart teaching.* Jossey-Bass.

Anderson, K. J., & Smith, G. (2005). Students' preconceptions of professors: Benefits and barriers according to ethnicity and gender. *Hispanic Journal of Behavioral Sciences*, 27(2), 184-201. https://doi.org/10.1177/0739986304273707

Anderson, L. W., & Krathwohl, D. R. (Eds.). (2001). *A taxonomy for learning, teaching, and assessing. A revision of Bloom's Taxonomy of Educational Objectives.* Addison-Wesley-Longman.

Anderson, T., Rourke, L., Garrison, D., & Archer, W. (2001). Assessing teaching presence in a computer conferencing context. *Journal of Asynchronous Learning Networks*, 5(2), 1-17. http://dx.doi.org/10.24059/olj.v5i2.1875

Andrews, T. C., Auerbach, A. J. H., & Andrews, T. C. (2019). Exploring the relationship between teacher knowledge and active-learning implementation in large college biology. *CBE Life Sciences Education*, 18(4), Article 48. https://doi.org/10.1187/cbe.19-01-0010

Angelo, T. A., & Cross, K. P. (1993). *Classroom assessment techniques* (2nd ed.). Jossey-Bass.

Appleton, J. J., Christenson, S. L., & Furlong, M. J. (2008). Student engagement with school: Critical conceptual and methodological issues of the construct. *Psychology in the Schools*, 45(5), 369-386. https://doi.org/10.1002/pits.20303

Armbruster, P., Patel, M., Johnson, E., & Weiss, M. (2009). Active learning and student-centered pedagogy improve student attitudes and performance in introductory biology. *CBE Life Sciences Education*, 8, 203-213. https://www.ncbi.nlm.nih.gov/pmc/articles/PMC2736024/

Aronson, J., Fried, C. B., & Good, C. (2002). Reducing the effects of stereotype threat on African American college students by shaping theories of intelligence. *Journal of Experimental Social Psychology*, 38(2), 113-125.

Arreola, R. A. (2000). *Developing a comprehensive faculty evaluation system* (2nd ed.). Anker.

Arreola, R. A. (2007). *Developing a comprehensive faculty evaluation system* (3rd ed.). Anker.

Ashar, H., & Skenes, R. (1993, Winter). Can Tinto's student departure model be applied to nontraditional students? *Adult Education Quarterly*, 43(2), 90-100.

Athens, W. (2018). Perceptions of the persistent: Engagement and learning community in underrepresented populations. *Online Learning*, 22(2), 27-57.

Atkins, S., & Murphy, K. (1994). Reflective practice. *Nursing Standard*, 8(39), 49-56.

Austin, A. E. (2002). Preparing the next generation of faculty: Graduate school as socialization to the academic career. *Journal of Higher Education*, 73(1), 94-122.

Axelrod, J., Bloom, B. S., Ginsburg, B. E., O'Meara, W., & Williams, J. C. (1949). *Teaching by discussion in the college program.* College of the University of Chicago.

Baddeley, A. (1998). Working memory (Mémoire de travail). *Comptes Rendus de l'Académie des Sciences-Series III - Sciences de la Vie*, 321(2-3), 167-173. https://doi.org/10.1016/S0764-4469(97)89817-4

Baeten, M., Dochy, F., & Struyven, K. (2013). The effects of different learning environments on students' motivation for learning and their achievement. *British Journal of Educational Psychology*, 83(3), 484-501. https://doi.org/ 10.1111/j.2044-8279.2012.02076.x

Bain, K. (2004). *What the best college teachers do.* Harvard University.

Bangert, A. (2008). The influence of social presence and teaching presence on the quality of online critical inquiry. *Journal of Computing in Higher Education*, 20(1), 34-61.

Barkley, E. F., & Major, C. H. (2016). *Learning assessment techniques: A handbook for college faculty.* Jossey-Bass.

Barkley, E. F., & Major, C. H. (2018). *Interactive lecturing: A handbook for college faculty.* Jossey-Bass.

Barkley, E. F., & Major, C. H. (2020). *Student engagement techniques: A handbook for college faculty* (2nd ed). Jossey-Bass.

Barkley, E. F., Major, C. H., & Cross, K. P. (2014). *Collaborative learning techniques: A handbook for college faculty* (2nd ed). Jossey-Bass.

Bartsch, R. A., & Cobern, K. M. (2003). Effectiveness of PowerPoint presentations in lectures. *Computers and Education*, 41(1), 77-78. https://doi.org/10.1016/S0360-1315(03)00027-7

Bautista, V. (2000). *Improve your grades: How to become an honor student.* Bookhaus Publishers.

Becher, T. (1987). The disciplinary shaping of the profession. In B. R. Clark (Ed.), *The academic profession: National, disciplinary, and institutional settings.* University of California Press. https://doi.org/10.1525/9780520311329-009

Bennett, J. M., & Bennett, M. J. (2004). Developing intercultural sensitivity: An integrative approach to global and economic diversity. In D. Landis, J. M. Bennett, & M. J. Bennett (Eds.), Handbook of intercultural training (3rd ed., pp.147-165). Sage. https://www.researchgate.net/publication/344750735_Developing_Intercultural_Sensitivity_An_Intercultural_Approach_to_Global_and_Domestic_Diversity

Bennett, R., Hobson, J., Jones, A., Martin-Lynch, P., Scutt, C., Strehlow, K., & Veitch, S. (2016). Being chimaera: A monstrous identity for SoTL academics. *Higher Education Research & Development*, 35(2), 217-228.

Benton, S. L., & Li, D. (2015). Response to a better way to evaluate undergraduate teaching: Editorial Note #1. *IDEA Center*, 1-8. https://www.ideaedu.org/Portals/0/Uploads/Documents/A_Better_Way_to_Evaluate.pdf

Beran, T., & Violato, C. (2010). Student ratings of teaching effectiveness: Student engagement and course characteristics. *Canadian Journal of Higher Education*, 39(1), 1-13. https://journals.sfu.ca/cjhe/index.php/cjhe/article/view/491

Berk, R. A. (2013). *Top 10 flashpoints in student ratings and the evaluation of teaching: What faculty administrators must know to protect themselves in employment decisions*. Stylus.

Bernard, R. M., Abrami, P. C., Borokhovski, E., Wade, C. A., Tamim, R., Surkes, M. A., & Bethel, E. (2009). A meta-analysis of three types of interaction treatments in distance education. *Review of Educational Research*, 79(3), 1243-1289. doi:10.3102/0034654309333844

Bernstein, D., & Bass, R. (2005). The scholarship of teaching and learning. *Academe*, 91(4), 37-42.

Bess, J. L. (1977). The motivation to teach. *Journal of Higher Education*, 48(3), 243-258. https://doi.org/10.2307/1978679

Bettez, S. C., & Hytten, K. (2013). Community building in social justice work: A critical approach. *Educational Studies*, 49(1), 45-66. https://doi.org/10.1080/00131946.2012.749478

Bigatel, P., & Edel-Malizia, S. (2018). Predictors of instructor practices and course activities that engage online students. *Online Journal of Distance Learning Administration*, 21(1). https://www.westga.edu/~distance/ojdla/spring211/bigatel_malizia211.html

Biggs, J. (1999). *Teaching for quality learning at university* (4th ed.). Society for Research into Higher Education, Open University Press.

Blakey, C. H., & Major, C. H. (2019). Student perceptions of engagement in online courses: An exploratory study. *Online Journal of Distance Learning Administration*, 22(4). https://www.westga.edu/~distance/ojdla/winter224/blakeymajor224.html

Blair, E. (2014). Academic development through the contextualization of the scholarship of teaching and learning: Reflections drawn from the recent history of Trinidad and Tobago. *International Journal for Academic Development*, 19(4), 330-340. http://dx.doi.org/10.1080/1360144X.2013.860032

Bligh, D. A. (1999). *What's the use of lectures?* Jossey-Bass.

Blikstein, P., & Wilensky, U. (2010). MaterialSim: A constructionist agent-based modeling approach to engineering education. In M. Jacobson & P. Reimann (Eds.), *Materialism: A constructionist agent-based modeling approach to engineering education* (pp. 17-60). Springer. https://doi.org/10.1007/978-0-387-88279-6_2

Bloom, B., Englehart, M., Furst, E., Hill, W., & Krathwohl, D. (1956). *Taxonomy of educational objectives, handbook 1: Cognitive domain.* Longman.

Bloome, D. (1986). Building literacy and the classroom community. *Theory into Practice,* 25(2), 71-76. https://doi.org/10.1080/00405848609543203

Boettcher, J. V, & Conrad, R. (2010). *The online teaching survival guide: simple and practical pedagogical tips.* Jossey-Bass.

Boniecki, K. A., & Moore, S. (2003). Breaking the silence: Using a token economy to reinforce classroom participation. *Teaching of Psychology,* 30(3), 224-227. https://doi.org/10.1207%2FS15328023TOP3003_05

Bonwell, C. C., & Eison, J. A. (1991). *Active learning: Creating excitement in the classroom* (ASHE-ERIC Higher Education Report No. 1). The George Washington University, School of Education and Human Development. https://files.eric.ed.gov/fulltext/ED336049.pdf

Booth, S., & Woollacott, L. C. (2018). On the constitution of SoTL: Its domains and contexts. *Higher Education,* 75(3), 537-551. https://doi.org/10.1007/s10734-017-0156-7

Boring, A., Ottoboni, K., & Starks, P. B. (2016). Student evaluations of teaching (mostly) do not measure teaching effectiveness. *Science Open Research.* https://doi.org/10.14293/S2199-1006.1.SOR-EDU.AETBZC.v1

Boston, W., Diaz, S., Gibson, A., Ice, P., Richardson, J., & Swan, K. (2009). An exploration of relationship between indicators of the community of inquiry framework and retention in online programs. *Journal of Asynchronous Learning Networks,* 13(3), 67-83.

Bowen, J., & Watkins, E. (2016). *Teaching naked techniques: A practical guide to designing better courses.* Jossey-Bass.

Bowen, S. (2005, Winter). Engaged learning: Are we all on the same page? *Peer Review.* https://www.aacu.org/publications-research/periodicals/engaged-learning-are-we-all-same-page

Boyer, E. L. (1990). *Scholarship reconsidered: Priorities of the professoriate.* Princeton University Press.

Bransford, J. D., Brown, A. L., & Cocking, R. R. (Eds.). (1999). *How people learn: Brain, mind, experience, and school.* National Academy Press.

Braun, V., & Clarke, V. (2006). Using thematic analysis in psychology. *Qualitative Research in Psychology,* 3(2), 77-101. https://doi.org/10.1191/1478088706qp063oa

Braxton, J. M., & Nordvall, R. C. (1985). Selective liberal arts colleges: Higher quality as well as higher prestige? *Journal of Higher Education,* 56(5), 538-544. https://doi.org/10.2307/1981210

Brent, R. & Felder, R. (2004). A protocol for peer review of teaching. Proceedings of the 2004 American Society for Engineering Education Annual Conference & Exposition. https://www.engr.ncsu.edu/wp-content/uploads/drive/1nsrTgNg0sR3rNGxZoLhU3cBUzWg1167e/2004-ASEE(Peer%20Review).pdf

Brookfield, S. A. (2000). Transformative learning as ideology critique. In J. Mezirow & Associates (Eds.), *Learning as transformation* (pp.125–148). Jossey-Bass.

Brookfield, S. D. (2017). *Becoming a critically reflective teacher* (2nd ed.). Jossey-Bass.

Brookfield, S. D., & Preskill, S. (2005). *Discussion as a way of teaching: Tools and techniques for democratic classrooms.* Jossey-Bass.

Brophy, J. (2004). *Motivating students to learn* (2nd ed.). Lawrence Erlbaum.

Brown, G., & Atkins, M. (1988). *Effective teaching in higher education.* Routledge.

Bruer, J.T (1997). Education and the brain: A bridge too far. *Educational Researcher,* 26: 4–16.

Buchanan, T. (2000). The efficacy of a World-Wide Web mediated formative assessment. *Journal of Computer Assisted Learning*, 16(3), 193-200. https://doi.org/10.1046/j.1365-2729.2000.00132.x

Bruer, J.T. (1997). Education and the brain: A bridge too far. Educational Researcher, 26: 4–16.

Bulu, S. T. (2012). Place presence, social presence, co-presence, and satisfaction in virtual worlds. *Computers & Education*, 58(1), 154-161.

Burns, K. (2017). Community college faculty as pedagogical innovators: How the scholarship of teaching and learning (SoTL) stimulates innovation in the classroom. *Community College Journal of Research and Practice*, 41(3), 153-167. http://dx.doi.org/10.1080/10668926.2016.1168327

Buskist, W., Sikorski, J., Buckley, T., & Saville, B. K. (2002). Elements of master teaching. In S. F. Davis & W. Buskist (Eds.), *The teaching of psychology: Essays in honor of Wilbert McKeachie and Charles L. Brewer* (pp. 27-39). Lawrence Erlbaum.

Cameron, J. (2001). Negative effects of reward on intrinsic motivation-- A limited phenomenon: Comment on Deci, Koestner, and Ryan. *Review of Educational Research*, 71(1), 29-42. https://doi.org/10.3102%2F00346543071001029

Carnegie Foundation (2021). Foundation history. https://www.carnegiefoundation.org/about-us/foundation-history/

Carney, R. N., & Levin, J. R. (2002). Pictorial illustrations still improve students' learning from text. *Educational Psychology Review*, 14(1), 5-26. https://link.springer.com/content/pdf/10.1023/A:1013176309260.pdf

Cashin, W. (2011). *Effective classroom discussions (IDEA paper, #49)*. The IDEA Center. https://www.ideaedu.org/Portals/0/Uploads/Documents/IDEA%20Papers/IDEA%20Papers/IDEA_Paper_49.pdf

Centra, J. A. (2003). Will teachers receive higher student evaluations by giving higher grades and less course work? *Research in Higher Education*, 44(5), 495-518.

Centra, J. A. (2009). *Differences in responses to the Student Instructional Report: Is it bias?* Educational Testing Service.

Chandler, P., & Sweller, J. (1991) Cognitive load theory and the format of instruction. *Cognition and Instruction*, 8(4), 293-332. https://doi.org/10.1207/s1532690xci0804_2

Chanpet, P., Chomsuwan, K., & Murphy, E. (2020). Online project-based learning and formative assessment. *Technology, Knowledge and Learning*, 25(3), 685-705.

Charbonneau-Gowdy, P., & Chavez, J. (2018). *Endpoint: Insights for theory development in a blended learning program in chile.* 17th European Conference on eLearning, ECEL 2018, 81-89.

Chen, P. D., Guidry, K. R., & Lambert, A. D. (2009). Engaging online learners: *A quantitative study of postsecondary student engagement in the online learning environment* [Paper presentation]. Annual meeting of the American Educational Research Association, San Diego, CA, United States.

Chen, Z., Jiao, J., & Hu, K. (2021). Formative assessment as an online instruction intervention: Student engagement, outcomes, and perceptions. *International Journal of Distance Education Technologies*, 19(1), 50-65.

Chew, S. L., & Cerbin. W. J. (2021). The cognitive challenges of effective teaching. *The Journal of Economic Education*, 52(1), 17-40. https://www.tandfonline.com/doi/full/10.1080/00220485.2020.1845266

Chick, N., & Poole, G. (2013). The necessary and dual conversations of a vibrant SoTL. Editors' introduction. *Teaching & Learning Inquiry,* 1(1), 1-4. https://doi.org/10.20343/teachlearninqu.2.1.1

Chickering, A. W., & Gamson, Z. F. (1987). Seven principles for good practice in undergraduate education. *AAHE Bulletin*, 9(2), 3-7. https://files.eric.ed.gov/fulltext/ED282491.pdf

Choe, R. C., Scuric, Z., Eshkol, E., Cruser, S., Arndt, A., Cox, R., Toma, S. P., Shapiro, C., Levis-Fitzgerald, M., Levis-Fitzgerald, M., Barnes, G., & Crosbie, R. H. (2019). Student satisfaction and learning outcomes in asynchronous online lecture videos. *CBE - Life Sciences Education*, 18(4). https://www.lifescied.org/doi/10.1187/cbe.18-08-0171

Church, E. B. (2015). *Building community in the classroom.* Scholastic. http://www.scholastic.com/teachers/article/building-community-classroom

Christensen, C. R., Garvin, D. A., & Sweet, A. (Eds.). (1991). *Education for judgment: The artistry of discussion leadership.* Harvard Business School Press.

Chisadza, C., Nicholls, N., & Yitbarek, E. (2019). Race and gender biases in student evaluations of teachers, *Economics Letters*, 179, 66-71. https://doi.org/10.1016/j.econlet.2019.03.022

Clark, B. R. (1980). *Academic culture.* Higher Education Research Group, Yale University.

Clark, R. E. (2000). Evaluating distance education: Strategies and cautions. *Quarterly Review of Distance Education*, 1, 3-16.

Clarke, J. H. (1988). Designing discussions as group inquiry. *College Teaching*, 36(4), 140-143. https://www.jstor.org/stable/27558299

Clayson, D. E. (2009). Student evaluations of teaching: Are they related to what students learn? A meta-analysis and review of the literature. *Journal of Marketing Education*, 31(1), 16-30. http://dx.doi.org/10.1177/0273475308324086

Clayson, D. E., Frost, T. E., & Sheffet, M. J. (2006). Grades and the student evaluation of instruction: A test of the reciprocity effect. *Academy of Management Learning & Education*, 5(1), 52-65. https://doi.org/10.5465/amle.2006.20388384

Clegg, S., Tan, J., & Saeidi, S. (2002). Reflecting or acting? Reflective practice and continuing professional development in higher education. *Reflective Practice*, 3, 131-146. https://doi.org/10.1080/14623940220129924

Cobb, S. C. (2011). Social presence, satisfaction, and perceived learning of RN-to-BSN students in Web-based nursing courses. *Nursing Education Perspectives*, 32(2), 115-119. https://doi.org/10.5480/1536-5026-32.2.115.

Coburn, C., & Turner, E. (2012). The practice of data use: An introduction. *American Journal of Education*, 118, 99-111. http://www.jstor.org/stable/10.1086/663272

Cohen, P. A. (1981). Student ratings of instruction and student achievement: A meta-analysis of multisection validity studies. *Review of Educational Research, 51*(3), 281-309. http://dx.doi.org/10.2307/1170209

Condon, W., Iverson, E. R., Manduca, C. A., Rutz, C., & Willett, G. (2016). *Faculty development and student learning. Assessing the connections.* Indiana University Press.

Corich, S. P., Kinshuk, D., & Hunt, L. M., (2004). Assessing discussion forum participation: In search of quality. *International Journal of Instructional Technology and Distance Learning, 1*(12), 1-12.

Cornell University's Teaching Center. (2020). *Universal design for learning.* https://teaching.cornell.edu/teaching-resources/designing-your-course/universal-design-learning

Cox, M. D. (2004). Introduction to faculty learning communities. *New Directions for Teaching & Learning, 2004*(97), 5-23. https://doi.org/10.1002/tl.129

Craig, J. (2014). What have we been writing about? Patterns and trends in the scholarship of teaching and learning in political science. *Journal of Political Science Education, 10*(1), 23-36. https://doi.org/10.1080/15512169.2013.859086

Cuseo, J. B. (1992). Cooperative learning: A pedagogy for diversity. *Cooperative Learning & College Teaching, 3*(1), 2-6.

Dallimore, E. J., Hertenstein, J. H., & Platt, M. B. (2006). Nonvoluntary class participation in graduate discussion courses: Effects on grading and cold calling. *Journal of Management Education, 30*(2), 354-377. https://doi.org/10.1177%2F1052562905277031

Dallimore, E. J., Hertenstein, J. H., & Platt, M. B. (2008). Using discussion pedagogy to enhance oral and written communication skills. *College Teaching, 56*(3), 163-172. https://doi.org/10.3200/CTCH.56.3.163-172

Dallimore, E. J., Hertenstein, J. H., & Platt, M. B. (2010). Class participation in accounting courses: Factors that affect student comfort and learning. *Issues in Accounting Education, 25*(4), 613-629. https://doi.org/10.2308/iace.2010.25.4.613

Dallimore, E. J., Hertenstein, J. H., & Platt, M. B. (2013). Impact of cold-calling on student voluntary participation. *Journal of Management Education, 37*(3), 305-341. https://doi.org/10.1177%2F1052562912446067

Darby, F. (2019). *How to be a better online teacher.* Chronicle Advice Guide. https://www.chronicle.com/interactives/advice-online-teaching?cid=cp234

Darabi, A., Nelson, D. W., Meeker, R., Liang, X., & Boulware, W. (2010). Effect of worked examples on mental model progression in a computer-based simulation learning environment. *Journal of Computing in Higher Education 22*(2), 135-147.

Darabi, A., Liang, X., Suryavanshi, R., & Yurekli, H. (2013). Effectiveness of online discussion strategies: A meta-analysis. American Journal of Distance Education, 27(4), 228-241. https://doi.org/10.1080/08923647.2013.837651

Davis, B. G. (1993). *Tools for teaching.* Jossey-Bass.

Davis, B. G. (2009). *Tools for teaching* (2nd ed.). Jossey-Bass.

Davis, D. J. (2010). The experiences of marginalized academics and understanding the majority: Implications for institutional policy and practice. *International Journal of Learning, 17*(6), 355-364. https://doi.org/10.18848/1447-9494/CGP/v17i06/47077

Davis, J. R. (1976). *Teaching strategies for the college classroom.* Westview Press.

Davis, M. (2003). Barriers to reflective practice: The changing nature of higher education. *Active Learning in Higher Education, 4*(3), 243-255. https://journals.sagepub.com/doi/10.1177/14697874030043004

Dawson, P. (2016). Are lectures a good way to learn? www.theedadvocate.org/lectures-good-way-learn/

Day, C. (1999). Professional development and reflective practice: Purposes, processes and partnerships. *Pedagogy, Culture and Society, 7,* 221-233. https://doi.org/10.1080/14681366.1999.11090864

Deci, E. L. (1971). Effects of externally mediated rewards on intrinsic motivation. *Journal of Personality and Social Psychology, 18*(1), 105-115. https://psycnet.apa.org/doi/10.1037/h0030644

Deslauriers, L., Schelew, E., & Wieman, C. (2011). Improved learning in a large enrollment physics class. *Science, 33*, 862. www.math.unm.edu/mctp/gstts/science.pdf

Dewey, J. (1910) *How we think*. Heath.

Dewey, J. (1933). How we think: A restatement of the relation of reflective thinking to the educative process. Heath.

Dietz-Uhler, B., & Lanter, J.R. (2009). Using the four-questions technique to enhance learning. *Teaching of Psychology, 36*, 38-41. https://doi.org/10.1080/00986280802529327

Dinham, S. (2002). NSW Quality Teaching Awards: Research, rigour and transparency. *Unicorn, 28*(1), 5-9. https://hdl.handle.net/1959.11/11782

Dinham, S. (2007a). *Leadership for exceptional educational outcomes*. Post Pressed.

Dinham, S. (2007b). The secondary Head of Department and the achievement of exceptional student outcomes. *Journal of Educational Administration, 45*(1), 62-79. http://dx.doi.org/10.1108/09578230710722458

Divan, A., Ludwig, L., Matthews, K., Motley, P., & Tomljenovic-Berube, A. (2017). Survey of research approaches utilized in the scholarship of teaching and learning publications. *Teaching & Learning Inquiry, 5*(2), 16-29. https://doi.org/10.20343/teachlearninqu.5.2.3

Driscoll, M. (2000). *Psychology of learning for instruction*. Allyn & Bacon.

Duchastel, P. C., & Brown, B. R. (1974). Incidental and relevant learning with instructional objectives. *Journal of Educational Psychology, 66*(4), 481-485. https://doi.org/10.1037/h0036743

Duell, O. K. (1974). Effect of type of objective, level of test question, and the judged importance of tested materials upon posttest performance. *Journal of Educational Psychology, 66*(2), 225-232. https://doi.org/10.1037/h0036272

Dunning, D. (2007). *Self-insight: Roadblocks and detours on the path to knowing thyself.* Taylor & Francis.

Dweck, C. S. (2006). *Mindset: The new psychology of success.* Random House.

Dweck, C., Chiu, C., & Hong, Y. (1995). Implicit theories and their role in judgments and reactions: A word from two perspectives, *Psychological Inquiry, 6*(4), 267-285. https://doi.org/10.1207/s15327965pli0604_1

Eagan, M. K., Stolzenberg, E. B., Berdan Lozano, J., Aragon, M. C., Suchard, M. R., & Hurtado, S. (2014). *Undergraduate teaching faculty: The 2013–2014 HERI faculty survey.* Higher Education Research Institute, UCLA. http://heri.ucla.edu/monographs/HERI-FAC2014-monograph.pdf

Eberly Center. (2020). *What is the difference between assessment and grading?* Carnegie Mellon University. https://www.cmu.edu/teaching/assessment/basics/grading-assessment.html

Ebert-May, D., Derting, T. L., Hodder, J., Momsen, J. L., Long, T. M., & Jardeleza, S. E. (2011). What we say is not what we do: Effective evaluation of faculty professional development programs. *BioScience, 61*(7), 550-558. https://bioscience.oxfordjournals.org/content/61/7/550.full.pdf

Eble, K. E. (1976). *The craft of teaching.* Jossey-Bass.

Eddy, S. L., & Hogan, K. A. (2014). Getting under the hood: How and for whom does increasing course structure work? *CBE Life Sciences Education, 13*(3), 453-468.

Eichelberger, A., & Leong, P. (2019). Using TPACK as a framework to study the influence of college faculty's beliefs on online teaching. *Educational Media International, 56*(2), 116-133. https://doi.org/10.1080/09523987.2019.1614246

Eiszler, C. F. (2002). College students' evaluations of teaching and grade inflation. *Research in Higher Education, 43*(4), 483-501. https://doi.org/10.1023/A:1015579817194

El-Shamy, S. (2004). *How to design and deliver training for the new and emerging generations.* Pfeiffer.

Elliot, D. L., Baumfield, V., & Reid, K. (2016). Searching for 'a third space': A creative pathway towards international Ph.D. students' academic acculturation. *Higher Education Research & Development, 35*(6), 1180-1195. https://doi.org/10.1080/07294360.2016.1144575

Esarey, M., & Valdes, N. (2020). Unbiased, reliable, and valid student evaluations can still be unfair. *Assessment & Evaluation in Higher Education, 45*(8), 1106-1120. https://doi.org/10.1080/02602938.2020.1724875

Exley, K., & Dennick, R. (2004). *Giving a lecture: From presenting to teaching.* Routledge Falmer.

Fanghanel, J., Pritchard, J., Potter, J., & Wisker, G. (2015). Defining and supporting the scholarship of teaching and learning (SoTL): A sector-wide study. Literature review. Higher Education Academy. https://repository.uwl.ac.uk/id/eprint/2066/1/literature_review.pdf

Farley, J., Risko, E. F., & Kingstone, A. (2013). Everyday attention and lecture retention: The effects of time, fidgeting, and mind wandering. *Frontiers in Psychology, 4*(4), 619. https://dx.doi.org/10.3389%2Ffpsyg.2013.00619

Favizza, S. M., Uitlugt, M. G., & Fenn, K. M. (2017). Logged in and zoned out: How laptop internet use relates to classroom learning. *Psychological Science, 28*(2), 171-180. https://doi.org/10.1177/0956797616677314

Feldman, K. A. (1988). Effective college teaching from the students' and faculty's view: Matched or mismatched priorities. *Research in Higher Education, 28*, 291-344.

Feldman, K. A. (1997). Identifying exemplary teachers and teaching: Evidence from student ratings. In R. P. Perry & J. C. Smart (Eds.), *Effective teaching in higher education: Research and practice.* Agathon Press.

Felton, P. (2013). Principles of good practice in SoTL. *Teaching & Learning Inquiry, 1*(1), 121-125. https://doi.org/10.2979/teachlearninqu.1.1.121

Fendler, L. (2003). Teacher reflection in a hall of mirrors: Historical influences and political reverberations. *Educational Researcher, 32*(3), 16-25.

Fernandez-Balboa, J-M., & Steihl, J. (1995). The generic nature of pedagogical content knowledge among college professors. *Teaching and Teacher Education, 11*(3), 293-306. https://doi.org/10.1016/0742-051X(94)00030-A

Filak, V. F., & Sheldon, K. M. (2008). Teacher support, student motivation, student need satisfaction, and college teacher course evaluations: Testing a sequential path model. *Educational Psychology, 28*(6), 711-724.

Fink, L. D. (2003). *Creating significant learning experiences: An integrated approach to designing college courses.* Jossey-Bass.

Fink, L. D. (2013). *Creating significant learning experiences: An integrated approach to designing college courses* (2nd ed.). Jossey-Bass.

Frederick, P. (1994). Classroom discussion. In K. W. Prichard & R. M. Sawyer (Eds.), *Handbook of college teaching* (pp. 99-109). Greenwood.

Fredericks, J. A., Blumenfeld, P. C., & Paris, A. H. (2004). School engagement: Potential of the concept, state of the evidence. *Review of Educational Research, 74*(1), 59-109. https://doi.org/10.3102%2F00346543074001059

Freeman, S., Eddy, S. L., McDonough, M., Smith, M. K., Okoroafor, N., Jordt, H., & Wenderoth, M. P. (2014). Active learning increases student performance in science, engineering, and mathematics. *Proceedings of the National Academy of Sciences, 111*(23), 8410-8415. https://doi.org/10.1073/pnas.1319030111

Freeman, T. M., Anderman, L. H., & Jensen, J. M. (2010). Sense of belonging in college: Freshmen at the classroom and college levels. *The Journal of Experimental Education, 75*(3), 203-220. https://www.jstor.org/stable/20157456

Freire, P. (1970). *Pedagogy of the oppressed.* Seabury.

Fulmer, S. (2017). *Should I share my learning outcomes with students?* The Learning Scientists. https://www.learningscientists.org/blog/2017/10/4-1

Gaff, J. G., & Wilson, R. C. (1971). Faculty cultures and interdisciplinary studies. *The Journal of Higher Education, 42*(3), 186-201. https://doi.org/10.2307/1980354

Gagne, R. M. (1984). Learning outcomes and their effects: Useful categories of human performance. *American Psychologist, 39*(4), 377-385. https://psycnet.apa.org/doi/10.1037/0003-066X.39.4.377

Gagne, E. D., & Rothkopf, E. Z. (1975). Text organization and learning goals. *Journal of Educational Psychology, 67*(3), 445-450. https://doi.org/10.1037/h0076617

Gardner, H. (1983). *Frames of mind.* Basic Books.

Garrison, D. R., Anderson, T., & Archer, W. (2000). Critical inquiry in a text-based environment: Computer conferencing in higher education model. *The Internet and Higher Education, 2*(2-3), 87-105.

Garside, C. (1996). Look who's talking: A comparison of lecture and group discussion teaching strategies in developing critical thinking skills. *Communication Education, 45*(3), 212-227. https://doi.org/10.1080/03634529609379050

Gayle, B. M., Randall, N., Langley, L., & Preiss, R., (2013). Faculty learning processes: A model for moving from scholarly teaching to the scholarship of teaching and learning. *Teaching and Learning Inquiry: The ISSOTL Journal, 1*(1), 81-93. https://doi.org/10.20343/teachlearninqu.1.1.81

Geertsema, J. (2016). Academic development, SoTL and educational research. *International Journal for Academic Development, 21*(2), 122-134. http://dx.doi.org/10.1080/1360144X.2016.1175144

Gibbs, G. (1988). *Learning by doing: A guide to teaching and learning methods.* Further Education Unit.

Gigliotti, R. J., & Buchtel, F. S. (1990). Attributional bias and course evaluations. *Journal of Educational Psychology, 82*(2), 341-351. https://psycnet.apa.org/doi/10.1037/0022-0663.82.2.341

Gilroy, M. (2007). Bias in student evaluations of faculty? *The Hispanic Outlook in Higher Education, 17*(19), 26-27.

Ginsberg, M. B., & Wlodkowski, R. J. (2009). *Diversity and motivation: Culturally responsive teaching college* (2nd ed.). Jossey-Bass.

Glass, A. L., & Kang, M. (2019). Dividing attention in the classroom reduces exam performance. *Educational Psychology, 39*(3), 395-408. https://doi.org/10.1080/01443410.2018.1489046

Glassick, C. E., Huber, M. T., & Maeroff, G. I. (1997). Scholarship assessed: Evaluation of the professoriate. *An Ernest L. Boyer project of The Carnegie Foundation for the Advancement of Teaching.* Jossey-Bass.

Goldsmid, C., & Wilson, E. K. (1980). *Passing on sociology: The teaching of a discipline.* Wadsworth.

Gonzalez, M., & Moore, N. (2020). A comparison of faculty and graduate students' perceptions of engaging online courses: A mixed-method study. *International Journal of Educational Methodology, 6*(1), 223-236. https://doi.org/10.12973/ijem.6.1.223

Good, C. V., & Merkel, W. R. (1959). *Dictionary of education* (2nd ed.). McGraw-Hill.

Good, J. J., Bourne, K. A., Drake, R. G., (2020). The impact of classroom diversity philosophies on the STEM performance of undergraduate students of color. *Journal of Experimental Social Psychology, 91*, Article 104026.

Goodman, D. J. (2011). *Promoting diversity and social justice: Educating people from privileged groups.* Routledge.

Goos, M. (2004). Learning mathematics in a classroom community of inquiry. *Journal of Research in Mathematics Education, 35*(4), 258-291. https://psycnet.apa.org/doi/10.2307/30034810

Grant, G. (1988). *Teaching critical thinking.* Praeger.

Gravestock, P., & Gregor-Greenleaf, E. (2008). *Student course evaluations: Research, models, and trends.* Higher Education Quality Council of Ontario.

Greaves, K. (2015). Is scholarship of teaching and learning in practical legal training a professional responsibility? *The Law Teacher, 49*(1), 22-38. https://doi.org/10.1080/03069400.2014.991203

Greene, K., & Mitcham, K. C. (2012). Community in the classroom. *English Journal, 101*(4), 13-15. https://library.ncte.org/journals/ej/issues/v101-4

Grossman, P. (1990). *The making of a teacher.* Teacher's College Press.

Grossman, P. L., Wilson, S. M., & Shulman, L. S. (1989). Teachers of substance: subject matter knowledge for teaching. In M. C. Reynolds, (Ed.), *Knowledge base for the beginning teacher* (pp. 23-36). Pergamon Press.

Gunawardena, C. N., & McIsaac, M. S. (2004). Distance education. In D. H. Jonasen (Ed.), *Handbook of research for educational communications and technology* (2nd ed., pp. 355-396). Erlbaum.

Gurin, P., Dey, E., Hurtado, S., & Durin, G. (2002). Diversity and higher education: Theory and impact on educational outcomes. *Harvard Educational Review, 72*(3), 330-367.

Gurung, R. A. R., Ansburg, P. I., Alexander, P. A., Lawrence, N. K., & Johnson, D. E. (2008). The state of the scholarship of teaching and learning in psychology. *Teaching of Psychology, 35*(4), 249-261.

Gurung, R. A. R., & Wilson, J. H. (Eds.). (2013). *Doing the scholarship of teaching and learning: Measuring systematic changes to teaching and improvements in learning.* Jossey-Bass.

Gunter, G. A. (2007). The effects of the impact of instructional immediacy on cognition and learning in online classes. *International Journal of Social Sciences, 2*(3), 196-202.

Haigh, N., Gossman, P., & Jiao, X. (2011). Undertaking an institutional 'Stock-Take' of SoTL: New Zealand University case studies. *Higher Education Research and Development, 30*(1), 9-23. https://doi.org/10.1080/07294360.2011.536969

Hanstedt, P. (2018). *Creating wicked students: Designing courses for a complex world.* Stylus.

Harland, T., Hussain, R., & Bakar, A. (2014). The scholarship of teaching and learning: Challenges for Malaysian academics. *Teaching in Higher Education, 19*(1), 38-48. http://dx.doi.org/10.1080/13562517.2013.827654

Harp, S. F., & Maslich, A. A. (2005). The consequences of including seductive details during lecture. *Teaching of Psychology, 32*(2), 100-103. https://doi.org/10.1207%2Fs15328023top3202_4

Harris, B. A. (2001). The importance of creating a "sense of community." *Journal of College Student Retention, 8*(1), 83-105. https://doi.org/10.2190%2FAMNM-2VKP-V6MH-D1GF

Hasweh, M. Z. (1987). Effects of subject matter knowledge in the teaching of biology and physics. *Teaching and Teacher Education, 3*(1), 109-120. https://doi.org/10.1016/0742-051X(87)90012-6

Hativa, N. (2000). Becoming a better teacher: A case of changing the pedagogical knowledge and beliefs of law professors. *Instructional Science, 29,* 491-523. https://doi.org/10.1023/A:1026521725494

Hativa, N. (2013). *Student ratings of instruction: A practical approach to designing, operating, and reporting.* Oron Publications.

Hatton, N., & Smith, D. (1995). Reflection in teacher education: Towards definition and implementation. *Teaching and Teacher Education, 11*(1), 33-49. https://doi.org/10.1016/0742-051X(94)00012-U

Hausmann, L. R. M., Ye, F., Schofield, J. W., & Woods, R. L. (2019). Sense of belonging and persistence in White and African American first-year students. *Research in Higher Education, 50*, 649-669. https://doi.org/10.1007/s11162-009-9137-8

Healey, M. (2000). Developing the scholarship of teaching in higher education: A discipline-based approach. *Higher Education Research and Development, 19*(2), 169-189. https://doi.org/10.1080/072943600445637

Hearn, M. C. (2012). Positionality, intersectionality, and power: Socially locating the higher education teacher in multicultural education. *Multicultural Education Review, 4*(2), 39-59. https://doi.org/10.1080/2005615X.2011.11102893

Hechter, M., & Opp, K-D. (Eds.). (2001). *Social norms.* Russell Sage Foundation.

Hedley, A. R. (1994). Interpersonal and interactional aspects of teaching. *Teaching Sociology, 18*(1), 32-38. https://www.jstor.org/stable/i256590

Henley, D. C. (2003). Use of web-based formative assessment to support student learning in a metabolism/nutrition unit. *European Journal of Dental Education, 7*(3), 116-122. https://doi.org/10.1034/j.1600-0579.2003.00310.x

Hew, K. F., Qiao, C., & Tang, Y. (2018). Understanding student engagement in large-scale open online courses: A machine learning facilitated analysis of student's reflections in 18 highly rated MOOCs. *The International Review of Research in Open and Distributed Learning, 19*(3). https://doi.org/10.19173/irrodl.v19i3.3596

Hockings, C. (2010). *Inclusive learning and teaching in higher education: A synthesis of research.* Higher Education Academy. https://www.plymouth.ac.uk/uploads/production/document/path/2/2735/Inclusive_teaching_and_learning_in_HEsynthesis_.pdf

Hodgson, V. (1984). Learning from lectures. In F. Marton, D. Hounsell, & N. Entwistle (Eds.), *The experiences of learning* (pp. 90-102). Scottish Academic Press.

Holbeck, R., Bergquist, E., & Lees, S. (2014). Classroom assessment techniques: Checking for student understanding in an introductory university success course. *Journal of Instructional Research, 3*, 38-42.

Hollander, J. (2002). Learning to discuss: Strategies for improving the quality of class discussion. *Teaching Sociology, 30*(3), 317-327. https://doi.org/10.2307/3211480

Hora, M. T., & Oleson, A. K. (2017). Examining study habits in undergraduate STEM courses from a situative perspective. *International Journal of STEM Education, 4*(1). https://link.springer.com/content/pdf/10.1186/s40594-017-0055-6.pdf

Hora, M. T., & Smolarek, B. (2018). Examining faculty reflective practice: A call for critical awareness and institutional support. *The Journal of Higher Education, 89*, 1-29. https://doi.org/10.1080/00221546.2018.1437663

Hostetter, C., & Busch, M. (2006). Measuring up online: The relationship between social presence and student learning satisfaction. *Journal of Scholarship of Teaching and Learning, 6*(2), 1-12.

Howard, W., Perrotte, G., Lee, M., & Frisone, J. (2017). A formative case evaluation for the design of an online delivery model providing access to study abroad activities. *Online Learning, 21*(3), 115-134.

Hu, S., & McCormick, A. C. (2012). An engagement-based student typology and its relationship to college outcomes. *Research in Higher Education, 53*(7), 738-754.

Huber, M., & Hutchings, P. (2005). *The advancement of learning: Building the teaching commons.* Jossey-Bass.

Huber, M., & Morreale, S. (Eds). (2002). *Disciplinary styles in the scholarship of teaching and learning: Exploring common ground.* American Association for Higher Education; The Carnegie Foundation for the Advancement of Teaching.

Hurtado, S., & Carter, D. F. (1997). Effects of college transition and perceptions of the campus racial climate on Latino students' sense of belonging. *Sociology of Education, 70*(4), 324-345. https://doi.org/10.2307/2673270

Huston, T. A. (2005). *Research report: Race and gender bias in student evaluations of teaching.* Seattle University Center for Excellence in Teaching and Learning. http://sun.skidmore.union.edu/sunNET/ResourceFiles/Huston_Race_Gender_TeachingEvals.pdf

Hutchings, P. (2000). Approaching the scholarship of teaching and learning. In P. Hutchings (Ed.), Opening lines: Approaches to the scholarship of teaching and learning (pp. 1-10). Carnegie Publications, the Carnegie Foundation for the Advancement of Teaching.

Hutchings, P., Huber, M. T., & Ciccone, A. (2011). *The scholarship of teaching and learning reconsidered: Institutional integration and impact.* Jossey-Bass.

Hutchings, P., & Shulman, L. S. (1999). The scholarship of teaching: New elaborations, new developments. *Change: The Magazine of Higher Learning, 31*(5), 10-15. https://doi.org/10.1080/00091389909604218

Imel, S. (1992). *Reflective practice in adult education.* (ED346319). https://eric.ed.gov/?id=ED346319

Isaias, P., McKimmie, B., Bakharia, A., Zornig, J., & Morris, A. (2017). How to flip a classroom and improve student learning and engagement: The case of PSYC1030. *International Association for Development of the Information Society, 18*, 60-69.

Jencks, C. J., & Reisman, D. (1969). *The academic revolution.* Doubleday Anchor Books.

Jenkins, J. J. (2014a). *The diversity paradox: Seeking community in an intercultural church.* Lexington Books.

Jenkins, J. J. (2014b). A "community" of discipline: The paradox of diversity within an intercultural church. *Western Journal of Communication, 78*(2), 134-154. https://doi.org/10.1080/10570314.2013.845793

Jeong, H., Hmelo-Silver, C., & Kihyuno, J. (2019). Ten years of computer-supported collaborative learning: A meta-analysis of CSCL in STEM education during 2005-2014. *Educational Research Review, 28*(2019), 100284, 1-17. https://doi.org/10.1016/j.edurev.2019.100284

Jervis, F. M., & Congdon, R. G. (1958). Student and faculty perceptions of educational values. *American Psychologist, 13*(8), 464-466. https://doi.org/10.1037/h0046996

Johnson, D. W., & Johnson, R. T. (1997). Academic controversy: Increase intellectual conflict and increase the quality of learning. In W. E. Campbell & K. A. Smith (Eds.), *New paradigms for college teaching* (pp. 212-242). Interaction Book.

Johnson, D. W., Johnson, R. T., & Smith, K. (1998). *Active learning: Cooperation in the college classroom.* Interaction Book Company.

Johnson, D. W., Johnson, R. T., & Smith, K. A. (1991). *Cooperative learning: Increasing college faculty instructional productivity* (ASHE-ERIC Higher Education Reports, No. 4). George Washington University. https://files.eric.ed.gov/fulltext/ED343465.pdf

Johnson, D. W., Johnson, R. T., & Smith, K. A. (2014). The power of cooperative learning for university classes: The interrelationships among theory, research, and practice. *Journal on Excellence in College Teaching, 25*(3-4), 85-118.

Johnson, D. W., Johnson, R. T., & Stanne, M. B. (2000). *Cooperative learning methods: A meta-analysis.* https://www.researchgate.net/profile/David_Johnson50/publication/220040324_Cooperative_learning_methods_A_meta-analysis/links/00b4952b39d258145c000000.pdf

Johnson-Bailey, J., & Lee, M-Y. (2005). Women of color in the academy: Where's our authority? *Feminist Teacher, 15*(2), 111-122. http://www.jstor.org/stable/40545917?origin=JSTOR-pdf

Jordi, R. (2011). Reframing the concept of reflection: Consciousness, experiential learning, and reflective learning practices. *Adult Education Quarterly, 61*(2), 181-197. https://doi.org/10.1177/0741713610380439

Joyce, A. (2017). Course difficulty and its association with student perceptions of teaching and learning--RESEARCH. *Kentucky Journal of Excellence in College Teaching and Learning, 14,* Article 4. https://encompass.eku.edu/kjectl/vol14/iss/4

Junco, R., Heiberger, G., & Loken, E. (2011). The effect of Twitter on college student engagement and grades. *Journal of Computer Assisted Learning, 27*(2), 119-132. https://doi.org/10.1111/j.1365-2729.2010.00387

Kane, R., Sandretto, S., & Heath, C. (2004). An investigation into excellent tertiary teaching: Emphasizing reflective practice. *Higher Education, 47*(3), 283-310.

Kanuka, H., Rourke, L., & Laflamme, E. (2007). The influence of instructional methods on the quality of online discussion. *British Journal of Educational Technology, 38*(2), 260-271.

Kaplan, R. (1976). Effects of grouping and response characteristics of instructional objectives when learning from prose. *Journal of Educational Psychology, 68*(4), 424-430. https://doi.org/10.1037/0022-0663.68.4.424

Karp, D. A., & Yoels, W. C. (1976). The college classroom: Some observations on the meanings of student participation. *Sociology and Social Research, 60*(4), 421-439.

Kember, D., & Gow, L. (1994). Orientations to teaching and their effect on the quality of student learning. *Journal of Higher Education, 65*(1), 58-74. https://doi.org/10.2307/2943877

Kern, B., Mettetal, G., Dixson, M. D., & Morgan, R. K. (2015). The role of SoTL in the academy: Upon the 25th anniversary of Boyer's Scholarship Reconsidered. *Journal of the Scholarship for Teaching and Learning, 15*(3), 1-14. http://dx.doi.org/10.14434/josotl.v15i3.13623

King, P. M., & Baxter Magolda, M. B. (2005). A developmental model of intercultural maturity. *Journal of College Student Development, 46*(6), 571-592. https://doi.org/10.1353/csd.2005.0060

Kloss, R. J. (1996). Writing things down vs. writing things up: Are research papers valid? *College Teaching, 44*(1), 3-7. https://www.jstor.org/stable/27558745

Ko, J., Sammons, P., & Bakkum, L. (2013). *Effective teaching: A review of research and evidence.* CfBT Education Trust.

Kohn, A. (1993/1999). *Punished by rewards.* Houghton Mifflin.

Kolb, D. A. (1984). *Experiential learning.* Prentice Press.

Korthagen, F. A. J. (2001). *Linking practice and theory: The pedagogy of realistic teacher education.* Lawrence Erlbaum Associates Publishers.

Kreber, C. (2001). Learning experientially through case studies? A conceptual analysis. *Teaching in Higher Education, 6*(2), 217-228. https://doi.org/10.1023/A:1020464222360

Kreber, C. (1999). A course-based approach to the development of teaching-scholarship: A case study. *Teaching in Higher Education, 4,* 309-325. https://doi.org/10.1080/1356251990040301

Kreber, C. (2002). Teaching excellence, teaching expertise, and the scholarship of teaching. *Innovative Higher Education, 27,* 5-23. https://doi.org/10.1023/A:1020464222360

Kuh, G. D., Cruce, T. M., Shoup, R., Kinzie, J., & Gonyea, R. M. (2008). Unmasking the effects of student engagement on first-year college grades and persistence. *Journal of Higher Education, 79*(5), 540-563.

Kuh, G.D., Ikenberry, S.O., Jankowski, N.A., Cain, T.R., Ewell, P.T., Hutchings, P., & Kinzie, J. (2015). *Using evidence of student learning to improve higher education.* National Institute for Learning Outcomes Assessment. San Francisco, CA: Wiley/Jossey-Bass

Kuh, G. D., Kinzie, J., Buckley, J. A., Bridges, B. K., & Hayek, J. C. (2007). *Piecing together the student success puzzle: Research, propositions, and recommendations.* Jossey-Bass.

Kuit, J. A., Reay, G., & Freeman, R. (2001). Experiences of reflective teaching. *Active Learning in Higher Education, 2*(2), 128-142. https://journals.sagepub.com/doi/10.1177/1469787401002002004

Kurfiss, J. G. (1988). *Critical thinking: Theory, research, practice, and possibilities* (ASHE-ERIC Higher Education Report Vol. 2). The George Washington University. http://dx.doi.org/10.2307/1317666

Kyndt, E., Raes, E., Lismont, B., Timmers, F., Cascallar, E., & Dochy, F. (2013). A meta-analysis of the effects of face-to-face cooperative learning. Do recent studies falsify or verify earlier findings? *Educational Research Review, 10*(2013), 133-149. http://dx.doi.org/10.1016/j.edurev.2013.02.002

Ladd, E. C., & Lipsett, S. M. (1975). *The divided academy: Professors and politics.* McGraw-Hill.

Laprade, K., Perkins, D., & Gilpatrick, M. (2014). Impact of reflective practice on online teaching performance in higher education. *MERLOT Journal of Online Learning and Teaching, 10*(4), 625-639.

Larrivee, B. (2000). Transforming teaching practice: Becoming the critically reflective teacher. *Reflective Practice, 1*(3), 293-307. https://doi.org/10.1080/713693162

Lattuca, L. R., & Stark, J. S. (1994). *Shaping the college curriculum: Academic plans in context* (2nd ed.). Jossey-Bass.

Lawrence, J. H., Hart, K. A., Mackie, C., Muniz, D., & Dickman, E. (1990). *A comparison of the teaching goals, assumptions, and practices of faculty in eight liberal arts disciplines* (ED326115) [Paper presentation]. Annual Meeting of the Association for the Study of Higher Education, Portland, OR, United States. ERIC. https://files.eric.ed.gov/fulltext/ED326115.pdf

Lawrie, G., Marquis, E., Fuller, E., Newman, T., Qiu, M., Nomikoudis, M., Roelofs, F., & van Dam, L. (2017). Moving towards inclusive learning and teaching: A synthesis of recent literature. *Teaching & Learning Inquiry, 5*(1), 9-21. http://dx.doi.org/10.20343/teachlearninqu.5.1.3

Layne, L. (2012). Defining effective teaching. *Journal on Excellence in College Teaching, 23*(1), 43-68. http://celt.muohio.edu/ject/issue.php?v=23&n=1

Lazos, S. R. (2011) Are student teaching evaluations holding back women and minorities? The perils of "doing" gender and race in the classroom. In G. Gutiérrez y Muhs, Y. F. Niemann, C. G. González, & A. P. Harris (Eds.), *Presumed incompetent: The intersections of race and class for women in academia* (pp. 164-185). Utah State University Press. http://dx.doi.org/10.2307/j.ctt4cgr3k.19

Lazowski, R. A., & Hulleman, C. S. (2016). Motivation interventions in education: A meta-analytic review. *Review of Educational Research, 86*(2), 602-640. https://doi.org/10.3102%2F0034654315617832

Leahy, W., & Sweller, J. (2011). Cognitive load theory, modality of presentation and the transient information effect. *Applied Cognitive Psychology, 25*(6), 943-951. https://doi.org/10.1002/acp.1787

Leahy, W., & Sweller, J. (2016). Cognitive load theory and the effects of transient information on the modality effect. *Instructional Science, 44*, 107-123. https://doi.org/10.1007/s11251-015-9362-9

Leber, J., Renkl, A., Nückles, M., & Wäschle, K. (2018). When the type of assessment counteracts teaching for understanding. *Learning: Research and Practice, 4*(2), 161-179. https://doi.org/10.1080/23735082.2017.1285422

Lee, A., Poch, R., Shaw, M., & Williams, R. (2012). *Engaging diversity in undergraduate classrooms: A pedagogy for development intercultural competence (ASHE Higher Education Report Volume 38, No. 2)*. Jossey-Bass.

Lee, J. J. (2004). Comparing institutional relationships with academic departments: A study of five academic fields. *Research in Higher Education, 45*(6), 603-624. https://doi.org/10.1023/B:RIHE.0000040265.86668.1a

Lee, S. J., & Huang, K. (2018). Online interactions and social presence in online learning. *Journal of Interactive Learning Research, 29*(1), 113-128.

Leibowitz, B., & Bozalek, V. (2016). The scholarship of teaching and learning from a social justice perspective. *Teaching in Higher Education, 21*(2), 109-122. https://doi.org/10.1080/13562517.2015.1115971

Leinhardt, G., & Smith, D. (1985). Expertise in mathematics instruction: Subject matter knowledge. *Journal of Educational Psychology 77*(3), 247-271. https://psycnet.apa.org/doi/10.1037/0022-0663.77.3.247

Lemov, D. (2010). *Teach like a champion: 49 techniques that put student on the path to college.* San Francisco: Jossey-Bass.

Lenze, L. F., & Dinham, S. M. (1994). *Examining pedagogical content knowledge of college faculty new to teaching* [Paper presentation]. The Annual Meeting of the American Educational Research Association, New Orleans, LA, United States. https://files.eric.ed.gov/fulltext/ED375139.pdf

Lenze, L. F., & Dinham, S. M. (1999). Learning what students understand. In R. J. Menges (Ed.), *Faculty in new jobs: A guide to settling in, becoming established, and building institutional support* (pp. 147-165). Jossey-Bass.

Leverenz, T. R., & Lewis, B. R. (1981). *An analysis of faculty consistency in the academic professions* (ED201254). ERIC. https://files.eric.ed.gov/fulltext/ED201254.pdf

Levine, L. E., Fallahi, C. R., Nicoll-Senft, J. M., Tessier, J. T., Watson, C. L., & Wood, R. M. (2008). Creating significant learning experiences across disciplines. *College Teaching, 56*, 247-254. http://www.tandfonline.com/doi/abs/10.3200/CTCH.56.4.247-254

Levitin, D. J. (2014). *The organized mind: Thinking straight in the age of information overload.* Plume/Penguin Books.

Li, D., & Benton, S. L. (2017). *The effects of instructor gender and discipline group on student ratings of instruction* (Report No. 10). The IDEA Center. https://www.researchgate.net/publication/325319979_IDEA_Research_Report_10_April_2017_The_Effects_of_Instructor_Gender_and_Discipline_Group_on_Student_Ratings_of_Instruction

Li, H., Xiong, Y., Hunter, C. V., Guo, X., & Tywoniw, R. (2020). Does peer assessment promote student learning? A meta-analysis. *Assessment & Evaluation in Higher Education, 45*(2), 193-211.

Liebert, R. J., & Bayer, A. E. (1975). Goals in teaching undergraduates: Professional reproductions and client-centeredness. *The American Sociologist, 10*(4), 195-204. https://www.jstor.org/stable/27702193

Lindberg-Sand, A., & Sonesson, A. (2008). Compulsory higher education training in Sweden: Development of a national standards framework based on the scholarship of teaching and learning. *Tertiary Education and Management, 14*(2), 123-139. https://doi.org/10.1080/13583880802053051

Little, O., Goe, L., & Bell, C. (2009). *A practical guide to evaluating teacher effectiveness.* National Comprehensive Center for Teacher Quality. https://files.eric.ed.gov/fulltext/ED543776.pdf

Locke, E. A. (1968). Toward a theory of task motivation and incentives. *Organizational Behavior and Human Performance, 3*(2), 157-189. https://doi.org/10.1016/0030-5073(68)90004-4

Locke, E. Shaw, K., & Saari, L., & Latham, G. (1981). Goal setting and task performance: 1969-1980. *Psychological Bulletin, 90,* 125-152. 10.1037//0033-2909.90.1.125.

Lockee, B., Moore, M., & Burton, J. (2001). Old concerns with new distance education research. *Educause Quarterly, 24*(2), 60-62.

Lowman, J. (1995). *Mastering the techniques of teaching* (3rd ed.). Jossey-Bass.

Lundvall, B-Å., & Johnson, B. (1994). The learning economy. *Journal of Industry Studies, 1*(2), 23-42. https://doi.org/10.1080/13662719400000002

Macnell, L., & Driscoll, A., & Hunt, A. (2015). What's in a name: Exposing gender bias in student ratings of teaching. *Innovative Higher Education, 40,* 291-303. 10.1007/s10755-014-9313-4.

Macsuga-Gage, A., Simonsen, B., & Briere, D. (2012). Effective teaching practices: Effective teaching practices that promote a positive classroom environment. *Beyond Behavior, 22*(1), 14-22. http://dx.doi.org/10.1177/107429561202200104

Major, C. H., & Braxton, J. (2020). SoTL in perspective: An inventory of the scholarship of teaching literature with recommendations for prospective authors. *Journal of the Professoriate, 11*(2), 1-30. https://caarpweb.org/wp-content/uploads/2021/01/SOTL-in-Perspective_Major_Braxton_11_2.pdf

Major, C. H. (2015). *Teaching online: A guide to theory, research, and practice.* Johns Hopkins University Press.

Major, C. H., & Dolly, J. (2003). The importance of graduate program experiences to faculty self-efficacy for academic tasks. *Journal of Faculty Development, 19*(2), 89-100.

Major, C., & McDonald, E. (2021). Developing instructor TPACK: A research review and narrative synthesis. *Journal of Higher Education Policy and Leadership Studies, 2*(2), 51-67. DOI: https://dx.doi.org/10.29252/johepal.2.2.51

Marcketti, S., VanDerZanden, A. M., & Leptien, J. R. (2015). SoTL champions: Leveraging their lessons learned. *International Journal for the Scholarship of Teaching and Learning, 9*(1), Article 4. https://doi.org/10.20429/ijsotl.2015.090104

Marks, H. M. (2000). Student engagement in instructional activity: Patterns in the elementary, middle, and high school years. *American Educational Research Journal, 37*(1), 153-184. https://doi.org/10.3102%2F00028312037001153

Marsh, H. W. (2007). Students' evaluations of university teaching: A multidimensional perspective. In P. Perr & J. C. Smart (Eds.), *The scholarship of teaching and learning in higher education: An evidence-based perspective* (pp. 319-384). Springer. https://doi.org/10.1007/1-4020-5742-3_9

Marsh, H. W., & Roche, L. A. (1997). Making students' evaluations of teaching effectiveness effective: The critical issues of validity, bias, and utility. *American Psychologist, 52*, 1187-1197. http://dx.doi.org/10.1037//0003-066X.52.11.1187

Mårtensson, K., Roxå, T., & Olsson, T. (2011). Developing a quality culture through the scholarship of teaching and learning. *Higher Education Research and Development, 30*(1), 51-62. http://dx.doi.org/10.1080/07294360.2011.536972

Martin, E., Prosser, M., Trigwell, K., Ramsden, P., & Benjamin, J. (2000). What university teachers teach and how they teach it. *Instructional Science, 28*, 387-412. https://doi.org/10.1023/A:1026559912774

Marton, F., & Säljö, R. (1976). On qualitative differences in learning: I. Outcome and process. *British Journal of Educational Psychology, 46*(2), 4-11. https://doi.org/10.1111/j.2044-8279.1976.tb02980.x

Maslow, A. H. (1943). A theory of human motivation. *Psychological Review, 50*(4), 370-396. https://psycnet.apa.org/doi/10.1037/h0054346

Mayer, R. E., & Moreno, R. (2003). Nine ways to reduce cognitive load in multimedia learning. *Educational Psychologist, 38*(1), 43-52. http://dx.doi.org/10.1207/S15326985EP3801_6

McAlpine, L., & Weston, C. (2000). Reflection: Issues related to improving professors' teaching and students' learning. *Instructional Science, 28*, 363-385. https://doi.org/10.1023/A:1026583208230

McAlpine, L., Weston, C., Beauchamp, C., & Wiseman, C. (1999). Building a metacognitive model of reflection. *Higher Education, 37*, 105-131. https://doi.org/10.1023/A:1003548425626

McCann, T. M., Johannessen, L. R., Kahn, E., & Flanagan, J. M. (2006). *Talking in class: Using discussion to enhance teaching and learning.* National Council of Teachers of English.

McGonigal, K. (2005). Teaching for transformation: From learning theory to teaching strategies. *Speaking of Teaching, 14*(2), 1-3. http://arrs.org/uploadedFiles/ARRS/Life_Long_Learning_Center/Educators_ToolKit/STN_transformation.pdf

McKeachie, W. J. (2002). *McKeachie's teaching tips: Strategies, research, and theory for college and university teachers.* Houghton Mifflin

McKinney, J. P., McKinney, K. G., Franiuk, R., & Schweitzer, J. (2006). The college classroom as a community. *College Teaching, 54*(3), 281-284. https://www.jstor.org/stable/27559284

McKinney, K. (Ed.). (2013). *The scholarship of teaching and learning in and across the disciplines.* Indiana University Press.

McLean, M., & Blackwell, R. (1997) Opportunity knocks? Professionalism and excellence in university teaching, *Teachers and Teaching, 3*(1), 85-99. https://www.tandfonline.com/doi/abs/10.1080/1354060970030106

McMillan, D. W., & Chavis, D. M. (1986). Sense of community: A definition and theory. *Journal of Community Psychology, 14*(1), 6-23. https://doi.org/10.1002/1520-6629(198601)14:1<6::AID-JCOP2290140103>3.0.CO;2-I

Means, B., Toyama, Y., Murphy, R., Bakia, M., & Jones, K. (2010, September). *Evaluation of evidence-based practices in online learning: A meta-analysis and review of online learning studies.* Monograph. https://www2.ed.gov/rschstat/eval/tech/evidence-based-practices/finalreport.pdf

Mengel, F., Sauermann, J., & Zölitz, U. (2019). Gender bias in teaching evaluations. *Journal of the European Economic Association, 17*(2), 535-566. https://doi.org/10.1093/jeea/jvx057

Meyers, R. A. (2007). *Guidelines for human research participants in scholarship of teaching and learning research.* http://sotl.ucalgaryblogs.ca/files/2015/11/Meyers-IRB-White-Paper_SoTL-Leadership-Site.pdf

Mezirow, J. (1990). How critical reflection triggers transformative learning. In J. Mezirow & Associates (Eds.), *Fostering critical reflection in adulthood.* Jossey-Bass. https://skat.ihmc.us/rid=1LW06D9V6-26428MK-1Z64/Mezirow's%20chapter,%20How%20Critical%20Refletion%20Triggers%20TL.pdf

Mezirow, J. (1997). Transformative learning: Theory to practice. In P. Cranton (Ed.), *Transformative learning in action: Insights from practice* (pp. 5-12). Jossey-Bass. https://doi.org/10.1002/ace.7401

Michaelsen, L. K., Davidson, N., & Major, C. H. (2014). Team-based learning practices and principles in comparison with cooperative learning and problem-based learning. *Journal on Excellence in College Teaching, 25*(3/4), 57-84. http://celt.miamioh.edu/ject/issue.php?v=25&n=3%20and%204

Miller, J. E., Groccia, J. E., & Wilkes, J. M. (1996). Providing structure: The critical element. In T. E. Sutherland & C. C. Bonwell (Eds.), *Using active learning in college classes: A range of options for faculty* (No. 67, pp. 17-30). *New Directions for Teaching and Learning*; John Wiley & Sons. https://doi.org/10.1002/tl.37219966705

Miller, J. E., Trimbur, J., & Wilkes, J. M. (1994). Group dynamics: Understanding group success and failure in collaborative learning. In K. Bosworth & S. J. Hamilton (Eds.), *Collaborative learning: Underlying processes and effective techniques* (No. 59, pp. 33-44). New Directions for Teaching and Learning; Jossey-Bass. https://doi.org/10.1002/tl.37219945906

Miller-Young, J., & Yeo, M. (2015). Conceptualizing and communicating SoTL: A framework for the field. *Teaching and Learning Inquiry, 3*(2), 37-53. https://doi.org/10.20343/teachlearninqu.3.2.37

Millis, B. J., & Cottell, P. G. (1998). *Cooperative learning for higher education faculty.* Oryx Press.

Mishra, P., & Koehler, M. J. (2006). Technological pedagogical content knowledge: A framework for integrating technology in teachers' knowledge. *Teachers College Record, 108*(6), 1017–1054.

Mitchell, K., & Martin, J. (2018). Gender bias in student evaluations. *PS: Political Science & Politics, 51*(3), 648-652. https://doi.org/10.1017/S104909651800001X

Mitchell, K. W., & Manzo, W. H. (2018). The purpose and perception of learning objectives. *Journal of Political Science Education, 14*(4), 456-472. DOI: 10.1080/15512169.2018.1433542

Morrison, G. R., Ross, S. M., Kemp, J. E., & Kalman, H. (2009). *Designing effective instruction* (6th ed.). Wiley.

Mousavi, S., Low, R., & Sweller, J. (1995). Reducing cognitive load by mixing auditory and visual presentation modes. *Journal of Educational Psychology, 87,* 319-334. https://doi.org/10.1037/0022-0663.87.2.319

Mtawa, N., Fongwa, S., & Wangenge-Ouma, G. (2016). The scholarship of university-community engagement: Interrogating Boyer's model. *International Journal of Educational Development, 49,* 126-133. https://doi.org/10.1016/j.ijedudev.2016.01.007

Murphy, K. P., Wilkinson, I. A. G., Soter, A. O., Hennessey, M. N., & Alexander, J. F. (2009). Examining the effects of classroom discussion on students' comprehension of text: A meta-analysis. *Journal of Educational Psychology, 101*(3), 740-764. https://doi.apa.org/doi/10.1037/a0015576

Murray, M. H. (1997). Better learning through curricular design at a reduced cost. *The Research Journal for Engineering Education, 86*(4), 309-313. https://doi.org/10.1002/j.2168-9830.1997.tb00303.x

Murray, R. (Ed.) (2008). *The scholarship of teaching and learning in higher education.* Open University Press.

Natasi, B. K., & Clements, D. H. (1991). Research on cooperative learning: Implications for practice. *School Psychology Review, 20*(1), 110-131. http://dx.doi.org/10.1080/02796015.1991.12085536

National Survey of Student Engagement. (2013). *A fresh look at student engagement – Annual Results 2013*. Indiana University Center for Postsecondary Research.

Nelson, C. E. (2003). Doing it: Examples of several of the different genres of the scholarship of teaching and learning. *Journal on Excellence in College Teaching, 14*(2), 85-94.

Newmann, F. M., Wehlage, G. G., & Lamborn, S. D. (1992). The significance and sources of student engagement. In F. Newmann (Ed.), *Student engagement and achievement in American secondary schools.* Teachers College Press. https://files.eric.ed.gov/fulltext/ED371047.pdf

Ng, C. (2018). "I learn for a job promotion!": The role of outcome-focused career goals in motivating distance learners to learn. *Distance Education, 39*(3), 390-410.

Nilson, L. B. (2010). Teaching at its best: *A research-based resource for college instructors.* Jossey-Bass.

Nilson, L. B. (2012). Time to raise questions about student ratings. In J. E. Groccia (Ed.), *To improve the academy: Resources for faculty, instructional, and organizational development* (Vol. 31, pp. 213-228). Jossey-Bass.

Nilson, L. B. (2013). *Creating self-regulated learners: Strategies to strengthen students' self- awareness and learning skills.* Stylus.

Noetel, M., Griffith, S., Delaney, O., Sanders, T., Parker, P. D., del Pozo Cruz, B., & Lonsdale, C. (2021). Video improves learning in higher education: A systematic review. *Review of Educational Research.* https://doi.org/10.3102/0034654321990713

Noteboom, J. T., & Claywell, L. (2010). *Student perceptions of cognitive, social, and teaching presence.* Paper presented at the 26th Annual Conference on Distance Teaching & Learning, USA.

Nusbaum, A. T., Swindell, S., & Plemons A. (2021). Kindness at first sight: The role of syllabi in impression formation. *Teaching of Psychology, 48*(2), 130-143. doi:10.1177/0098628320959953

Onwuegbuzie, A. J., Dickinson, W. B., Leech, N. L., & Zoran, A. G. (2009). A qualitative framework for collecting and analyzing data in focus group research. *International Journal of Qualitative Methods, 8*(3), 1-21. doi:10.1177/160940690900800301

Osterman, K. F. (1990). Reflective practice: A new agenda for education. *Education and Urban Society, 22*(2), 133-152. https://doi.org/10.1177/0013124590022002002

O'Sullivan, S. (2011). Applying the scholarship of teaching and learning in an Irish context: Mission impossible? *Teaching Sociology, 39*(3), 303-319. https://doi.org/10.1177%2F0092055X11407287

Page, S. (2007). *The difference: How the power of diversity creates better groups, firms, schools, and societies.* Princeton University Press.

Palmquist, B. (2011). Star motions with sky simulators. *The Classroom Astronomer, 3*(1), 20-23.

Pan, D., Tan, G. S. H., Ragupathi, K., Booluck, K., Roop, R., & Ip, Y. K. (2009). Profiling teacher/teaching using descriptors derived from qualitative feedback: Formative and summative applications. *Research in Higher Education, 50*(1), 73-100. https://doi.org/10.1007/s11162-008-9109-4

Pani, J. R., Chariker, J. H., Naaz, F., Mattingly, W., Roberts, J., & Sephton, S. E. (2014). Learning with interactive computer graphics in the undergraduate neuroscience classroom. *Advances in Health Sciences Education, 19*, 507-528. https://doi.org/10.1007/s10459-013-9483-3

Papadima-Sophocleous, S., & Giannikas, C. N. (2019). Time to evaluate: The students' perspective of an online MA in CALL programme. In F. Meunier, J., Van d Vyver, L., Bradley, & S. Thouësny (Eds.), *CALL and complexity – short papers from EUROCALL 2019* (pp. 334-339). https://research-publishing.net/publication/chapters/978-2-490057-54-2/1032.pdf

Pascarella, E. T., & Terenzini, P. T. (2005). *How college affects students: A third decade of research.* John Wiley & Sons.

Patterson, M. C. (2017). A naturalistic investigation of media multitasking while studying and the effects on exam performance. *Teaching of Psychology, 44*(1), 51-57. https://doi.org/10.1177%2F0098628316677913

Paulsen J., & McCormick A. C. (2020). Reassessing disparities in online learner student engagement in higher education. *Educational Researcher, 49*(1), 20-29. doi:10.3102/0013189X19898690

Paunesku, D., Walton, G. M., Romero, C., Smith, E. N., Yeager, D. S., & Dweck, C. S. (2015). Mind-set interventions are a scalable treatment for academic underachievement. *Psychological Science, 26*(6), 784-793.

Peeck, J. (1993). Increasing picture effects in learning from illustrated text. *Learning and Instruction, 3*(3), 227-238. https://doi.org/10.1016/0959-4752(93)90006-L

Platt, G. M., Parsons, T., & Kirshstein, R. (1976). Faculty teaching goals, 1968-1973. *Social Problems, 24*, 298-307. https://doi.org/10.2307/800347

Pollock, P. H., Hamann, K., & Wilson, B. M. (2011). Learning through discussions: Comparing benefits of small-group and large class setting. *Journal of Political Science Education, 7*(1), 48-64. https://doi.org/10.1080/15512169.2011.539913

Prince, M. (2004). Does active learning work? A review of the research. *Journal of Engineering Education, 93*(3), 223-231. https://doi.org/10.1002/j.2168-9830.2004.tb00809.x

Pugh, K. (Author), & Alsukairi, Z. (Designer). (2019). *The big ideas of motivation* [Infographic]. Learning and Experience. https://learningandexperienceblog.files.wordpress.com/2019/09/motivationbigideas-infographic.pdf

Rabe-Hemp, C., Woollen, S., & Humiston, G. S. (2009). A comparative analysis of student engagement, learning, and satisfaction in lecture hall and online learning settings. *Quarterly Review of Distance Education, 10*(2), 207-218.

Raffini, J. P. (1996). *150 ways to increase intrinsic motivation in the classroom.* Allyn and Bacon.

Ravenscroft, B., Luhanga, U., & King, B. (2017). Adapting Bangert's online teaching effectiveness evaluation tool to a Canadian context. *Innovations in Education and Teaching International, 54*(4), 355-363. https://doi.org/10.1080/14703297.2016.1231618

Reid, L. D. (2010). The role of perceived race and gender in the evaluation of college teaching on RateMyProfessors.com. *Journal of Diversity in Higher Education, 3*(3), 137-152. https://www-sciencedirect-com.libdata.lib.ua.edu/science/article/pii/S0191491X16300232?via%3Dihub#bbib0665

Reschly, A. L., Huebner, E. S., Appleton, J. J., & Antaramian, S. (2008). Engagement as flourishing: The contribution of positive emotions and coping to adolescents' engagement at school and with learning. *Psychology in the Schools, 45*(5), 419-431. https://doi.org/10.1002/pits.20306

Rice, R. E. (1991). *Rethinking what it means to be a scholar. Teaching excellence: Toward the best in the academy.* POD Network.

Richardson, J. C., & Ice, P. (2010). Investigating students' level of critical thinking across instructional strategies in online discussions. *Internet and Higher Education, 13*(1), 52-59. Elsevier Ltd. from https://www.learntechlib.org/p/108359/.

Richardson, J. C., Koehler, A., Besser, E., Caskurlu, S., Lim, J., & Mueller, C. (2015). Conceptualizing and investigating instructor presence in online learning environments. *The International Review of Research in Open and Distance Learning, 16*(3), 256-297.

Richmond, A., Boysen, G., & Gurung, R. A. R. (2016). An evidence-based guide to college and university teaching: *Developing the model teacher* (1st ed.). Routledge. https://doi.org/10.4324/9781315642529

Rink, J. (2013). Measuring teacher effectiveness in physical education. *Research Quarterly for Exercise and Sport, 84*(4), 407-418. https://doi.org/10.1080/02701367.2013.844018

Risko, E. F., Anderson, N., Sarwal, A., Engelhardt, M., & Kingstone, A. (2012). Everyday attention: Variation in mind wandering and memory in a lecture. *Cognitive Psychology, 26*(2), 234-242. https://doi.org/10.1002/acp.1814

Robinson, C. C., & Hullinger, H. (2008). New benchmarks in higher education: Student engagement in online learning. *Journal of Education for Business, 84*(2), 101-109.

Rose, D. H., & Meyer, A. (2002). *Teaching every student in the digital age: Universal design for learning.* Association for Supervision and Curriculum Development.

Rovai, A. P. (2001). Building classroom community at a distance: A case study. *Educational Technology Research and Development, 49*(4), 33-48. https://doi.org/10.1007/BF02504946

Rovai, A. P. (2002). Building sense of community at a distance. *International Review of Research in Open and Distance Learning, 3*(1). https://doi.org/10.19173/irrodl.v3i1.79

Royal, K. D. (2010). Evaluating faculty perceptions of student learning outcomes: A Rasch measurement analysis. *Journal of MultiDisciplinary Evaluation, 6*(114), 18-31. https://eric.ed.gov/?id=EJ909610

Royal, K. D., Eli, J. A., & Bradley, K. D. (2010). Exploring community college faculty perceptions of student outcomes: Findings of a pilot study. *Community College Journal of Research & Practice, 34*(7), 523-540. https://doi.org/10.1080/10668920701827025

Royer, P. N. (1977). Effects of specificity and position of written instructional objectives on learning from lecture. *Journal of Educational Psychology, 69*(1), 40-45. https://doi.org/10.1037/0022-0663.69.1.40

Rust, C., Price, M., & O'Donovan, B. (2003). Improving students' learning by developing their understanding of assessment criteria and processes. *Assessment & Evaluation in Higher Education, 28*, 147-164. http://area.fc.ul.pt/artigos%20publicados%20internacionais/Improving%20students%20learning.pdf

Rutherford, P. (2012). *Active learning and engagement strategies.* Just ASK Publications.

Ryman, S., Burrell, L., & Richardson, B. (2009). Creating and sustaining online learning communities: Designing environments for transformative learning. *International Journal of Pedagogies and Learning, 5*(3), 46-58.

Säljö, R. (1979). Learning about learning. *Higher Education 8*(4), 443-451. https://doi.org/10.1007/BF01680533

Saville, B. K., Lambert, T., & Robertson, S. (2011). Interteaching: Bringing behavioral education into the 21st century. *Psychological Record, 61*(1), 153-166. https://doi.org/10.1007/BF03395752

Sax, L. J. (1996). The dynamics of "tokenism:" How college students are affected by the proportion of women in their major. *Research in Higher Education, 37*(3), 389-425. https://doi.org/10.1007/BF01730108

Scerbo, M. W., Warm, J. S., Dember, W. N., & Grasha, A. F. (1992). The role of time and cuing in a college lecture. *Contemporary Educational Psychology, 17*(4), 312-328. https://doi.org/10.1016/0361-476X(92)90070-F

Schinske, J., & Tanner, K. (2014). Teaching more by grading less (or differently). *CBE Life Sciences Education, 13*(2), 159-166. https://doi.org/10.1187/cbe.cbe-14-03-0054

Schön, D. A. (1983). *The reflective practitioner: How professionals think in action.* Basic Books, Inc.

Schwartz, D. L., Tsang, J. M., & Blair, K. B. (2016). *The ABCs of how we learn: 26 scientifically proven approaches, how they work, and when to use them* (1st ed.). W.W. Norton & Company.

Shaffer, C., & Anundsen, K. (1993). *Creating community anywhere: Finding support and connection in a fragmented world.* Putnam Publishing Group.

Shea, P., & Bidjerano, T. (2009). Community of inquiry as a theoretical framework to foster "epistemic engagement" and "cognitive presence" in online education. *Computers & Education, 52*(3), 543-553. from https://www.learntechlib.org/p/66906/.

Shea, P., Sau Li, C., & Pickett, A. (2006). A study of teaching presence and student sense of learning community in fully online and web-enhanced college courses. *The Internet and Higher Education, 9,* 175-190. doi:10.1016/j.iheduc.2006.06.005

Shelton, C. C., Warren, A. E., & Archambault, L. M. (2016). Exploring the use of interactive digital storytelling video: Promoting student engagement and learning in a university hybrid course. *TechTrends, 60*(5), 465-474.

Short, F., & Martin, J. (2011). Presentation vs. performance: Effects of lecturing style in higher education on student preference and student learning. *Psychology Teaching Review, 17*(2), 71-82. https://files.eric.ed.gov/fulltext/EJ959028.pdf

Shulman, L. S. (1986). Those who understand: Knowledge growth in teaching. *Educational Researcher, 15*(2), 4-14. https://doi.org/10.3102%2F0013189X015002004

Shulman, L. S. (1987). Knowledge and teaching: Foundations of the new reform. *Harvard Educational Review, 57*(1), 1-23. https://doi.org/10.17763/haer.57.1.j463w79r56455411

Shulman, L. S. (1991). Ways of seeing, ways of knowing: Ways of teaching, ways of learning about teaching. *Journal of Curriculum Studies, 23*(5), 393-395. https://doi.org/10.1080/0022027910230501

Shulman, L. S. (2002). Making differences: A table of learning. *Change, 34*(6), 36-44. http://dx.doi.org/10.1080/00091380209605567

Silberman, M. (1996). *Active learning: 101 strategies to teach any subject.* Allyn & Bacon.

Simmons, N., & Poole, G. (2016). The history of SoTL in Canada: Answering calls for action. *New Directions for Teaching and Learning, 146,* 13-22. https://doi.org/10.1002/tl.20182

Sing, C. C., & Khine, M. S. (2006). An analysis of interaction and participation patterns in online community. *Educational Technology and Society, 9*(1), 250-261

Singh, C. (2006). *Introduction to educational technology.* Lotus Press.

Skinner, E. A., Kindermann, T. A., & Furrer, C. J. (2009). A motivational perspective on engagement and disaffection: Conceptualization and assessment of children's behavioral and emotional participation in academic activities in the classroom. *Educational and Psychological Measurement, 69*(3), 493-525. https://doi.org/10.1177%2F0013164408323233

Slagter van Tyron, P. J., & Bishop, M. J. (2009). Theoretical foundations for enhancing social connectedness in online learning environments. *Distance Education, 30*, 291-315.

Slavin, R. E. (1990). *Cooperative learning: Theory, research, and practice.* Allyn & Bacon.

Smart, J. C., & Ethington, C. A. (1995). Disciplinary and institutional differences in undergraduate education goals. In N. Hativa & M. Marincovich (Eds.), *Disciplinary differences in teaching and learning: Implications for practice* (pp. 49-57). Jossey-Bass. https://doi.org/10.1002/tl.37219956408

Smart, J. C., Feldman, K. A., & Ethington, C. A. (2000). *Academic disciplines: Holland's theory and the study of college students and faculty.* Vanderbilt University Press.

Smith, B. P. (2007). Student ratings of teaching effectiveness: An analysis of end-of-course faculty evaluations. *College Student Journal, 41*(4), 788-800. https://eric.ed.gov/?id=EJ816803

Smith, B. P. (2009). Student ratings of teaching effectiveness for faculty groups based on race and gender. *Education, 129*(4), 615-624. https://eric.ed.gov/?id=EJ871612

Smith, B. P., & Hawkins, B. (2011). Examining student evaluations of black college faculty: Does race matter? *The Journal of Negro Education, 80*(2), 149-162. https://www.jstor.org/stable/41341117

Smith, B. P., & Johnson-Bailey, J. (2011/2012). Implications for non-white women in the academy. *The Negro Educational Review, 62-63*(1-4), 115-140.

Smith, K. A. (1996). Cooperative learning: Making "group work" work. In T. E. Sutherland & C. C. Bonwell (Eds.), *Using active learning in college classes: A range of options for faculty* (No. 67, pp. 71-82). *New Directions for Teaching and Learning*; Jossey-Bass. https://karlsmithmn.org/wp-content/uploads/2020/07/Smith-Making_Groupwork_Work-NDTL-67-1996-draft.pdf

Smith, K. A. (2000). Going deeper: Formal small-group learning in large classes. In J. MacGregor, J. L. Cooper, K. A. Smith, & P. Robinson (Eds.), *New directions for teaching and learning: Strategies for energizing large classes; From small groups to learning communities, 81*, 25-46. https://doi.org/10.1002/tl.8103

Smith, K. A., Sheppard, S. D., Johnson, D. W., & Johnson, R. T. (2005). Pedagogies of engagement: Classroom-based practices. *Journal of Engineering Education, 94*(1), 87-101. https://doi.org/10.1002/j.2168-9830.2005.tb00831.x

Sodhi, M. K., & Cohen, H. L. (2012). The manifestation and integration of embodied knowing into social work practice. *Adult Education Quarterly, 62*(2), 120-137. https://doi.org/10.1177%2F0741713611400302

Solórzano, D., Ceja, M., & Yosso, T. (2000). Critical race theory, racial microaggressions, and campus racial climate: The experiences of African American college students. *Journal of Negro Education, 69*(1-2), 60-73. https://www.jstor.org/stable/2696265

Song, H., & Schwarz, N. (2008). If it's hard to read, it's hard to do: Processing fluency affects effort prediction and motivation. *Psychological Science, 19*(10), 986-988. https://journals.sagepub.com/doi/10.1111/j.1467-9280.2008.02189.x

Sousa, D. A. (2006). *How the brain learns.* Corwin Press.

Spillane, J. P. (2012). Data in practice: Conceptualizing the data-based decision-making phenomena. *American Journal of Education, 118*(2), 113-141. http://dx.doi.org/10.1086/663283

Spooren, P., Brockx, B., & Mortelmans, D. (2013). On the validity of student evaluation of teaching: The state of the art. *Review of Educational Research, 83*(4), 598-642. https://doi.org/10.3102/0034654313496870

Springer, L., Stanne, M. E., & Donovan, S. S. (1999). Effects of small-group learning on undergraduates in science, mathematics, engineering, and technology: A meta-analysis. *Review of Educational Research, 69*, 21-51. https://doi.org/10.3102%2F00346543069001021

Stark, J. S. (2000). Planning introductory college courses: Content, context, and form. *Instructional Science, 28*, 413-438.

Stark, J. S., & Morstain, B. R. (1978). Educational orientations of faculty in liberal arts colleges: An analysis of disciplinary differences. *Journal of Higher Education, 49*(5), 420-437. https://www.jstor.org/stable/1980507

Steele, C. M. (2011). Foreword: Pursuing effective integrated education. *Journal of Social Issues, 67*(3), 431-434.

Stevens, D. D., & Levi, A. J. (2005). Leveling the field: Using rubrics to achieve greater equity in teaching and assessment. *Essays on Teaching Excellence, Professional and Organizational Development Network in Higher Education, 17*(1). https://pdxscholar.library.pdx.edu/cgi/viewcontent.cgi?article=1087&context=edu_fac

Stephens, N. M., Fryberg, S. A., Markus, H. R., Johnson, C. S., & Covarrubias, R. (2012). Unseen disadvantage: How American universities' focus on independence undermines the academic performance of first-generation college students. *Journal of Personality and Social Psychology, 102*(6), 1178-1197. https://psycnet.apa.org/doi/10.1037/a0027143

Strobel, J., & van Barneveld, A. (2009). When is PBL more effective? A meta-synthesis of meta-analyses comparing PBL to conventional classrooms. *Interdisciplinary Journal of Problem-Based Learning, 3*(1), 44-58. https://doi.org/10.7771/1541-5015.1046

Sue, D. W. (2010). *Microaggressions in everyday life: Race, gender, and sexual orientation.* John Wiley & Sons.

Suskie, L. (2009). *Assessing student learning: A common sense guide* (2nd ed.). Jossey-Bass.

Svinicki, M. D. (2004). Authentic assessment: Testing in reality. *New Directions for Teaching and Learning, 2004*, 23-29. https://doi.org/10.1002/tl.167

Svinicki, M., & McKeachie, W. E. (2013). *McKeachie's teaching tips: Strategies, research, and theory for college and university teachers.* Cengage.

Swan, K., Matthews, D., Bogle, L., Boles, E., & Day, S. (2012). Linking online course design and implementation to learning outcomes: A design experiment. *The Internet and Higher Education, 15*(2), 81-88. https://doi-org.libdata.lib.ua.edu/10.1016/j.iheduc.2011.07.002

Swaner, L. E. (2007). Linking engaged learning, student mental health and well-being, and civic development: A review of the literature. *Liberal Education, 93*(1), 16-25.

Sweller, J., van Merriënboer, J. J. G., & Paas, F. (2019). Cognitive architecture and instructional design: 20 years later. *Educational Psychology Review, 31*(2), 261-292. https://link.springer.com/article/10.1007/s10648-019-09465-5

Swinton, O. H., (2010). The effect of effort grading on learning. *Economics of Education Review, 29*(6), 1176-1182.

Szabo, M., & Kanuka, H. (1999). Effects of violating screen design principles of balance, unity, and focus on recall learning, study time, and completion rates. *Journal of Educational Multimedia and Hypermedia, 8*(1), 23-42.

Taylor, A. K., & Kowalski, P. (2014). *Student misconceptions: Where do they come from and what can we do?* In V. A. Benassi, C. E. Overson, & C. M. Hakala (Eds.), *Applying science of learning in education: Infusing psychological science into the curriculum* (pp. 259-273). Society for the Teaching of Psychology. https://files.eric.ed.gov/fulltext/EJ1085109.pdf

Tebben, S. L. (1995). Community and caring in a college classroom. *Journal for a Just and Caring Education, 1*(3), 335-344. https://eric.ed.gov/?id=EJ517754

Terenzini, P. T., Springer, L., Yaeger, P. M., Pascarella, E. T., & Nora, A. (1996). First-generation college students: Characteristics, experiences, and cognitive development. *Research in Higher Education, 37*(1), 1-22. https://eric.ed.gov/?id=ED387004

Theall, M., & Franklin, J. (2001). Looking for bias in all the wrong places: A search for truth or a witch hunt in student ratings of instruction? In M. Theall, P. C. Abrami, & L. A. Mets (Eds.), *The student ratings debate: Are they valid? How can we best use them? New directions for Institutional Research* (No. 109, pp. 45-56). Jossey-Bass. https://doi.org/10.1002/ir.3

Theobald, E. J., Hill, M. J., Tran, E., Agrawal, S., Arroyo, E. N., Behling, S., Chambwe, N., Cintrón, D. L., Cooper, J. D., Dunster, G., Grummer, J. A., Hennessey, K., Hsiao, J., Iranon, N., Jones, L., II, Jordt, H., Keller, M., Lacey, M. E., Littlefield, C. E., Lowe, A., & Freeman, S. (2020). Active learning narrows achievement gaps for underrepresented students in undergraduate science, technology, engineering, and math. *PNAS, 117*(12), 6476-6483. https://doi.org/10.1073/pnas.1916903117

Thistoll, T., & Yates, A. (2016). Improving course completions in distance education: An institutional case study. *Distance Education, 37*(2), 180-195.

Tight, M. (2018). Tracking the scholarship of teaching and learning. *Policy Reviews in Higher Education, 2*(1), 61-78. https://doi.org/10.1080/23322969.2017.1390690

Trigwell, K. (2013). Evidence of the impact of scholarship of teaching and learning purposes. *Teaching & Learning Inquiry: The ISSOTL Journal, 1*(1), 95-105. doi:10.2979/teachlearninqu.1.1.95

Trigwell, K., Martin, E. Benjamin, J., & Prosser, M. (2000). Scholarship of teaching: A model. *Higher Education Research and Development, 19*(2), 155-168. https://doi.org/10.1080/072943600445628

Trigwell, K., & Shale, S. (2004). Student learning and the scholarship of university teaching. *Studies in Higher Education, 29*(4), 523-536. https://doi.org/10.1080/0307507042000236407

Trochim, W. M. K. (2006). *Research methods knowledge base.* http://www.socialresearchmethods.net/kb/qualmeth.php

Tuckman, B. (1965). Developmental sequence in small groups. *Psychological Bulletin, 63*(6), 384-389. https://psycnet.apa.org/doi/10.1037/h0022100

Uttl, B., White, C. A., & Gonzalez, D. W. (2017). Meta-analysis of faculty's teaching effectiveness: Student evaluation of teaching ratings and student learning are not related. *Studies in Educational Evaluation, 54*, 22-42. https://doi.org/10.1016/j.stueduc.2016.08.007

van Manen, M. (1990). *Researching lived experience: Human science for an action sensitive pedagogy.* Albany, NY: SUNY.

Vekiri, I. (2002). What is the value of graphical displays in learning? *Educational Psychology Review, 14*(3), 261-312. https://doi.org/10.1023/A:1016064429161

Velan, G. M., Rakesh, K. K., Mark, D., & Wakefield, D. (2002). Web-based self-assessments in pathology with questionmark perception. *Pathology, 34*, 282-284. https://doi.org/10.1080/00313020220131372

Verschelden, C. (2017). *Bandwidth recovery: Helping students reclaim cognitive resources lost to poverty, racism, and social marginalization.* Stylus Publishing.

Voelker, D., & Martin, R. (2013). *Wisconsin teaching fellows & scholars program assessment project: Final report.* University of Wisconsin System, Office of Professional & Instructional Development. https://www.uwgb.edu/UWGBCMS/me dia/CATL/pdf/WTFSStudy2013.pdf

Walton, G. M., & Cohen, G. L. (2011). A brief social-belonging intervention improves academic and health outcomes of minority students. *Science, 331*(6023), 1447–1451. https://doi.org/10.1126/science.1198364

Waterman, M., Weber, J., Pracht, C., Conway, K., Kunz, D., Evans, B., & Starrett, D. (2010). Preparing scholars of teaching and learning using a model of collaborative peer consulting and action research. *International Journal of Teaching and Learning in Higher Education, 22*(2), 140-155. http://files.eric.ed.gov/fulltext/EJ930146.pdf

Weiman, C. (2015). A better way to evaluate undergraduate teaching. *Change: The Magazine of Higher Learning, 47*(1), 6-15. https://doi.org/10.1080/00091383.2015.996077

Weimer, M. (2002). *Learner-centered teaching: Five key changes to practice.* Jossey-Bass.

Weimer, M. (2006). *Enhancing scholarly work on teaching and learning: Professional literature that makes a difference.* Jossey-Bass.

Weimer, M. (2014). Teaching effectiveness: The definitions of teachers and students. *Faculty Focus.* https://www.facultyfocus.com/articles/teaching-and-learning/teaching-effectiveness-definitions-teachers-students/

Wiggins, G., & McTighe, J. (1998). Backward design. *In Understanding by Design* (pp. 13-34). ASCD. https://educationaltechnology.net/wp-content/uploads/2016/01/backward-design.pdf

Willingham-McLain, L. (2015). Using a scholarship of teaching and learning approach to award faculty who innovate. *International Journal for Academic Development, 20*(1), 58-75. https://doi.org/10.1080/1360144X.2014.995661

Willits, F., & Brennan, M. (2017). Another look at college student's ratings of course quality: data from Penn State student surveys in three settings. *Assessment & Evaluation in Higher Education, 42*(3), 443-462. https://doi.org/10.1080/02602938.2015.1120858

Wilson, R. C., Gaff, J. G., Dienst, E. R., Wood, L., & Bavry, J. L. (1975). *College professors and their impact on students.* John Wiley & Sons.

Wilson-Doenges, G., & Gurung, R. A. R. (2013). Benchmarks for scholarly investigations of teaching and learning. *Australian Journal of Psychology, 65*(1), 63-70. http://dx.doi.org/10.1111/ajpy.12011

Winer, L., DiGenova, L., Costopoulos, A., & Cardoso, K. (2016). Addressing common concerns about online student ratings of instruction: A research-informed approach. *Canadian Journal of Higher Education, 46*(4), 115-131. https://doi.org/10.47678/cjhe.v46i4.186112

Winkelmes, M-A., Bernacki, M., Butler, J., Zochowski, M., Golanics, J., & Weavil, K. H. (2016). A teaching intervention that increases underserved college students' success. *Peer Review, 18*(1/2), 31-36. https://cte.ku.edu/sites/cte.ku.edu/files/docs/Branding/Winkelmes%20et%20al%20 2016%20Transparency%20and%20Underserved%20Students.pdf

Wininger, S. R. (2005). Using your tests to teach: Formative summative assessment. *Teaching of Psychology, 32*(3), 164-166. https://doi.org/10.1207/s15328023top3203_7

Wlodkowski, R. J. (2008). *Enhancing adult motivation to learn: A comprehensive guide for teaching all adults* (3rd ed.). Jossey-Bass.

Wlodkowski, R. J., & Ginsberg, M. B. (1995). A framework for culturally responsive teaching. *Educational Leadership, 54*(1), 17-21. https://eric.ed.gov/?id=EJ511715

Wong, A. K., Remin, R., Love, R., Aldred, R., Ralph, P., & Cook, C. (2013). Building pedagogical community in the classroom. *Christian Higher Education, 12*(4), 282-295. https://doi.org/10.1080/15363759.2013.805635

Wright, S. L., & Jenkins-Guarnieri, M. A. (2012). Student evaluations of teaching: Combining the meta-analyses and demonstrating further evidence for effective use. *Assessment & Evaluation in Higher Education, 37*(6), 683-699. https://doi.org/10.1080/02602938.2011.563279

Yeager, D. S., & Dweck, C. S. (2012). Mindsets that promote resilience: When students believe that personal characteristics can be developed. *Educational Psychologist, 47*(4), 302-314. https://doi.org/10.1080/00461520.2012.722805

Yeager, D. S., Hanselman, P., Walton, G. M., Murray, J. S., Crosnoe, R., Muller, C., Tipton, E., Schneider, B., Hulleman, C. S., Hinojosa, C. P., Paunesku, D., Romero, C., Flint, K., Roberts, A., Trott, J., Iachan, R., Buontempo, J., Yan, S. M., Carvalho, C. M., & Dweck, C. S. (2019). A national experiment reveals where a growth mindset improves achievement. *Nature, 573*(7774), 364-369. https://doi.org/10.1038/s41586-019-1466-y

Young, S. (2006). Student views of effective online teaching in higher education. *American Journal of Distance Education, 20*(2), 65-77. http://dx.doi.org/10.1207/s15389286ajde2002_2

Zayac, R. M., Poole, B. D., Gray, C., Sargent, M., Paulk, A., Haynes, E. (2021). No disrespect: Student and faculty perceptions of the qualities of ineffective teachers. *Teaching of Psychology, 48*(1), 55-62.

Zeichner, K. M., & Liston, D. P. (2014). *Reflective teaching: An introduction* (2nd ed.). Routledge.

Zumbrunn, S., McKim, C., Buhs, E., & Hawley, L. R. (2014). Support, belonging, motivation, and engagement in the college classroom: A mixed method study. *Instructional Science, 42*(5), 661-684. https://doi.org/10.1007/s11251-014-9310-0

# About the Authors

## ELIZABETH F. BARKLEY

Dr. Elizabeth Barkley is a best-selling author whose books have been translated into multiple languages. They include four in the Jossey-Bass/Wiley College Teaching Techniques Series: *Student Engagement Techniques: A Handbook for College Faculty* (2nd ed., with Claire H. Major, 2020), *Interactive Lecturing: A Handbook for College Faculty* (with Claire H. Major, 2018), *Learning Assessment Techniques: A Handbook for College Faculty* (with Claire H. Major, 2016), and *Collaborative Learning Techniques: A Handbook for College Faculty* (2nd ed., with Claire H. Major and K. Patricia Cross, 2014). She also wrote *Crossroads: The Roots of America's Popular Music* (2nd ed., Prentice Hall, 2007) and three interactive digital textbooks for Kendall Hunt in conjunction with Great River Learning: *Crossroads: The Music of American Cultures* (2019), *World Music: Roots to Contemporary Global Fusions* (2012), and *Great Composers and Music Masterpieces of Western Civilization* (with Robert Hartwell, 2015). Based on her books, she has been invited to present keynotes and conduct workshops at conferences and post-secondary institutions in the United States and internationally.

With more than four decades' experience as an innovative and reflective teacher, Elizabeth has received numerous honors and awards, most recently the League for Innovation's Terry O'Banion Lifetime Achievement Prize for Inspiring Significant Change to Teaching and Learning. She was also named California's Higher Education Professor of the Year by the Carnegie Foundation for the Advancement of Teaching, formally recognized by the California state legislature for her contributions to undergraduate education, chosen as one of two Carnegie Scholars in the discipline of music to conduct pioneering work in the Scholarship of Teaching and Learning, selected as "Innovator of the Year" in conjunction with the National League for Innovation, presented with the Hayward Award for Educational Excellence, and honored by the Center for Diversity in Teaching and Learning in Higher Education. Additionally, her Music of American Cultures course — a comparative and integrative study of U.S. multicultural musical styles exploring the music of Native Americans, European Americans, African Americans, Hispanic/Latino Americans, and Asian Americans from their historical roots to the present — was selected as "Best Online Course" by the California Virtual Campus.

She is currently Executive Director of the K. Patricia Cross Academy, a web-based professional development site for college faculty (*kpcrossacademy.org*), and professor emerita of music history at Foothill College, Los Altos, California.

## CLAIRE HOWELL MAJOR

Dr. Claire Howell Major is a leading scholar in the areas of instructional methods and online learning. She has authored and co-authored several books, including four in the Jossey-Bass/Wiley College Teaching Techniques Series: *Student Engagement Techniques: A Handbook for College Faculty* (2nd ed., with Elizabeth Barkley, 2020), *Interactive Lecturing: A Handbook for College Faculty* (with Elizabeth Barkley, 2018), *Learning Assessment Techniques: A Handbook for College Faculty* (with Elizabeth Barkley, 2016), and *Collaborative Learning Techniques: A Handbook for College Faculty* (2nd ed., with Elizabeth Barkley and Pat Cross, 2014). She has also published *Teaching for Learning: 101 Intentionally Designed Educational Activities Designed to Put Students on the Path to Success* (2nd ed., with Michael Harris and Todd Zakrajsek, Routledge, 2021), and *Online Learning: A Guide to Theory, Research, and Practice* (Johns Hopkins University Press, 2015). In addition to her books on teaching, she has published works on qualitative methods, including *Qualitative Research: The Essential Guide to Theory and Practice* (with Maggi Savin-Baden, Routledge, 2013) and *An Introduction to Qualitative Research Synthesis: Managing the Information Explosion in Social Science Research* (with Maggi Savin-Baden, Routledge, 2010). She also publishes her scholarship in leading education journals, such as *Teachers College Record, The Journal of Higher Education, Research in Higher Education*, and *Higher Education.*

Claire has extensive teaching experience in higher education. Early in her career, working as a teaching assistant and then adjunct faculty member, she taught more than 40 sections of developmental studies English, freshman composition, and sophomore literature. During this time, she taught across institutional types, including at a large urban community college, a two-year historically black college, a two-year technical institution, a four-year public institution, and a large research institution. After completing her doctorate, she worked as director of a center for teaching, then focused specifically on problem-based learning, at a small private four-year religious institution. Her work there involved helping faculty across the university integrate innovative teaching methods into their courses. Now, she teaches master's and doctoral level courses on college teaching, technology in higher education, and reading research in the field of higher education.

She is currently Chief Information Officer of the K. Patricia Cross Academy, a web-based professional development site for college faculty, and professor of higher education administration at The University of Alabama.

Made in the USA
Las Vegas, NV
24 May 2023